MALE JEALOUSY

CONTINUUM LITERARY STUDIES SERIES

Also available in the series:

Forthcoming titles:

MALE JEALOUSY
Literature and Film

LOUIS LO

continuum

Continuum International Publishing Group
The Tower Building, 11 York Road, London SE1 7NX
80 Maiden Lane, Suite 704, New York, NY 10038
www.continuumbooks.com

British Library Cataloguing-in-Publication Data
A catalogue record for this book is available from the British Library.

ISBN: 978-0-8264-9955-4 (hardback)

Library of Congress Cataloguing-in-Publication Data
A catalog record for this book is available from the Library of Congress.

Typeset by Aarontype Limited, Easton, Bristol
Printed and bound in Great Britain by Biddles Ltd, King's Lynn, Norfolk

For my parents, Hui Shun-oi (許信愛) and Lo Wing-fat (勞榮發).

Contents

Acknowledgements

I want to acknowledge the real help, given by many people, which made the writing of this book possible. It would not be possible for me to acknowledge fully the encouragement and intellectual generosity from Jeremy Tambling, then at the University of Hong Kong (HKU), whose passionate scholarship, wit and friendship have influenced me to undertake the initial research. He has improved many pages of this book with his comments. The studentship offered by HKU allowed me to work on this project between the years 2001 and 2005. The conference grant sponsored by Hong Kong ShueYan University made possible my trip to Manchester, where I was able to do further research, and to meet Chris Perriam who gave valuable comments on the relationship between revenge and jealousy (topics discussed in Chapter 8) that I developed from the paper ' "Your Life Didn't Belong to You": Jealousy in Almodóvar's *Carne Trémula* [Live Flesh]', presented at the *Rhetoric, Politics, Ethics* conference in Ghent (April 2005). This trip to Ghent was sponsored by the conference grant offered by HKU. I owe special thanks to Susan Ingram for her comments on an earlier version of Chapter 1, entitled ' "Gambling and Women do not Mix": *Gilda* and Jealousy', presented at the conference *Hong Kong/Hollywood at the Borders: Alternative Perspective, Alternative Cinemas* (April 2004).

I would also like to thank Peter Evans, Otto Heim and Paul Smethurst for their useful advice and criticism on my work. Paul Kong and Law Wing-yee read an early version of the work and gave valuable suggestions. Anna Sandeman's comments on the manuscript have resulted in firm improvements. Fong Ho-yin's friendship and infinite conversations directly or indirectly contributed to many ideas and arguments. I have received help from Fung Ka-ming who provided me with sources of films, especially Buñuel's *El*. Yue Lui, Siu Ki, Ching Mei, Paul Funge, Isaac Hui and Angus Cheng offered me supports of various sorts, making my life smoother and fuller. The students and my teaching assistant made my course on Proust at The School of Professional And Continuing Education at HKU an unforgettable experience.

Introduction

Jealousy: *This Strange Passion*

Buñuel was right to call it a 'strange passion': jealousy, as discussed here, is an affectual state triggered by the fear of the potential loss of the beloved. Being jealous has been said to be the sign of being in love – suggesting that if love is undetectable, we must look for jealousy, as jealousy is more visible. According to St Augustine, 'He that is not jealous is not in love'.[1] Being in love is a state mixed with jealousy: as the French dictionary, *Littré*, defines it, it is '*Sentiment qui naît dans l'amour et qui est produit par la crainte que la personne aimée ne préfère quelque autre*' [Jealousy: sentiment which is born in love and which is produced by the fear that the person loved may prefer someone else.][2]

But jealousy is not as simple as some group psychologists portray it. Titles such as *Justifying Emotions: Pride and Jealousy*, or *Jealousy: What is It and Who Feels It?* imply an attitude which says: jealousy is a crystal-clear emotion, we know it well, it is negative and sometimes destructive, and we will teach you how to control it.[3] The problem with this view is that it excludes challenges from Marxist criticism, which stresses the working of false consciousness, and in turn, the Marxist sense of ideology as affecting the subjectivity and the emotional life of the jealous person. This view also pays no consideration to the area explored by psychoanalytic criticism, which argues that the unconscious is the more influential area of human psyche than reason or common sense, those conscious aspects of thinking which can be inspected. Criticism motivated by Michel Foucault brings into play the importance of political aspects of knowledge, which are ignored in the more simple view, where knowledge is believed to be transparent and objective. Deconstruction brings the idea of the inside and outside into question, and challenges the notion of the proper and property. The challenge posed by 'queer theorists', that no pre-existing gender position and sexuality can be taken as normal, is also crucial to the analysis of jealousy. These viewpoints challenge the idea that human beings are rational, consistent, homogeneous and normatively bourgeois. In *The Psychological Structure of Fascism* (1985), George Bataille defines *homogeneous* society as 'productive society' and 'useful society' (p. 138). What is homogeneous belongs to the realm of possession and of the bourgeois. Whereas 'the *heterogeneous* world includes everything result-ing from *unproductive* expenditure' (ibid., p. 142) and it belongs to the realm of experience that shocks, and also to the unconscious. Furthermore, '*hetero-geneous* existence can be represented as something *other*, as *incommensurate*, by charging these words with the *positive* value they have in affective experi-ence' (ibid., p. 143). Throughout the book I use the terms homogeneous and heterogeneous as Bataille uses them.

Before we can define jealousy, we have to consider how the idea of person-hood has become the way we understand it. We have to bear in mind that what we understand as jealousy, as love, as possession, as being the owning subject, even owing our own body, are concepts that need to be brought into consideration. Using these conceptual tools we can start the search of what a 'cure of jealousy' could be, assuming that we need one. If we do not under-stand the assumptions behind the society which make jealousy possible, the cures offered may turn out to be non-cures.

The Cure of Jealousy [*Desengaño de cellos*] is one of the books in the library of Don Quixote, by Bartolomeó López de Enrinco (1586) as discussed by the narrator in *Don Quixote* (first published 1605) in Part One, Chapter Nine. The following are varying translations of the title:

> *The Cure of Jealousy* (Jarvis 1742/1998a, p. 67)
> *The Disenchantments of Jealousy* (Putnam 1949/1976, p. 121)
> *The Unveiling of Jealousy* (Cohen 1950, p. 75)
> *Jealousy's Home Truths* (Raffel 1999, p. 50)
> *The Undeceptions of Jealousy* (Rutherford 2000, p. 74)
> *The Deceptions of Jealousy* (Grossman 2003, p. 51)

The dictionary definition for *desengaño* is 'disillusion', but *engaño* means 'delusion' or 'deception'. It is curious to note that the last two translations seem to contradict each other.[4] Why is *desengaño* rendered as both undecep-tion and deception? Disillusion, in English, means 'the action of freeing or becoming freed from illusion; the condition of being freed from illusion; dis-enchantment' (*OED*), but it also means 'illusion, delusion' (*OED*). 'Disillu-sion' means what it means and also the opposite. So, to play tricks with language, *desengaño* (disillusion) could be analogous to Derrida's notion of the *pharmakon*, which means poison and medicine at the same time (2004, pp. 67–186). Is illusion the poison and disillusion the medicine? We do not know which is which. The disillusion of jealousy could be its dis-illusion, that is to say, the undoing, unveiling or disenchantment of the 'tricks' of jealousy (as the translations of Putnam, Cohen, Jarvis and Rutherford imply), or the illusion(s) of jealousy (as with Raffel and Grossman).[5]

What is the cure of jealousy? The translation of the title as 'the cure of jealousy' renders this ambiguity of Cervantes' title, since it could be the cure for jealousy as a disease, and thus implying an undoing of that influence. But the cure of jealousy also means the cure which is performed by jealousy. It suggests that love is enchantment and jealousy a disenchantment that undoes this enchantment. Jealousy as a cure evokes a positive view of jealousy, as contrary to the view that jealousy is a negative emotion. So, the cures turn out to be the non-cures, which renders the idea of the two-folded or antithetical nature of jealousy.

This book is a theory-based study of male jealousy in Western culture, in order to unveil and discuss the existence of possessive assumptions in love relations. The works include those by Cervantes, Shakespeare, Proust, Buñuel, Vidor and Almodóvar, in which different forms of jealousy in different kinds of love relations are portrayed. By tracing the meanings of jealousy and the representation of jealous men (married or unmarried, heterosexual or homosexual), I argue that jealousy is promoted within patriarchy and logocentrism, where to love is the desire to be loved, and love cannot be guaranteed in any form of sexual relationship. Treating jealousy as a 'symptom' of modernity, this book explores causes and (non)-cures of jealousy, in order to show that the conditions basic to jealousy coincide with beliefs which are made normal in the history of modernity.

The book is in three parts. The first chapter begins with Charles Vidor's film *Gilda* (1946), as a paradigmatic discussion of the potentialities and different aspects of jealousy, and I follow in Chapter 2, with the theoretical framework which Freud uses to discuss paranoia – which I connect with jealousy, for both terms are associated with an anxiety concerning the other, and in some cases perhaps jealousy may be understood as paranoia and paranoia as jealousy. Freud's analysis of the memoir written by Daniel Schreber, whom Freud judged to be paranoid, lays out a theoretical framework for analysing jealousy. The four symptoms of paranoia, namely, delusion of persecution, erotomania, delusion of jealousy and megalomania, are seen by Freud as possible reactions to a homosexual wishful phantasy. Special attention is given to the implication and significance for a man to say, or more importantly deny saying, 'I (a man) love him (a man).' From there I segue to the jealousy portrayed among characters in Dickens' *Little Dorrit*, two women and one man, and three men in *Our Mutual Friend* to illustrate what has been discussed at the level of theory.

The second part analyses works by Cervantes and Shakespeare, and so historicizes jealousy by looking at the concept in the early modern period, where it conflates with codes of honour. Chapter 3 discusses possession, concentrating on jealousy which is evoked by an imagined third party.

In such a case jealousy is characterized by paranoia, anxiety about the invasion of the other on the self. Borders become the main concern for paranoia; these extend to borders of the house and in turn national boundaries; internally, paranoia is obsessed with bodily borders and thus with personal identity. Cervantes' jealous old man from Extremadura, Carrizales, is an example from the early modern period; his jealousy has to do more with the idea of property than with love. A more complicated, but more common type of jealousy (also portrayed by Cervantes), appears in Chapter 4: that which involves a 'real' third party: in the tradition of *Los dos amigos* [The two friends] in *El curioso impertinente*. The second part of this book ends with a chapter on the *dos amigos* idea in *Othello*. The standing-in, or place-holding, nature of 'lieutenancy' in Iago and Othello is discussed in relation to the marginality of the split identity of the person that is by this means constructed as jealous. And it reverts to the subject of envy, if we take Othello as a figure of possession, and therefore jealousy, and Iago as illustrating non-possession, and therefore envy.

The third part deals with jealousy in modern times. Here, the focus is on Proust's *À la recherche du temps perdu*, which is read through two chapters. Reverting to the subject of male homosexuality as Freud discussed this in relation to Schreber, who is taken as the case study of paranoia, Chapters 6 and 7 re-situate the discussion of jealousy in Proust, looking now not at jealous husbands, but at lovers and their anxiety concerning male homosexuality and – a new subject, not discussed in Freud's analysis – lesbianism. The seduction of reading the signs given from the beloved complicates the issue of jealousy: to be in love is to expose ourselves to the risk of being jealous, so much so that jealousy overthrows love. If we follow Foucault, homosexuality in the modern period becomes a separate issue from whatever its status was in the early modern. The category of 'the homosexual' as a character type had not yet emerged in Cervantes' and Shakespeare's time, even if homosexual acts were the subject of repression.[6] Proust's *À la recherche du temps perdu* is primarily a first person narrative. The narrator is jealous for quite a different reason from Swann, who appears in several volumes and is the protagonist of an interpolated novel in the first volume. Swann's jealousy is to do with the mobility of signs given by the beloved, whereas the narrator's jealousy is to do with the beloved's putative lesbianism. Jealousy becomes anxiety about the sexuality of the beloved. It is the problem also associated with Saint-Loup, and perhaps Charlus. In these cases involving Swann, the narrator and Saint-Loup, jealousy has to do with oneself, instead of the beloved. Discussing jealousy in Almodóvar's film *Carne Trémula* (1997), Chapter 8, the last chapter, deals with a more complex structure, the structure of three, and aims at giving a conclusion on male jealousy. The book ends, via discussion of revenge, that which is so often inseparable from jealousy, with an attempt to think beyond jealousy, and to find a cure.

Cervantes' two novellas and Buñuel's and Almodóvar's films, are chosen for their construction of jealousy in Spanish contexts. Shakespeare's Othello and Proust are chosen for their emphasis on love and its relation to jealousy. I could have included many other examples from Shakespeare, such as *The Two Gentlemen of Verona*, *Much Ado about Nothing*, *The Winter's Tale*, and also Alain Robbe-Grillet's *Jealousy* (1957), as well as Asian texts such as Oshima Nagisa's film *Realm of the Senses*, and Cao Xueqin's *The Story of the Stone* (1754–91) The last two Asian texts are excluded for two reasons: I want to concentrate on how jealousy is understood in the history of modernity in Western civilization, and the texts are more about female jealousy, which will have to be the subject of another project.

The Gender of Jealousy

What is the gender of jealousy? By this I do not mean its grammatical gender in any particular language. In Bronzino's painting, *An Allegory of Venus and Cupid*,[7] Jealousy is personified as, in Erwin Panofsky's words, an 'elderly woman madly tearing her hair', who combines 'the terrifying aspects of Envy and Despair' (1972, p. 88). Standing behind Venus and Cupid, Jealousy is a woman with green skin. Her mouth is open wide, and she is suffering from great pain.

Let us consider another figure of jealousy, taken from Buñuel's film *El* or *This Strange Passion* (1953), which connects the analysis of materials ranging from the seventeenth to the twentieth century. *El* is about the love affair of a jealous man, who ends up retreating to a monastery in a half-mad state. At the beginning, Francisco falls in love with his childhood friend Raúl's fiancée Gloria, whose feet in shoes he sees first in church, on a Maundy Thursday ritual washing of the feet of the poor. Eventually he marries her but becomes increasingly tormented by the thought that they are being looked at, or rather, being humiliated, first when they are on honeymoon in Francisco's home town, Guanajuato, where he is engaged in a lawsuit with the government, fighting for the land his family once owned. At one point he seeks the comfort of his servant Pablo. When Gloria escapes from a life-threatening 'punishment', she encounters her ex-fiancée Raúl in the street. She tells him about her sufferings and about Francisco's jealous and paranoid acts, including an attempt to 'punish' her by pushing her from the top of a church bell tower. After another failed attempt to punish her by first

tying her up while she is sleeping, Gloria leaves his house, which is like a
fortress, designed by Francisco's grandfather, an engineer, and has almost
the power of another character in the film. Francisco decides to retreat to
a monastery after his breakdown in the church where he first saw Gloria.
He beats his friend Father Velasco in the middle of a service, at the peak of
his delusion, which has driven him to think that people around him are
laughing at him. Gloria finally marries Raúl, and gives birth to a child who
is named Francisco. The film ends with Francisco's zigzagging walk after he
tells the priest, 'time has proven my point', in response to the news that his
ex-wife Gloria has married her ex-fiancée Raúl.

The motif of foot fetishism is important in *El*. The *mise-en-scene* in the
beginning suggests that Francisco is 'saved' from falling in love with boys'
bare feet, which are kissed by Father Velasco. He falls in love with Gloria,
or rather with her feet in shoes. He seems to be interested in shod feet
rather than bare feet. At one point when Francisco is very jealous and revengeful, he re-falls in love with her when he sees her shod feet under the dining
table. For Francisco, fetishism is the cure for jealousy. But it is also a non-
cure, as fetishists require women' bodies to be supplemented. Freud argues
that fetishism saves men from homosexuality (1991b).[8] I will discuss the
issue of fetishism in relationship to homosexuality in Chapter 7 (pp. 146–7).

'This Strange Passion' was the English 'translation' of the film title.
'Passion' has plural meanings (*OED*): it is related to passivity, that which
is produced from an external force; it means suffering, as in the Passion
of Jesus; it can mean a painful disorder, physical pain, or sexual desire;
it also means an intense feeling or emotion, or even madness. We could
play with the title of *El*, a film about jealousy, as 'This Strange Suffering', 'This Strange Disorder', 'This Strange Madness', 'This Strange
Desire', or 'This Strange Passivity'. Calling a film about jealousy 'He' or
'The' – meanings of 'El' – may even evoke the sense that jealousy is the
dominant emotion (or passion) in patriarchal society.

The gender of jealousy is 'masculine' for several reasons: first, the concept of possession is premised upon the belief in the subject possessing a
single (and usually masculine) identity. Second, the insistence on truth as
single and unified, and belief in wholeness and rationality, is also what
is imbricated in jealousy. Third, curiosity, as a quality always associated
with jealousy, has to do with the desire for control, which is masculine.
If the gender of jealousy is masculine, it suggests that a jealous woman is
masculinized. If we could find a way to love without jealousy, it would be
purely feminine, as falling in love is to lose the desire for control, to open up
oneself to others, which is opposite to having masculine identity. How to
love without becoming jealous? This question leads to the criticism of these

basic beliefs in patriarchal society, such as possessive individualism and its derivatives, including such founding beliefs since the Enlightenment as human rights, freedom and rationality. So, possessing (having power), knowing (curiosity and the will to truth), seeing (ocularcentric understanding), and collecting (a belief in wholeness) may all be vicissitudes of jealousy.[9] It may be objected that this book disregards female jealousy, especially in the light of Freud's comment in 'Some Psychical Consequences of the Anatomical Distinction between the Sexes', that jealousy 'plays a far larger part in the mental life of women than of men' (1991e, p. 338). However, matters are not so easy because Freud suggests that woman's jealousy is an 'easy displacement' (ibid.) of her penis-envy, a problematic concept in itself. To quote Freud:

> Even after penis-envy has abandoned its true object, it continues to exist: by an easy displacement it persists in the character-trait of *jealousy*. Of course, jealousy is not limited to one sex and has a wider foundation than this, but I am of opinion that it plays a far larger part in the mental life of women than of men and that is because it is enormously reinforced from the direction of displaced penis-envy. (ibid.)

So Freud would agree that envy is the emotion resulting from non-possession, and that envy and jealousy are easily confused — a view which will be followed up in Chapter 5. In this way, he cannot be said to side with the view that jealousy is primarily feminine. Having said that, I will discuss more aspects of male jealousy by using a woman's name: Gilda.

Chapter One

Amigos: *Gilda*

This chapter takes *Gilda* as an example to examine different aspects of jealousy. Because of the complex nature of the relationship between Mundson, Gilda and Farrell, a short synopsis of Charles Vidor's 1946 film will be useful. 'Gambling and women do not mix', says Ballin Mundson, who saves Johnny Farrell's life with his 'little friend': his stick with a hidden dagger. This 'little friend' is, in Mundson's words, the 'most faithful and obedient friend in the world'. Farrell soon runs a casino in Buenos Aires for Mundson, who is also secretly the head of a cartel monopolizing a tungsten company. Mundson marries a woman he has known for only one day. She is Gilda (played by Rita Hayworth), the former lover of Farrell, who, having been declared Mundson's most faithful friend, has to look after his master's possessions, including the beautiful Gilda. Attempting to make Farrell jealous, Gilda goes out with other men. Farrell, not wanting Mundson to know Gilda's 'infidelity', covers for her by telling fake stories to Mundson about what they have been up to (going swimming, for instance) and in order to make him believe, has to pretend it is he who has been out with Gilda. Mundson is investigated by Detective Maurice Obregon for murdering a German who threatens his tungsten monopoly; Mundson decides to fake his death. After this event (which even Farrell does not know is fake), Gilda marries Farrell, who punishes her by not seeing her and not letting her go out with other men. The film ends with a reunion of Gilda and Farrell after Mundson's real death. Uncle Pio kills Mundson with the 'little friend' because Mundson tries to take Gilda with him before escaping from Argentina.

Three aspects of jealousy are to be considered: first, jealousy as an emotion involving three parties; secondly, curiosity and voyeurism provoked by jealousy as a way of possession; finally, Gilda as an example of a jealous woman.

Triangular Relationships and Homoeroticism

Gilda opens with an encounter between two men: the casino owner Mundson saves the life of the gambler Farrell, who later becomes Mundson's right-hand man. The structure of the film is one of repetition: Gilda and Farrell knew each other before they met in Buenos Aires, when Gilda becomes Mrs Mundson. Gilda has no family name in the film: she is Gilda, Mrs Mundson and Mrs Farrell as the film moves on. Getting married twice indicates a pattern of repetition. The triangular relationship of Farrell – Mundson – Gilda is important. According to René Girard's notion of 'triangular desire', a man falls in love with the beloved not because he loves the other spontaneously, but because of a mimetic desire which is induced by a third party who loves the beloved in the first place (1976, p. 24).[1] The homoerotic, or homosocial (the term is taken from Eve Sedgwick in *Between Men*) attraction between Mundson and Farrell fulfils the triangle: the desire involved is 'between men' and not between Gilda and the two men in her life only. Eve Sedgwick begins *Between Men* by arguing that 'homophobia' and homosociality construct patriarchal institutions such as marriage, as well as being their consequence. Mundson's marrying of Gilda (his heterosexuality) can be an unconscious token of his homoerotic desiring of Farrell.

In the beginning, Farrell has a toast with Mundson, who says, 'to the three of us', the third one being his 'little friend', 'the most faithful, obedient friend'. His walking stick with a hidden dagger is pointing up and the hidden dagger is 'turned on', both literally (the blade is out) and symbolically (sexually aroused). This gesture and his famous maxim, 'gambling and women do not mix', are homoerotically charged. Richard Dyer argues that masculinity and normality are problematized in the portrayal of the relationship between Mundson and Farrell (1998, p. 117). The toasting sequence when Mundson marries Gilda repeats the first toasting between Mundson and Farrell:

Mundson: To the three of us.
Gilda: To the three of us.
Mundson: What's the matter, Johnny?
Farrell: I've got confused.
Mundson: Confused! Why?
Farrell: Just a few weeks ago we drank a toast to the three of us.
Gilda: Well, who was the third one then? Should I be jealous?
Mundson: Darling, just a friend of mine.
Gilda: Is it a him or a her?
Mundson: That's very interesting. What do you think, Johnny?
Farrell: A her.
Gilda: Oh . . . !
Mundson: Why . . . that conclusion?
Farrell: Because it looks like one thing, and right in front of your eyes it becomes another thing.

Mundson: Well, you haven't much faith in women's stability, have you, Johnny?

For Farrell a hidden dagger is not simply a phallic symbol (as most people expect), but rather, an emblem of femininity. He sees it as feminine and deceptive, but he himself is also a figure of deception: he is a gambler who is good at playing tricks on people, for he could 'look like one thing and right in front of your eyes become another'. He tells lies to Mundson in order to make him believe that Gilda is not seeing other men. So Farrell accuses the other (Gilda) of the deceptiveness he has been practising. For Gilda, jealousy is a structure involving three people. However, in this sequence we do not know who the third party is. Is Gilda the third party to the two men? Or Mundson the third party to the loving-hating couple? Or perhaps jealousy has to do with the unknown other, who is emblemized by Gilda as a feminine figure, or by the stick with a hidden dagger, which is both the 'most obedient friend' and a she who 'looks like one thing and right in front of your eyes becomes another'? Nevertheless there is something 'queer' in the relation between Farrell, Mundson and the stick, more than in the relation with Gilda; it is as if saying there will be no jealousy in a relationship between men only. Of course, an example taken from Wong Kar-wai's *Happy Together* (1997), a film set in Argentina, contradicts this assumption that there is no jealousy between men. The two male lovers, Lai Yiu-fai and Ho Po-wing go to Argentina to 'start over again'. But soon Ho leaves Lai, due to his jealousy, and Ho begins making a living by becoming a male prostitute. Lai and Ho are a modern version of the *dos amigos* motif. Towards the end Lai goes to a club called '3 Amigos' with another man, Chang, before Lai leaves Buenos Aires for Hong Kong, which means Lai will end the relationship with his beloved Ho. The name '3 Amigos' can be a reminder that there are always more than two people within a group of two, (Chang and Lai) even if the other one, namely Ho, is not there.[2] The three 'friends' suggests a relationship is actually a structure of three: there is a third party involved, though sometimes imaginary.

Farrell understands Gilda as a phallic woman. We can argue that Mundson is killed by his ignorance of the nature of femininity, or by his inability to understand women, for he thinks women are as dangerous as a hidden dagger, but actually he winds up killed by a man (Uncle Pio). But to see women as unknowable and dangerous can be a construction of patriarchal ideology; to understand women as phallic could be (within patriarchal ideology) a paranoid misreading of the situation.

Gilda is not just good at speaking in a way which opens up different interpretations, she is also good at dancing and singing. The emphasis on the visual image of Gilda is suggestive: on the one hand she dances and sings in a way that invites spectators; but on the other hand, she is the figure of the unknowable. The first awareness of her is of her voice, and through the eyes of Farrell we hear her singing. Mundson asks, 'Gilda, are you decent?' The sight of her face is deferred because we see her hair first: she is facing downward with her hair flowing towards the floor. She replies, 'Me? Yes, I *am* decent.' From her expression the audience knows she is punning on the word 'decent', which means both 'fully dressed' and 'conforming to accepted standards of behaviour', in which the latter meaning evokes her potential infidelity. She repeats the gesture of 'hair flowing' when she sings 'Put the Blame on Mame, Boys' for the third time together with an interrupted striptease show which aims to make Farrell jealous, and where he misunderstands her again.

Music is associated with Gilda throughout the film, starting with the background music Gilda is listening to when she first appears. It stops when she finds out that Farrell is her husband's right-hand man. The second time is when she is singing to Uncle Pio, which is also interrupted by Farrell. It opens as follows:

'When Mrs O'Leary's cow kicked the lantern in Chicago town,
They said that started the fire,
That burned Chicago down,
That's the story that went around,
But here's the real lowdown,
Put the blame on Mame, boys,
Put the blame on Mame'

Each stanza ends with putting the blame on 'Mame', for example, her 'kiss' created fire in Chicago in 1871 and ice in Manhattan in 1886. The cause of the fire that burns Chicago town was 'they say' Mrs O'Leary's cow, but this is not the *real* 'cause', which is to do with the destabilizing presence of the woman. Although it is sung to Uncle Pio, Farrell is the assumed listener because the song begins heard as a voiceover while he is shown sleeping. Through the eyes of the awakened Farrell, who sees through the window (with blinds now opened), we find out that Gilda is singing with an acoustic guitar while she sits on a green gambling table, listened to by Uncle Pio. Farrell is angry with him (is he jealous or envious?) and tells him to go back to the toilet 'where he belongs'. Farrell misses the point that a song could be sung *for* him although it is sung *to* somebody else. He doubly misunderstands Gilda by thinking she did go out with somebody (to swim!) before she sings in the casino. After they say that they hate each other so much, the sequence ends with Gilda throwing the guitar through a glass partition, and Farrell appearing behind the broken glass with revengeful smile. The third song 'Put the Blame on Mame, Boys' does not repeat the previous one. But it goes on with a natural disaster:

When they had the earthquake in San Francisco back in nineteen-six [...]

which is referred back to 'Old Mother Nature'. Gilda also refers to the 'hootchie-coo' dance while she is dancing for people in the casino. Her ability in pluralizing meaning comes to its climax during the striptease show, because the song is complaining about men putting the blame on women once things go wrong. (The viewer will notice how each verse of the song is a celebration of America.) But the music and the way she sings go in the opposite direction: she is seductive, as if saying she as a woman could indeed be a source of trouble – like an earthquake – and several men do indeed try to fight for the chance of undressing her.

Possession and Voyeurism

The film becomes a study of how to possess a woman like Gilda. The film shows Gilda marrying different men, but they are marked by what Martin Jay calls 'ocularcentric' culture, which links closely to the understanding of the world (1994). The very expression 'I see' pinpoints the relation between understanding and watching, or between knowledge and spectatorship. In other words: to possess is to know, and to know is to watch. Mundson and Farrell (and later on, the detective) are obsessed with looking through the blinds (French: *jalousie*, as in Alain Robbe-Grillet's novel *La Jalousie* (*Jealousy* in the English edition), *jalousie* being both 'jealousy' and 'window with blinds'). (The *OED* cites 1591 as the first appearance of *jalousie* as 'jealousy window'.) Their acts of watching are highlighted by showing the beholders from a reverse point of view: the closing blinds are shown from the outside. So, the film is marked out by the motif of watching. Farrell thinks:

I wanted to go back and see them together with me not watching. I wanted to know.

The camera then shows exactly what Farrell wanted to see (and know). In the dark, by identifying with Farrell, the audiences are also fed with Farrell's desired spectacle. The pleasure of watching in secret refers both to the desire of the protagonists (at least including Farrell and Pio), as well as the audiences. It evokes a sense of voyeurism because it translates exactly into watching other people making love in private. Right after this sequence Uncle Pio remarks:

It's interesting to watch.

If frequent references to the act of watching are self-reflective, maybe we can regard Farrell's comments as self-reflexive, and the film as a meta-text. Together with the theory of the male gaze that is argued for by Laura Mulvey discussing narrative film, to watch films in the dark guarantees the pleasure of 'seeing them [the protagonists] together with me [the audience] not watching'. (1975, pp. 6–18). To make a comparison, in Michael Powell's film *Peeping Tom* (1960), the serial killer Mark Lewis kills people using a tripod with a hidden dagger while recording with a video camera. He is obsessed with filming people's expressions of terror. Lewis' father, a scientist, had used him as the subject to research how he would react to fear. The desire to watch (recording with a video) and to know (scientific research) coincide with murdering.

However, the striptease show is a reminder of the non-possessible quality of sound, as if saying the idea of possessing Gilda is as impossible as possessing the voice. Sound is always in excess, and Mundson thinks that he can screen out the carnival by closing the window. In *The Four Fundamental Concepts of Psychoanalysis* (1998b), Lacan thinks of the 'drive' (*Trieb* in Freud: the 'instincts') as pursuing an imaginary object which it is hoped will confer a complete identity on the subject. The *objet petit a*, as he calls it, is everywhere and nowhere, and is thought of as inhering in that which is at the borders of what is desired. For example, he writes, 'These are the *objets a* – the breasts, the faeces, the gaze, the voice' (1998b, p. 242). The voice, as the *objet a*, is what the drive seeks to hold, or to compass. But Farrell is seduced by the singing voice of Gilda even though the blinds are closed. Or, in other words, to possess Gilda in terms of the visual is not complete, because nobody can possess her voice, including the singer, whose voice goes as it comes, in what Lacan calls an *aphanisis* (the fading of the subject) (ibid., p. 218).

Mundson has warned Farrell that 'gambling and women do not mix', and yet he marries Gilda. Perhaps Mundson has not contradicted himself because when he is accused by Farrell of betraying him, he defends himself, 'Gilda does not come under the category of women'. This statement can mean that Gilda is so special that she is not an ordinary woman, and therefore is capable of mixing with gambling. But what if it means that Gilda is not a woman in the way a man usually understands a woman? Lacan would enable the existence of the latter meaning; for him, the category of woman is created and described by the 'symbolic order', which is dominated by patriarchal language. The category of women, seeing women as in a category, neglects the question of the woman's desire, which cannot be named within the symbolic order. For Lacan, woman's desire might be for a *jouissance* beyond the phallus (1998a, p. 74).

Farrell's relationship with Gilda is marked out by love and hatred, two words which are apparently in opposition, and which are at least not mutually exclusive. The affect called 'hate' is very strange in the film. At least four characters use it.

1. Gilda tries to comfort Mundson by telling him that she hates Farrell.
   Mundson: Hate can be a very exciting emotion. [...] It warms me. [...] There is a heat that one can feel. [...] Hate is the only thing that ever warms me.
2. After Gilda sings the song 'Put the Blame on Mame, Boys' the first time,
   Gilda: I hate you so much that I'd destroy myself to take you down with me.
3. In the kissing sequence, immediately before the kiss:
   Gilda: You do hate me, don't you.
   Farrell: I don't think you have any idea how much.
   Gilda: Hate is very exciting. I hate you so much that I think I will have to die from it ... Darling ...
4. After Gilda's song and dance with striptease show.
   Detective Maurice Obregon: You two kids love each other pretty terribly.
   Farrell: I hate her.
   Obregon: Yes, that's what I mean. It's the most curious love-hate pattern I've ever had the privilege of witnessing. As long as you're as sick in the head as you are about her, you're not able to think anything clearly.

Let me single out the last one. The affect which Obregon calls a 'love-hate' pattern is 'curious'. For Obregon it does not matter whether Farrell loves or hates, for they are talking about an exciting emotion. It makes one zealous and extreme, the opposite of being indifferent (which is the detective's attitude). Freud discussed the interchangeability of love and hatred – that love and hatred are not opposite, but ambivalent states – when he says, in a discussion to be examined in the next chapter, 'it is a remarkable fact that the familiar principal forms of male paranoia can all be represented as contradictions of the single proposition: I (a man) *love* him (a man)' in his study of Schreber's *Memoir*. For example, it can be contradicted unconsciously and reformulated as 'I do not love him − I hate him', or ' I do not love him − I love her, because she loves me', or 'I do not love her − I hate her, because she hates me' − the case of Farrell and Gilda.

Gambling and Women do not Mix

According to the *OED*, envy also means 'active evil' or 'harm' which fits Lacan's notion of 'the evil eye' in *The Four Fundamental Concepts of Psychoanalysis* (1998b), as characterized by its power of destroying the good. He writes, 'The powers that are attributed to it, of drying up the milk of an animal on which it falls [...] of bringing with it disease or misfortune − where can we better picture this power than in *invidia*' (ibid., p. 115), the Latin for envy? For Lacan, envy is 'not at all necessarily what he might want [...] Everyone knows that envy is usually aroused by the possession of goods which would be of no use to the person who is envious of them' (ibid., p. 116). He quotes St Augustine's example, that he as a child was envious of his little brother who was being breastfed by his mother:

> I have personally watched and studied a jealous baby. He could not yet speak, pale with jealousy and bitterness, glared at his brother sharing his mother's milk. [...] But it can hardly be innocence, when the source of milk is flowing richly and abundantly, not to endure a share going to one's blood-brother, who is in profound need, dependent for life exclusively on that one food. (1991, I.vii.11)[3]

Victor Burgin, in his *In/Different Spaces* (1996), uses the phrase 'jealous envy' to signify an envy where one wants to possess a particular quality of the other. He writes, 'jealous envy is an unavoidable component of our relation to the other, the one who is different, who knows something we do not, who experiences things we shall never know. There is always something we want, and it is easy to believe that the other has it' (ibid., p. 135). Burgin singles out a desire for the other's possession by putting jealousy and envy together in order to signify that envy has a possessive component. But however it may be that jealousy and envy are not clearly differentiated, they are different. If we follow Burgin, there can only be jealous envy, but no envious jealousy. It would be better to maintain a distinction between envy and jealousy. The jealous person, Mundson, is envious in the sense that he doesn't feel he possesses Gilda when he marries her. But Farrell, who has possessed Gilda before, only feels jealous, even though Gilda is Mundson's wife. Envy has to do with lack of possession, jealousy with anxiety of losing possession.

In Lacan, envy is not jealous, and not aimed at possessing the other's 'good', but rather with ruining it, as we will see with Iago.

Both Burgin and Lacan point out the importance of vision and its relationship to knowledge. The gaze is either envious or evil, or both, aiming at destroying the beloved. In this sense, the envious gaze behind the *jalousie* is not jealous but envious, as it aims at destroying the beloved. The 'jealousy window' constructs the beholder's gaze, but it allows for either jealousy or envy. Mundson is the supervisor looking over his casino through the blinds, the *jalousie*. His gaze is not evil but jealous, because he is the owner and the husband. Farrell, who has been made 'the supervisor', is jealous because he is the one who desires his boss's possession (he possesses, even though he does not possess the little friend).

We could say Farrell is jealous at first because he is emotionally attached to Gilda and also because he works for (and so identifies with) Mundson the husband, who is jealous. But nevertheless Farrell *is* envious when he himself is the husband dreaming of possessing (but unable to possess) Gilda, and he is hopelessly haunted by the risk of Gilda's potential infidelity. Is Farrell jealous or envious at the end when Mundson is dead and he reunites with Gilda? The third man looking behind the 'jealousy window' is Detective Obregon, who speaks to Farrell after 'inspecting' the jealousy window and tells him about his view of the 'curious love-hate pattern'. He is neither jealous nor envious, but indifferent, 'I feel safe to be on the side of the police.' His empathy (with Farrell) shows a contradictory relationship with patriarchy, as if saying the police are on the side of Farrell the old lover, not because Mundson is a criminal figure, but because to associate with Mundson implies a kind of homosociality, if not homosexuality. It is as if saying no matter how odd the love-hate relationship of Farrell and Gilda is, to be a policeman is to avoid an association with such homosociality.

The film opens with a professional gambler Farrell winning dice games, and ends with the reunion of a woman and a man who no longer gambles. It echoes and challenges Mundson's maxim 'gambling and women do not mix', making the attitude of the film very ambiguous. Does the 'happy ending' contradict Mundson's maxim? It starts with a revolutionary homosexual undercurrent, but ends with a rather reactionary attitude by showing the death of Mundson through his 'little friend', which implies the end of homosocial relations. Farrell, a gambler, no longer gambles, together with Gilda, he is going back to America to become bourgeois. Walter Benjamin, in his book of the 1930s, *Charles Baudelaire* (1997), argues that gambling is the replacement of experience, which a modern man lacks and longs for. He quotes Émile Chartier Alain, 'gambling cares about no assured position', and it 'gives short shrift to the weighty past on which work bases itself' (ibid., p. 134). So work – not gambling – is on the side of history, time and identity. Benjamin writes, 'Gambling became a shock diversion of the bourgeoisie only in the nineteenth century' (ibid., p.135), so one gambles because of the lack of experience possible in modernity and gambling becomes a replacement to divert people from the shock 'experienced' in modern society. A gambler 'cannot make much use of experience' (ibid., p. 136) because gambling is 'a game of chance' and 'it is experience that accompanies one to the far reaches of time, that fills and divides time' (ibid., p. 136). So gambling might be associated with modernity, failure of experience to provide a narrative, destabilization of status, anti-history, non-memory, division of time, criminality (if we consider Mundson as a criminal figure), and homosexuality. Here, when contrasted with 'gambling' in Mundson's maxim, 'women' stand for the non-modern, for experience, establishment of status, history, memory, time, and heterosexuality. However, in 'Dostoevsky and Parricide' (1990b), Freud argues that to gamble is to fulfil the desire to lose, in order to submit oneself to the power of patriarchy. Gambling is a mode of self-punishment in order to relieve the sense of guilt aroused by the wish to kill the father in order to compete for the mother in the Oedipus complex. So for Freud, gambling and women *do* mix, while gambling and mother do *not* mix.

Benjamin's idea about gambling implies that gambling is feminine, because it is submissive to fate (Freud 1990b, p. 450). The gambler in Wong Kar-wai's film *2046* (2004) is a woman with a black glove (Su Li-zhen), and she always wins. She helps Chow Mo-wan, a writer from Hong Kong, who meets her in Singapore, and who is stuck there because he loses in the casino. Chow asks Su to come with him to Hong Kong, and he asks about her black glove. Su agrees that she will tell him her secret if he wins at cards, and come with him to Hong Kong – and of course he loses. Chow is even more feminine than the professional gambler because he submits to her and to fate, though he knows that he will lose anyway.

That gambling and women do not mix, could mean for Mundson that women are the enemy of his business and gambling has nothing to do with the game of chance because he is the boss of the casino and the house always wins. It can mean, though in an anti-feminist way, that to love a woman is already a kind of gambling, so 'gambling and women do not mix' may mean that the risk is too high to gamble twice. The film agrees with the maxim in a curious way: Mundson cannot mix gambling and women because Gilda leads him to his death. For Farrell, giving up gambling allows him to establish a stable status, which is patriarchal, heterosexual and reactionary.

The Jealous Woman

Gilda thinks that the reason to go out with other men is to make Farrell jealous, as comes out in the following dialogue:

Farrell: Doesn't it bother you at all that you're married?
Gilda: What I want to know is, does it bother you?

Gilda's concern shows that she is jealous. And her jealousy drives her to make Farrell jealous. Farrell feels jealous even though Gilda is Mundson's wife. When Farrell accuses her of being unfaithful to Mundson, Gilda replies:

All the things I did were just to make you jealous.

What does jealous mean in this context? The *OED* defines it as the 'solicitude or anxiety for the preservation or well-being of something; vigilance in guarding a possession from loss or damage'. Jealousy, apart from the anxiety to one's own possession, is as Ayala Malach Pines puts it, as a reaction to a perceived threat to a valued relationship,[4] which can also mean envy, which is 'a longing for the advantages enjoyed by another person' (*OED*). On the tendency of confusing envy with jealousy, Hanna Segal writes, in *Introduction to the Work of Melanie Klein* (1975), that:

in analytical writing one finds the same confusion as in everyday speech, where envy is commonly called jealousy. On the other hand, it is very rare indeed for jealousy to be described as envy; everyday speech [...] seems to avoid the concept of envy and tends to replace it by that of jealousy. (ibid., p. 39)

So, envy is always replaceable by jealousy in everyday speech, but, confirming the point made above about Victor Burgin, not the other way round. If Gilda sees jealousy as the anxiety over one's own possession, it implies that being married to the other is not enough to make Farrell envious. Gilda is emotionally attached to Farrell, who is not her husband, and in order to 'make [him] jealous' she pretends to have affairs with others. Farrell, being a jealous lover, pretends he is not jealous and that all he does is to protect the non-jealous man Mundson from knowing about Gilda's 'affairs'. Nevertheless after Farrell marries Gilda, he unjustifiably (as Gilda was unfaithful because of Farrell) punishes Gilda for her unfaithfulness to his ex-boss, her ex-husband. While this is the apparent reason, the real reason may be that he cannot deal with the burden of being Gilda's husband, partly because he feels that marriage does not guarantee possession, and partly because of the disappearance of Mundson, which destabilizes the Girardian triangle. Marriage at least in this instance connotes jealousy, or the desire to possess, rather than love.

Working from *Gilda*, we have introduced three problems involved in jealousy: its triangular structure, its voyeurism and curiosity, and its questioning of gender, and we have discussed the point that jealousy is an anxiety related to a crisis of whether there can be possession or not, which is aroused with a third party. Jealousy as a form of curiosity, related to voyeurism, has to do with the eye, or the desire to look. Jealousy may be the denial of homoeroticism between men. Finally, it may be caused by the anxiety of the realization of the 'queerness' of sexuality. But in the next chapter we will examine a theoretical framework for considering paranoia, as put forward by Freud in the Schreber Case analysis: a discussion of paranoia will lead us into considering what structures jealousy.

Chapter Two

Paranoia: Freud and the Schreber Case

> I thought I could feel nerves of voluptuousness on my body like those of a
> female body.
>
> Daniel Schreber, *Memoirs* (2000, p. 362)

Freud's so-called Schreber Case is perhaps the most commented-on case study for considering what is meant by the term 'paranoia'. In 1911 Freud wrote the case study 'Psychoanalytic Notes on an Autobiographical Account of a Case of Paranoia (Dementia Paranoides)'[1] (1990c) on the German jurist Daniel Paul Schreber (1842–1911), though he had never been his patient; Lacan states insightfully that Freud 'was initially and essentially interested in paranoia' (1993, p. 4).[2] Freud analyses the case solely by reading Schreber's *Denkwürdigkeiten eines Nervenkranken* [Memoirs of my Nervous Illness] (2000), which was written during the course of his mental breakdown, and published in 1903. Although Schreber claimed that he 'started this work without having publication in mind', yet he wrote, 'I believe that expert examination of my body and observation of my personal fate during my lifetime would be of a value both for science and the knowledge of religious truths' (2000, p. 3).

Daniel Paul Schreber was born in Leipzig. His father, Moritz Schreber, died at age 53 when Daniel was 19. Schreber married at the age of 36. His first illness began in 1884 after he stood as a candidate for the election to the Reichstag while he was *Landgerichtsdirektor* [Judge presiding over the Landgericht, a court of inferior jurisdiction] at Chemnitz. Confined at Sonnenstein Clinic and then at Leipzig Psychiatric Clinic, he was completely recovered by the end of 1885 and took up an appointment in the Landgericht in Leipzig next year. During that period of his illness, from autumn 1884 to the end of 1885, his doctor was Paul Flechsig, Professor of Pyschiatry at Leipzig University. In 1893 Schreiber took up an appointment as *Senatspräsident* [Judge presiding over a division of an Appeal Court] in Dresden, but his second illness started a few months later. On 21 November 1893 he was re-admitted to Leipzig Clinic, and then to Lindenhof Clinic, and finally (in June 1894) transferred to Sonnenstein Asylum in which he wrote the

Memoirs in the period from February to September 1900. After he was discharged from this asylum at the end of 1902 he published his *Memoirs* the next year. Four years later his third illness started and he died in the asylum at Leipzig-Dösen in April 1911. In September of the same year Freud finished his analysis of the Schreber Case.

Schreber's memoirs show that he had the delusion that he had been chosen by God to redeem and restore the world to its lost 'state of Bliss' (2000, p. 29), by giving birth to a new race of men, and that he had the idea that he was being transformed into a woman. Freud considered the delusion of being transformed into a woman, 'of being emasculated', as primary (*SC*, p. 148), even more so than Schreber's 'assumption of the role of Redeemer', which Freud felt was a standard delusion in paranoia. It should be noted that Freud assumes that becoming a woman and being emasculated are equivalents.

Schreber had written, in relation to a dream of 1893 before he was confined 'It really must be rather pleasant to be a woman succumbing to intercourse' (2000, p. 46) (which is translated in the English edition of Freud as 'after all it really must be very nice to be a woman submitting to the act of copulation' (*SC*, p. 142)).

Although Schreber lived in the asylum with such a delusional system, he '[gave] evidence of a lively interest, a well-informed mind, a good memory, and a sound judgment' to topics concerning 'events in the field of administration and law, of politics, art, literature or social life' (*SC*, p. 145), in other words, he was 'normal' in many aspects. His doctor, Flechsig, was his 'only enemy', the 'soul-murderer' in his monomaniacal delusional system.

Freud argues that Schreber's 'emasculation phantasy', is independent of the 'Redeemer motif'. The phantasy of being transformed into a woman, argues Freud, was the earliest within his delusional system (*SC*, pp. 148–9). In his memoirs Schreber admitted that he wore sundry feminine adornments such as ribbons and necklaces when he was alone in front of a mirror. Schreber's phantasy included being impregnated by divine rays, which connects with the thought of what it would be to be a woman. Freud interprets it as a wish to be penetrated. 'I will enjoy in advance that Blessedness granted to other human beings only after death', wrote Schreber:

This state of Blessedness is mainly a state of voluptuous enjoyment, which for its full development needs the phantasy of either being or wishing to be a female being, which naturally is not to my taste. (2000, p. 291) [The Standard Edition transcribes this as 'voluptuousness may be regarded as a fragment of the state of bliss given in advance, as it were, to men and other living creatures' (*SC*, p. 161).]

Here, Schreber claims that wishing to be a woman, is 'naturally' not his taste, but this contradicts his earlier phantasy of becoming a woman succumbing to intercourse. Freud concludes that the state of bliss is to be understood as being in its essence an intensified continuation of sensuality upon earth. To explain Schreber's sexualization of the state of heavenly 'bliss', which implies a state of death in relation to the earth, Freud suggests that it may be due to his condensation of the two principal meanings of the German word *'selig'*, which can mean 'dead' and 'sensually happy' (*SC*, p. 162). This double meaning of words had been discussed a year before in his essay 'The Antithetical Meaning of Primal Words' (1910), and is picked up again in "The 'Uncanny'" (1919). It is curious to note that Freud did not further discuss the ambiguity of this particular word in the Schreber Case, which here more than anywhere overthrows the identity of the speaking subject (and in that sense, can be thought of as paranoia-inducing). Freud writes:

> The exciting cause of his illness [...] was an outburst of homosexual libid.o; the object of his libid.o was probably from the very first his doctor, Flechsig, and his struggles against the libid.inal impulse produced the conflict which gave rise to the symptom. (*SC*, p. 177)

Schreber resisted this phantasy and the defensive struggle takes up several possible shapes, one of which is a delusion of persecution. Freud suggests that the conflict between Schreber's personality and his passive homosexual phantasy towards Flechsig was first resolved by turning the phantasy into persecution (*SC*, p. 182). This is because, suggests Freud, Schreber's affection towards Flechsig became an erotic desire, a feminine phantasy, and was immediately met with a 'repudiation', a 'masculine protest' (*SC*, pp. 176–7), possibly by Schreber himself, though Freud leaves this open. Later, Flechsig was replaced by the superior figure of God, and that seemingly intensified the conflict. However, it actually paved the way to a solution to the 'unbearable persecution'. Freud continues:

> It was impossible for Schreber to become reconciled to playing the part of a female wanton towards his doctor; but the task of providing God Himself with the 'voluptuous' sensations that He required called up no such resistance on the part of his ego. Emasculation was no longer a disgrace; it became 'consonant with the Order of Things'. (*SC*, p. 183)

This developed into Schreber's megalomania, by which Freud means 'the sexual overvaluation of the ego' (*SC*, p. 203). Schreber's feminine wishful phantasy demanded that he accept emasculation, but the unacceptability of this meant that it had to be expressed in the feeling, in his delirium, that he was being made into a woman.

In the third section of the analysis called 'On the Mechanism of Paranoia', Freud generalizes from the Schreber Case to suggest that the following are four possible symptoms resulting from reactions to the 'homosexual wishful phantasy of loving a man' (*SC*, p. 200):

1. Delusion of persecution.
2. Erotomania.
3. Delusion of jealousy.
4. Megalomania.

So the single proposition 'I (a man) *love* him (a man)' can be contradicted in four ways yielding four forms of paranoia (*SC*, pp. 200–3). The definition given by the *OED* calls paranoia a 'mental illness characterized by a persistent delusional system, usually on the theme of persecution, exaggerated personal importance, or sexual phantasy or jealousy, often as a manifestation of schizophrenia'. R.D. Laing in *The Divided Self* (1960) says that the family structure leads to schizophrenia, as the child has to submit to absolutely contradictory demands from the parents. Deleuze and Guattari (1984), who speak for schizophrenia as opposed to paranoia, see Schreber's delirium as a case of schizophrenia. They criticize Freud for not seeing the creative side of Schreber's desire to become woman and Freud's determination to cast it in a paranoid mode by confining it as an Oedipal struggle with the father (ibid., pp. 57 and 89). Delusions (or hallucinations) of grandeur are what Freud calls 'megalomania'. No matter how contradictory these two forms of paranoia are, Freud argues that they are the symptoms of reaction against a homosexual wishful phantasy.

Delusions of Persecution

After suggesting that the four principal forms of paranoia (including jealousy) could be represented as contradictions of the single proposition 'I (a man) *love* him (a man), Freud explains in detail how his hypothesis works in each case. The first one is the delusions of persecution. He writes:

> The proposition 'I (a man) *love* him (a man)' is contradicted by:
> (a) Delusions of *persecution*; for they loudly assert:
> 'I do not *love* him – I *hate* him.'

This contradiction, which must have run thus in the unconscious, cannot, however, become conscious to a paranoiac in this form. The mechanism of symptom-formation in paranoia requires that internal perceptions – feelings – shall be replaced by external perceptions. Consequently the proposition 'I hate him' becomes transformed by *projection* into another one:

> 'He *hates* (persecutes) me, which will justify me in hating him.' And thus the impelling unconscious feeling makes its appearance as though it were the consequence of an external perception:
>
>   'I do not *love* him – I *hate* him, because HE PERSECUTES ME.'
>
> Observation leaves room for no doubt that the persecutor is someone who was once loved.
>
> <div align="right">(<i>SC</i>, pp. 200–1)</div>

For the diagrams following, to illuminate this, four conventions are used:

1. Solid line represents love.
2. Broken line represents hatred.
3. Single line represents interior affect.
4. Double line represents exterior affect.

So a solid single line represents love towards the other, while a double solid line represents love (perceived by the subject) coming from the outside. Also, a single broken line represents hatred towards the other, while a double broken line represents hatred (perceived) from the outside. They are tabulated as follows:

Affect Arrow	Feature	Affect
——————▶	Solid line	Love
– – – – – ▷	Broken line	Hatred
::::::::::::▷	Double broken line	Hatred from the exterior
══════▶	Double solid line	Love from the exterior
——⊗——▶	Solid line with ⊗	Denial of love

Figure 2.1 Key to Diagrams

In the case of delusions of persecution, the verb 'love' is contradicted. The proposition 'I (a man) *love* him (a man)' (see Diagram 1a) becomes 'I do not *love* him – I *hate* him' (see Diagram 1b).

Diagram 1a:
'I (a man) *love* him (a man)'

Diagram 1b:
'I do not *love* him (1), I *hate* him (2)'

Freud argues that the love towards the man who is desired cannot become conscious, with paranoid results: 'what lies at the core of the conflict in cases of paranoia among males is a homosexual wishful phantasy of *loving a man*' (*SC*, p. 200). The statement is unacceptable, and an 'external perception' is then needed to rationalize the proposition 'I hate him' to avoid the fact that the hatred is actually love. The external perception is regarded as objective reality, as distinguished from an internal mechanism. So in order to have such an external perception, 'he hates me', the proposition 'I hate him' becomes transformed by projection into 'He *hates* me, which will justify me in *hating* him' (see Diagram 1c).

By projection, the internal feeling has acquired a corresponding external 'reality', which Freud calls the 'mechanism of symptom-formation'. In Laplanche and Pontalis's *The Language of Psychoanalysis* (1973), projection is defined as the

> operation whereby qualities, feelings, wishes or even 'objects,' which the subject refuses to recognize or rejects in himself, are expelled from the self and located in another person or thing. Projection so understood is a defence of very primitive origin which may be seen at work especially in paranoia, but also in 'normal' modes of thought such as superstition. (ibid., p. 349)

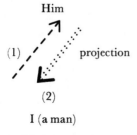

Diagram 1c:
'I hate him' (1) because 'He hates me' (2)

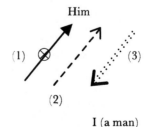

Diagram 1d:
'I do not *love* him (1) − I *hate* him (2), because he persecutes me (3)'

That is to say, an external perception from the outside is interpreted as the 'cause' of the paranoid hatred towards the one hated, who is actually loved. So there are three levels of transformation undergone:

1. From love to hate.
2. From 'I hate him' to 'he hates me' (by projection), the subject and object are reversed.
3. From the interior (love or hate) to the exterior (perception of being hated).

The formula thus becomes: 'I do not *love* him I *hate* him, because he persecutes me' (see Diagram 1d).

The delusion of persecution is the displaced fear of love towards the other. So the delusion of persecution can be the reaction to the subject's masculinity crisis, as exemplified in Schreber's anxiety towards Dr. Flechsig, whom Freud argues that Schreber once loved (*SC*, p. 201) and who becomes the figure of the 'soul murderer' later. (Schreber's wife kept Dr. Flechsig's portrait standing upon her writing-table for years, perhaps unconsciously provoking jealousy by creating a Girardian triangle.)

Schreber's phantasy, 'it really must be rather pleasant to be a woman succumbing to intercourse' (2000, p. 46), could be a wishful phantasy of turning into a woman, in which case it would be a desire for a Deleuzian form of schizophrenia (as opposed to paranoia), or a wish for what Foucault calls, with reference to the hermaphrodite status of Herculine Barbin, 'the happy limbo of a non-identity' (1980, p. xiii). Or it could be, as Freud seems to read it, a displacement of a homosexual wishful phantasy, as a defence mechanism against the fear/attraction of being penetrated as a man. The phantasy of turning into a woman and having sexual intercourse with a man could be a wish fulfilment of homosexuality, only the gender of the subject has been contradicted. If that is the case, activity (homosexual wishful phantasy) now turns into passivity (turning into a woman and succumbing to intercourse). That phantasy, under the same token, now turns into a fear of the subject's bodily boundary being invaded. But it could also be a desire for de-territorialization for a non-authoritarian, 'nomadic' state.

If the proposition 'I *love* him' could be transformed into 'I *hate* him', then the proposition 'He *hates* me' could also be 'recovered' to 'He *loves* me' by the same token. So the mechanism of the delusions of persecution (He persecutes me) becomes 'He loves me'. However, we can never be sure what is the starting proposition, since 'He hates me' is projected from 'I hate him', which is not necessarily transformed from 'I love him'. So love and hatred could both be an initial, ambivalent, relationship with objects, though Freud suggests 'hate, as a relation to objects, is older than love' (1984b, p. 137). If we come back to what we have discussed about love and jealousy, it is as if saying love is heterogeneous, indefinable, and perhaps includes hatred. This is what Freud calls ambivalence. Perhaps to be jealous is to attempt to refuse ambivalence, to fix 'love' as a single affect.

Erotomania

Having delusions of being loved by somebody is erotomania, and it is one of the possible reactions against the homosexual wishful phantasy. Freud writes:

> (b) Another element is chosen for contradiction in *erotomania*, which remains totally unintelligible on any other view:
> 'I do not love *him* − I love *her*.'
> And in obedience to the same need for projection, the proposition is transformed into:
> 'I observe that *she* loves me.'
> 'I do not love *him* − I love *her*, because SHE LOVES ME.'
>
> (*SC*, p. 201)

In the case of erotomania, it is first, the object 'him (a man)' who is denied. But the proposition 'I (a man) *love* him (a man)' (see Diagram 2a) is contradicted not only by the pronoun: him to her − but also by the source: the love comes from the outside. We start with 'I do not love *him* − I love *her*' (see Diagram 2b).

But this becomes, under the same token of the demand of projection, 'she loves me' (see Diagram 2c). Freud adds that the contradiction of the gender of the loved one ('I love *him*' vs. 'I love *her*') is not as 'diametrical' as love and hatred, so the interiorizing 'I love her' might not need an external perception ('she loves me') to justify it. But an external perception *is* needed to rationalize 'she loves me', and therefore signs of 'she loves me' (being loved by the other) are constructed in the external world: 'I observe that she loves me.' The formula thus becomes: 'I do not love *him* − I love *her* (because she loves me)' (see Diagram 2d).

Being loved by a woman could also be a displacement of the wish of being loved by the man, love for whom has been repressed. So the homosexual wishful phastany has undergone a gender change (man to woman), and a direction change (love to being loved). There are three levels of transformation undergone:

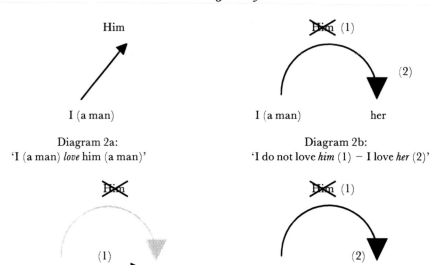

Diagram 2a:
'I (a man) *love* him (a man)'

Diagram 2b:
'I do not love *him* (1) − I love *her* (2)'

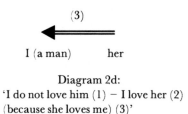

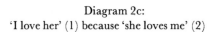

Diagram 2c:
'I love her' (1) because 'she loves me' (2)

Diagram 2d:
'I do not love him (1) − I love her (2)
(because she loves me) (3)'

1. From him to not him, the loved object is negated.
2. From the male 'him' to the female 'her', the gender of the loved object is inverted.
3. From the interior (I love) to the exterior (perception of 'she loves').

Though the word 'mania' dates back to the fourteenth century, and means, according to the *OED*, 'madness, particularly of a kind characterized by uncontrolled, excited, or aggressive behaviour', it is redefined in a new chapter of the *histoire de la folie* at the beginning of the nineteenth century (as the word 'psychiatry' appears first in 1808). Mania could be seen as the opposite to melancholia, which is characterized as non-activity or lack of action. But in the nineteenth century, melancholia is also mania.[3] In modern usage, melancholia is one side of a bipolar (manic depressive) mood disorder. (The second definition the *OED* offers for mania is 'a personal obsession, compulsion, or obsessive need; excessive excitement or enthusiasm'.) In melancholia there is a sense of the lost object, but *what* is lost is unknown. Since 'in mourning it is the ego which has become poor and empty; in melancholia it is the ego itself' (Freud 1984c, p. 254), it means that the lost object is not separate from the subject's sense of completeness.

The definition of erotomania offered by the *OED* is 'Melancholy or madness arising from passionate love', and it first appeared in 1874. Another definition adds: 'By some authors the term is restricted to those cases in which the imagination alone is affected; by others the grosser forms nymphomania and satyriasis are included.' However, the word 'Erotomania' is used in 1640 as a book title: *Traité de l'essence et guérison de l'amour*, which is translated as *Erotomania, or A Treatise Discoursing of the Essence, Causes, Symptomes, Prognosticks, and Cure of Love, or Erotique Melancholy*, written by Jacques Ferrand. As 'love madness', it is a word constantly reinvented, again most critically at the beginning of the nineteenth century by Philippe Pinel (1745–1826). His pupil Esquirol (1772–1840) defined erotomania as the 'chronic cerebral condition characterized by an excessive love for a person who may be imaginary or known to the subject, and by the delusion of being loved by that person'.[4] Lacan further explains:

> erotomania implies the choice of a person who is, to some extent, famous, and the idea that that person is concerned with no one but you. (quoted in Lacey 1988, p. 183)

The idea of being loved exclusively by someone famous is suggestive: First, it is a form of narcissism. Second, it evokes a sense of megalomania ('I am the only one who is worth loving'). Finally, it suggests that the desire to be loved is a form of paranoia, and that desire is homosexual in character, which is opposite to what the paranoiac disavows at the beginning. Paranoia refuses to acknowledge desire for another man. I will return to erotomania by discussing Dickens' *Little Dorrit* after finishing Freud's Schreber Case.

Delusions of Jealousy

Now we move on to Freud's discussion of the 'delusions of jealousy' as a symptom of Schreber's denial of 'I (a man) *love* him (a man)':

> (c) The third way in which the original proposition can be contradicted would be by delusions of jealousy, which we can study in the characteristic forms in which they appear in each sex.
>
> (α) Alcoholic delusions of jealousy. The part played by alcohol in this disorder is intelligible in every way. We know that that source of pleasure removes inhibitions and undoes sublimations. It is not infrequently disappointment over a woman that drives a man to drink – but this means, as a rule, that he resorts to the public-house and to the company of men, who

afford him the emotional satisfaction which he has failed to get from his wife at home. If now these men become the objects of a strong libid.inal cathexis in his unconscious, he will ward it off with the third kind of contradiction:

'It is not *I* who love the man − *she* loves him' and he suspects the woman in relation to all the men whom he himself is tempted to love.

Distortion by means of projection is necessarily absent in this instance, since, with the change of the subject who loves, the whole process is in any case thrown outside the ego. The fact that the woman loves the men is a matter of external perception to him; whereas the facts that he himself does not love but hates, or that he himself loves not this but that person, are matters of internal perception.

(*SC*, p. 202)

In the case of delusions of jealousy, rejection of the subject 'I' takes place, so the proposition 'I (a man) *love* him (a man)' (see Diagram 3a) becomes, '*she* loves him' (see Diagram 3b). So the statement 'It is not *I* who love the man', becomes, 'It is *she* who loves the man.'

Freud points out that projection does not take place because it is the subject ('I') who is contradicted and is therefore already outside the ego. The formula becomes: 'It is not *I* who love the man − *she* loves him.' So three levels of transformation take place:

1. From 'I' to 'not I', the loving subject is negated.
2. From the male 'I' to the female 'she', the gender of the loving subject is inverted.
3. From the interior (love) to the exterior (perception of somebody who loves).

Freud calls these kind of delusions 'alcoholic', perhaps because the scenario he uses is that when a man is driven by his wife to the public-house, where

Him

I (a man)

Diagram 3a:
'I (a man) *love* him (a man)'

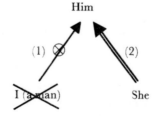

Him

(1)   (2)

I (a man)   She

Diagram 3b:
'It is not *I* who love the man (1)
− *She* loves him (2)'

the man is in the company of other men, who offer him pleasure, which he then has to defend in his unconscious. The result is that it must be the other, in this case, other women who love that man (as he is so desirable), instead of the subject who finds the men attractive.

The reactions to the homosexual wishful phantasy of the other men are discussed by Freud using the male as the example of paranoia. But for this particular symptom, delusions of jealousy, Freud discusses women's jealousy:

(β) Delusions of jealousy in women are exactly analogous.

'It is not *I* who love the women – *he* loves them.' The jealous woman suspects her husband in relation to all the women by whom she is herself attracted owing to her homosexuality and the dispositional effect of her excessive narcissism. The influence of the time of life at which her fixation occurred is clearly shown by the selection of the love-objects which she imputes to her husband; they are often old and quite inappropriate for a real love relation – revivals of the nurses and servants and girls who were her friends in childhood, or sisters who were her actual rivals.

(*SC*, p. 202)

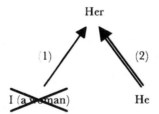

Diagram 3c: 'It is not *I* who love the women (1) – *he* loves them (2)'

The delusions of jealousy in women are exactly analogous. So the woman, who has the homosexual wishful phantasy, denies 'I (a woman) *love her* (a woman)' which becomes, 'It is not *I* who love the women – *he* loves them' (see Diagram 3c).

Megalomania

Freud writes:

Now it might be supposed that a proposition consisting of three terms, such as 'I love him', could only be contradicted in three different ways.

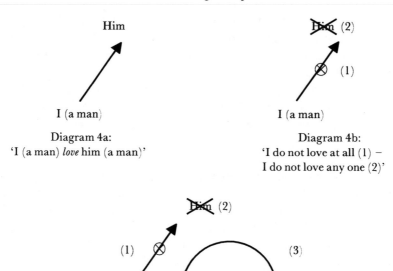

Diagram 4a:
'I (a man) *love* him (a man)'

Diagram 4b:
'I do not love at all (1) –
I do not love any one (2)'

Diagram 4c: 'I do not love him' (1) and (2); 'I love no one' (3) – 'I love only myself' (4).

Delusions of jealousy contradict the subject, delusions of persecution contradict the verb, and erotomania contradicts the object. But in fact a fourth kind of contradiction is possible – namely, one which rejects the proposition as a whole:

'*I do not love him at all – I do not love any one.*' And since, after all, one's libid.o must go somewhere, this proposition seems to be the psychological equivalent of the proposition: 'I love only myself.' So that kind of contradiction would give us megalomania, which we may regard as a *sexual overvaluation of the ego* and may thus set beside the overvaluation of the love-object with which we are already familiar.

(*SC*, p. 203)

Finally, megalomania is the rejection of the proposition 'I (a man) *love* him (a man)' (see **Diagram 4a**) as a whole: 'I do not love at all – I do not love any one' (see Diagram 4b). Freud explains that the subject's libid.o has to go somewhere, and therefore the contradiction becomes, 'I love only myself' (see Diagram 4c), which is defined as 'sexual overvaluation of the ego' (*SC*, p. 203). Four levels of transformation take place:

1. From love to 'not love', the action is reversed.
3. From 'him' to 'no one', the object is changed.
2. From 'do not love' back to 'love', the action is reversed again.
4. From 'no one' to 'myself', the loved object is inverted.

In his *Memoirs*, Schreber said he was called 'The seer of spirits', which means 'a man who sees, and is in communication with, spirits or departed souls' (2000, p. 81). He was usually referred to by Flechsig's soul (who appeared in Schreber's illusions, his 'soul-language') as 'the greatest seer of spirits of all centuries' (ibid.). To this Schreber retorted, 'from a wider point of view, one ought at least to speak of the greatest seer of spirits of all *millennia*' (ibid.). Phrases like 'from a wider point of view', 'one ought at least', and 'millennia (instead of centuries)', show a sense of excessive superiority mixed with a masochistic tendency. The excessive superiority could be a reaction to his masculinity crisis. Schreber's response shows the contradictory affects of bitterness and a sense of inferiority.

But nevertheless, if one is the greatest 'seer', he is also the wisest, the one who understands, the most powerful person. The German title of Schreber's memoirs, *Denkwürdigkeiten eines Nervenkranken*, literally means 'Memorabilia (or Noteworthy Thoughts) of a Nervous Patient', and echoes his megalomania. Louis Sass sees Schreber as a quasi-solipsist, and suggests that Schreber is a case showing the symptoms of modern emphases on personal initiative, especially on impersonality within social relationships. For Sass, Schreber is the victim of panopticism, a term derived from Jeremy Bentham, which exposes the subject to a constant normalizing gaze, from which a socialized authority is ultimately internalized (1987, pp. 101–47). By reading Schreber and Wittgenstein together, Sass addresses the problem of Schreber's megalomania and sees Schreber and Wittgenstein as cases of modern thought, which produces, using Wittgenstein's word, 'solipsism'. In *The Paradoxes of Delusion*, Sass defines madness as that 'what might be called the mind's perverse self-apotheosis' (1994, p. 12). William Niederland (1974) consolidates Freud's argument and suggests that Schreber's problem with his father was an 'early traumatic relationship' which contributed to his mental illness.[5] Schreber's father, Moritz Schreber, was an educator famous for creating machines to control the boy's body. Niederland argues that the greatest dread of Schreber is to stand in the place of the father, that is, to take up an active masculine role. Schreber's choice is rather to stay mad than to replace his father. Whereas in *Crowds and Power* (1978), Elias Canetti relates paranoia to power phantasies, and argues that the phantasy of a new world order and the motif of redeeming the world is the result of a desire to assert masculinity at a time of proto-fascism, of a national inferiority complex. Eric Santner, in *My Own Private Germany* (1996), however, posits Schreber's investiture crisis 'in the domain of symbolic authority and the production of "deviant" sexuality and gender identities' (p. 17). For Santner, Schreber's paranoia turns out to be a rejection of the authority of the law just when he had been promoted into it. So Santner sees Schreber as the victim of para-noia, which a fascist nation 'suffers', as fascism is the neurotic fear of the other. Schreber's madness resists full investiture in that state, and in that sense opposes megalomania. If he turns into a woman it would be in order to escape, so there is ambivalence in his delusions; they are both paranoid, thinking himself as a redeemer, and anti-paranoid.

If we follow Freud's connection of paranoia with a crisis of masculinity, as a reaction to a homosexual wishful phantasy which questions the stability of identity and gender, this reaction takes the form of two contradictory direc-tions: either as passive, feminine or as active, masculine. The passive form is represented as a phantasy of being a woman, whereas the active form becomes the megalomaniac phantasy, as a way of coping with the fear of the other. For Freud, the overvaluation of self could be a denial of the love of other men. When God is asked by Moses what His name is, He replies:

> I am who I am.
>
> (Exodus 3: 14)

which evokes a sense of the self-existent being. I will discuss this further in the chapter on Shakespeare's *Othello* (p. 92), in which Iago claims, solipsis-tically, in contrast to God:

> I am not what I am.
>
> (I.i.64)

Also, in Shakespeare's *Richard III*, King Richard says:

> Richard loves Richard; that is, I am I.
>
> (V.iii.183)

In *Henry VI, Part Three*, after stabbing Henry VI, Richard says:

> I am myself alone.
>
> (V.vi.83)

Another example is Shakespeare's 'Sonnet 121', which asserts male identity by putting the poet's signature throughout the poem, in 'vile', 'wills' and

'I am'. There is insistent punning on 'Will – I am', 'William', and God's name for himself, 'I am that I am'. In saying 'I am that I am' the 'I' is comparing himself with God, while the 'vil' in 'evil' (which also means the same as 'vile', its anagram) makes him (and his 'will', and God) evil, though in this sonnet these may be only rhetorical tropes:

> 'Tis better to be vile than vile esteemed,
> When not to be receives reproach of being,
> And the just pleasure lost, which is so deemed,
> Not by our feeling but by others' seeing.
> For why should others' false adulterate eyes
> Give salutation to my sportive blood?
> Or on my frailties why are frailer spies,
> Which in their wills count bad what I think good?
> No, I am that I am, and they that level
> At my abuses reckon up their own;
> I may be straight though they themselves be bevel.
> By their rank thoughts my deeds must not be shown,
> Unless this general evil they maintain –
> All men are bad and in their badness reign.

(1977, pp. 408–12)

On Ambivalence

Freud does not further develop the issue of jealousy among the four contradictions, beyond referring to 'alcoholic delusions of jealousy' which turn out to be the only symptom which relates to women. This seems to imply that as distinct from other forms of paranoia (such as delusions of persecution, erotomania or megalomania), jealousy is a subset of paranoia.

We have discussed the point in Chapter One that jealousy is fear of losing one's possession, and we also have introduced the problem involved in the distinction of jealousy and envy, that envy is the anxiety about another's possession. For Freud, the symptoms of paranoia may be the reaction to a homosexual wishful phantasy, jealousy as a form of paranoia has to do with non-possession (phantasy), which is in the realm of lack. The dominant emotion concerning possession might be envy, instead of jealousy.

However, we do not need to accept the conclusions of Freud's analysis on these symptoms. I would suggest that Freud's insight – that all the symptoms of paranoia are a denial of the homosexual wishful phantasy 'I (a man) *love* him (a man)', is more interesting than the conclusions. Peter van Sommers, in *Jealousy* (1988), a book on sexual jealousy written from a psychological approach, comments on Freud with regard to this issue:

> If it [the delusion] is so ready to convert love to hate and hate to love, why not change your delusion to make your lover hate your rival, for example, and put your mind at ease? My answer to that is that jealousy may very well be jealousy and not converted love at all. (ibid., p. 137)

Van Sommers' criticism misses the point, because the mechanism of paranoia is working under the token of the denial of a homosexual wishful phantasy, which has nothing to do with delusions of love, or the hatred of one person towards another. In addition, van Sommers does not agree with Freud that homosexuality, or fear of homosexuality, is integral to paranoia, and also for delusional jealousy (ibid., p. 139). However, van Sommers' answer is interesting: jealousy may not be an emotion converted from love. It may be independent of love, as contrary to what most people think, the idea that love is the sufficient and necessary condition for jealousy.

At the end of the Schreber Case, Freud writes 'Observation leaves room for no doubt that the persecutor is some one who was once loved' (*SC*, p. 201). However, as discussed in the Introduction, the reverse of love is not necessarily hate. In Freud's 'Instincts and their Vicissitudes' he writes:

> As the first of these [sexual] aims we recognize the phase of *incorporating* or *devouring* – a type of love which is consistent with abolishing the object's separate existence and which may therefore be described as ambivalent. At the higher stage [...] the striving for the object appears [...] an urge for mastery, to which injury or annihilation of the object is a matter of indifference. Love [...] is hardly to be distinguished from hate in its attitude towards the object. Not until the genital organization is established does love become the opposite of hate. (1984b, p. 137)

Borrowed from Bleuler, the word 'ambivalence', was used by Freud in 'Instincts and their Vicissitudes' (1915), and then in a revision of 'Three Essays on Sexuality' (originally 1905). There, ambivalence is the state of affairs in which 'the opposing pairs of instincts are developed to an approximately equal extent' (1991f, p. 118). So love and hatred are not opposite to each other. Freud argues that 'hate, as a relation to objects, is older than love' (ibid., p. 137). Jealousy and love are usually mixed. If love and hatred are not opposite to each other, perhaps that is the reason for the misuse of jealousy for envy in everyday language.

Self-punishing Paranoia: Miss Wade's Case in *Little Dorrit*

The gender of paranoia for Freud is primarily masculine. But for Lacan, erotomania, which in Freud is a displacement of the denied desire of another man, is enlarged, and its gender now becomes feminine.[6] The most famous case of erotomania for Lacan is Aimée. He reads Aimée as a case of 'self-punishing paranoia'(1989, p. 16). She thinks that others are persecuting her, and she knifes an actress in order to be punished, to justify her sense of guilt. The more negligent she is to her child, the more she needs to be punished, and by attacking the actress, she ensures punishment, like Freud's 'Criminals from a Sense of Guilt' (1990a). This is the inversion of how Freud talks about paranoia in relationship to men. Here, 'I (a woman) *love* her (a woman)' is contradicted as discussed above.

Lacan was influenced by de Clérambault (1872–1934), arguing that erotomania is the illusion that someone the subject loves is secretly in love with her. In *Lacan & Co.* (1990), Elisabeth Roudinesco quotes Lacan's doctoral thesis, *De la psychose paranoïaque*, discussing the case of Aimée and her belief that the actress Mme Z (Huguette Duflos) loved her. Aimée was arrested because she tried to kill Mme Z with a knife. Lacan argues that Aimée internalized Mme Z into her ego, and that what seemed to be murder was in fact an attempt at suicide (in Roudinesco 1990, pp. 112–13). Lacan suggests:

> The sexes have different positions with respect to the object, which is owing to the distance that separates the fetishistic form of love from the erotomanical form of love. (1989, p. 617)[7]

The difference between the fetishistic and erotomanical forms of love can be seen in Francisco in *El*, who pursues his wife as a result of fetishistic love (starting with her shoes) – fetishism being, according to Freud, a reaction to cover up the fear of castration, and to repress homosexuality. Francisco remains a masculine, single subject till the end, while the erotomaniacal form of love, as with Aimée, desires punishment while being as paranoid as Francisco is. Both forms of paranoia attack the other, but the paranoia characterized by fetishism remains unchanged, and when Francisco thinks he is being laughed at (punished) he attacks the priest, while the paranoia characterized by erotomania is cured after the 'self-punishment' and after treatment.[8]

So a person in a state of erotomania wants is to be loved by the one she desires. If we follow Lacan (and Freud), that erotomania is gender-specific, it will be a female-female relationship. What the person needs in the other is to supply the narcissism that they need and which (in the case of a woman) gives her identity. So, jealousy and erotomania are both related

to paranoia: jealousy is the paranoid reaction to the threat of loss of possession, whereas erotomania invests its ego in the other. One is primarily
masculine, and one perhaps feminine.

However, Lacan and de Clérambault do not limit erotomania to the
feminine. Erotomania is associated with nymphomania, 'uncontrollable
or excessive sexual desire' especially in woman (*OED*). In Ian McEwan's
Enduring Love (1997), a man, Jed, phantasies that another man, Joe, the
hero, is secretly in love with him after witnessing a balloon accident.
De Clérambault is referred to in Appendix I of the novel, which says it is
'Reprinted from the *British Review of Psychiatry*' under the names of the
authors Robert Wenn and Antonio Camia with the title 'A Homoerotic
Obsession, with Religious Overtones: A Clinical Variant of de Clérambault's Syndrome' (ibid., p. 233). But this review seems to be fictional: a fictional and scientific narrative is put together, or, perhaps, science is made as
fictional as a novel is. Or even, no scientific account of erotomania can be
given – or, perhaps it can. McEwan's version of erotomania seems to
ignore psychoanalysis (there is no reference to Lacan). Jed is in love with a
man (and becomes violent). So for McEwan, erotomania is derived from
male homosexual phantasy. Heterosexual love is involved here, as opposed
to both Freud and Lacan.[9]

There is a case of incipient erotomania described in Dickens' *Little Dorrit*
(1855–57) which involves two women, Tattycoram and Miss Wade. Miss
Wade stalks Tattycoram and persuades her to live with her, and she gives
Arthur Clennam an autobiographical account of her life, called 'The History of a Self Tormentor' (II.21.674–83), which is Dickens' version of
seeing the self in terms of being a self-punishing paranoid. Her first paragraph shows her paranoia:

> I have the misfortune of not being a fool. From a very early age I have
> detected what those about me thought they hid from me. If I could have
> been habitually imposed upon, instead of habitually discerning the truth,
> I might have lived as smoothly as most fools do. (II.21.674)

She is seduced by Henry Gowan, the worthless artist, and in jealous revenge
she stalks the woman he is about to marry, Pet Meagles. In the course of
doing so she comes across Tattycoram, the patronized servant of Pet, and
we can see how Tattycoram is fascinated by her in I.16.201–2. She tells of
her love affair with Henry Gowan to Arthur Clennam:

> He [Mr Gowan] had been intimate there for a long time, but had been
> abroad. He understood the state of things at a glance, and he under-
> stood me.

He was the first person I had ever seen in my life who had understood me. [...]

You will understand, then, that when your dear friend complimented me,
he really condoled with me [...] (II.21.680)

The idea of being 'understood' is stressed here. Miss Wade is called a 'self
tormentor' in the absence of the word 'masochist', which first appeared in
1892 (*OED*).[10] Miss Wade's need to be understood, which is important to
her feeling of love, contributes to a modern form of subjectivity: there is an
underlying, deeper self which needs to be understood, but not from the surface. Miss Wade integrates her paranoia with a desire for self torment (it is a
case of self-punishing paranoia) and this makes her take up with Tattycoram, who will, nonetheless, eventually reject her. Freud discusses the
compulsion to repeat by referring to a case of a patron repeatedly being
abandoned by his protégés, thus bringing together masochism, repetition,
and the desire to dominate, which is a form of paranoia, and the death
drive (1984a, p. 292).

Our Mutual Friend

After comparing the difference between the fetishistic and erotomanical
form of paranoia by discussing an episode involving female-female relationships in Dickens' *Little Dorrit*, I will close by illustrating Freud's idea of the
delusion of jealousy as the denial of loving another man through another
Dickens' novel, *Our Mutual Friend* (1865), a text full of male-male relationships, one of them between Bradley Headstone and Eugene Wrayburn.
Bradley Headstone, an ex-pauper and now a *petit bourgeois* schoolmaster, is
in love with Lizzie Hexam, a poorer woman who does not love him. To prevent herself from being seduced by Eugene Wrayburn, a barrister who hates
the class to which he belongs, Lizzie runs away from him even though she
is attracted to him.[11] Headstone proposes to Lizzie:

'You know what I am going to say. I love you. What other men may mean
when they use that expression, I cannot tell; what I mean is, that I am
under the influence of some tremendous attraction which I have resisted
in vain, and which overmasters me. You could draw me to fire, you could
draw me to water, you could draw me to the gallows, you could draw me
to any death, you could draw me to anything I have most avoided, you
could draw me to any exposure and disgrace. This and the confusion of

my thoughts, so that I am fit for nothing, is what I mean by your being the ruin of me. [. . .]'

'Mr. Headstone –'

'Stop! I implore you, before you answer me, to walk round this place once more. It will give you a minute's time to think, and me a minute's time to get some fortitude together.'

Again she yielded to the entreaty, and again they came back to the same place, and again he worked at the stone. (1997, pp. 389–90)

This is an extraordinary love scene. Headstone's proposal is almost an invitation to a refusal as his idea of love means he is willing to be destroyed by his beloved. He is dominated by a strong sense of self-destruction or hatred towards himself. He starts his proposal with a sense of self-devaluation, and he immediately thinks of other men even as he is saying 'I love you' to Lizzie – 'What other men may mean when they use that expression, I cannot tell.' It will be remembered that René Girard, in *Deceit, Desire & the Novel* (1976) says desire is imitative, induced by a third party, 'the mediator of desire' (p. 11). The triangular relationship, Headstone – Wrayburn – Lizzie, is Girardian, with Wrayburn as the mediator, Headstone as the desiring subject and Lizzie as the loved object. This helps us to understand the hatred of Headstone towards Wrayburn. 'The impulse toward the object is ultimately an impulse toward the mediator,' argues Girard, and:

[. . .] this impulse is checked by the mediator himself since he desires, or perhaps possesses, the object. [. . .] The subject is torn between two opposite feelings toward his model – the most submissive reverence and the most intense malice. This is the passion we call *hatred*.

Only someone who prevents us from satisfying a desire which he himself has inspired in us is truly an object of hatred. The person who hates first hates himself for the secret admiration concealed by his hatred. In an effort to hide this desperate admiration from others, and from himself, he no longer wants to see in his mediator anything but an obstacle. (1976, pp. 10–11)

Headstone's hatred towards Wrayburn and towards himself could be explained by Girard: Headstone 'first hates himself for the secret admiration concealed by his hatred'. The primary relationship in the erotic triangle is thus between the subject and the mediator. This is almost echoing Freud's idea of the denial of 'I (a man) *love* him (a man).' In *Between Men* (1985), Eve

Sedgwick puts forward a complicated version of the triangular relationship. She argues that Headstone's desire towards Lizzie is induced by Lizzie's brother Charley Hexam. Sedgwick writes:

> Yet an intense bond soon develops between the schoolmaster and young Charley. [...] Charley begs Bradley to come meet Lizzie first, however, and Bradley finds himself, as if by compulsion, violently in love with her. (ibid., p. 165)

So the mediator in the triangle Headstone – Charley – Lizzie is Charley. Sedgwick adds that this triangle is further complicated by Eugene Wrayburn, which forms the triangle Headstone – Wrayburn – Lizzie. I add Sedgwick here in order to show that the erotic triangle is not necessarily a static one. It could start off with one triangle and then change into another, with different people as the mediator. In addition, it is worth noting that the way Headstone woos in his proposal to Lizzie seems to suggest that his need to be refused is as compulsive as his falling in love with her. When Headstone is refused by Lizzie:

> 'Then,' said he, suddenly changing his [Headstone's] tone and turning to her, and bringing his clenched hand down upon the stone with a force that laid the knuckles raw and bleeding; 'then I hope that I may never kill him [Eugene Wrayburn]!' (II.15, p. 390)

Headstone thinks that Wrayburn is the obstacle between him and Lizzie, but nonetheless it is an unusual response to a failed proposal. It is as if he is inviting the refusal, so that he could blame it on Wrayburn. Girard would argue that Headstone proposes to Lizzie in order to be refused, so that he could imitate his secret admirer Eugene Wrayburn. Girard paraphrases Max Scheler's *Ressentiment*, that:

> there would be no envy, if the envious person's imagination did not transform into concerted opposition to the passive obstacle which the possessor puts in his way by the mere fact of possession. 'Mere regard at not possessing something which belongs to another and which we covet is not enough in itself to give rise to envy, since it might also be an incentive for acquiring the desired object or something similar ... *Envy* occurs only when our efforts to acquire it fail and we are left with a feeling of impotence.' (1976, p. 13)

So Headstone is trying (unconsciously) to put himself in the situation where he could be envious. Of course we know that it is only Headstone who thinks that Lizzie is in love with Wrayburn. But in his belief system it does not matter, as he has to fail in order to involve Wrayburn, even if the passion is not love but hatred. Or if we follow Sedgwick, Girard or Freud, Lizzie is only a token since his relationship with Wrayburn is more primary.

Headstone is indeed hostile to Wrayburn, and because he thinks that Wrayburn knows where Lizzie is, he tries to follow him in the dark. Freud would argue that it does not matter whether Lizzie falls in love with Wrayburn or not, nor whether Wrayburn knows where Lizzie is, since they are only tokens concealing his secret. Wrayburn and Headstone first meet when Headstone, as Charles Hexam's schoolmaster, visits Wrayburn and Mortimer Lightwood, asking Wrayburn about Lizzie:

> Composedly smoking, he [Wrayburn] leaned an elbow on the chimney-piece, at the side of the fire, and looked at the schoolmaster [Headstone]. It was a cruel look, in its cold disdain of him, as a creature of no worth. The schoolmaster looked at him, and that, too, was a cruel look, though of the different kind, that it had a raging *jealousy* and fiery wrath in it.

> Very remarkably, neither Eugene Wrayburn nor Bradley Headstone looked at all at the boy. Through the ensuing dialogue, those two, no matter who spoke, or whom was addressed, looked at each other. There was some secret, sure perception between them, which set them against one another in all ways. (2.6, p. 285, my emphasis)

There is a fascination between the cold Wrayburn and the hot Headstone. The 'jealousy' that Headstone has seems also echoed in Wrayburn's compulsion of playing a 'game' which he could not refuse, a compulsion which could also be a token concealing his secret fascination with Headstone. He enjoys being followed – before he reveals it to his friend Mortimer Lightwood he says, 'I am a little excited by the glorious fact that a southerly wind and a cloudy sky proclaim a hunting evening' (3.10, p. 534). His trick is to allow himself to be followed by Headstone, spending the whole night walking in the labyrinth of London, and at one point turning around, making himself present (It is Freud's *Fort*! *Da*! game). He tells Lightwood, who lives with him, that:

> I study and get up abstruse No Thoroughfares in the course of the day. With Venetian mystery I seek those No Thoroughfares at night, glide into them by means of dark courts, tempt the schoolmaster to follow, turn suddenly, and catch him before he can retreat. Then we face one another, and I pass him as unaware of his existence, and he undergoes

grinding torments. [...] Thus I enjoy the pleasures of the chase, and derive great benefit from the healthful exercise. (3.10, p. 533)

Being chased is passive, but Wrayburn is active in being chased by Headstone, who is 'undergoing grinding torments' (3.10, 534). For Wrayburn, being chased is a passive activity: in the sense that it is both active and passive. There is a kind of sadistic and masochistic attraction between them, but it would be difficult to say who is sadistic and who is masochistic. Wrayburn could be masochistic since he enjoys the dangerous pleasures of being chased. But it would be equally sound to say that Wrayburn is also sadistic since he enjoys seeing Headstone being humiliated – that he 'undergoes grinding torments'. Also, Headstone could equally be sadistic as much as masochistic. He could be sadistic to chase Wrayburn, and he could be masochistic to submit himself in situations in which Wrayburn could humiliate him – '[Headstone looks] like the hunted and not the hunter' (3.10, 534). It is almost impossible to differentiate whether Wrayburn is active or passive, as he is actively doing something in order to be passive (being chased). During the time when Wrayburn is chased, he is actively searching No Thoroughfares – the no-go zones in the heart of the city, the dead end in the labyrinths which turn one into passivity. But Wrayburn actively finds the 'No Thoroughfares' and by using them he turns himself active, from 'the hunted to the hunter'. Dickens writes:

Looking like the hunted and not the hunter, baffled, worn, with the exhaustion of deferred hope and consuming hate and anger in his [Headstone's] face, white-lipped, wild-eyed, draggle-haired, seamed with *jealousy* and anger, and torturing himself with the conviction that he showed it all and they exulted in it, he went by them in the dark, like a haggard head suspended in the air: so completely did the force of his expression cancel his figure. (3.10, 534, my emphasis)

Recalling Headstone's masochistic gesture of forcing his hand on a tombstone when his proposal to Lizzie is refused, he here seems guillotined, both at the level of the imaginary ('like a haggard head suspended in the air') and at the level of the signifier: as if saying that in his name 'Head/stone' there is also a sign of separation, like a castration. Using Freud's hypothesis, Headstone's hatred towards Wrayburn could be a reaction against the homosexual wishful phantasy, 'I (Headstone) love him (Wrayburn)', which could be projected into the following:

1. 'I do not *love* him – I *hate* him', which becomes 'I do not love him – I hate him, because he persecutes me' (delusions of persecution) or;

2. 'I do not love *him* – I love *her* (Lizzie)' which becomes 'I do not love him – I love her, because she (Lizzie) loves me' (which might explain why he proposes to Lizzie, as discussed earlier), or;
3. 'It is not *I* who love the man, *she* loves him', thus comes the 'jealousy and anger', or;
4. 'I do not love anyone – I love only myself.'

Headstone's 'conviction' of being tortured could be another example of his masochistic (and yet sadistic) character, but it could also be a reaction to the megalomaniac proposition 'I love only myself' in Case 4, which could be contradicted as 'I do not love anyone – including myself, I hate myself.'

The erotomaniacal proposition 'I love her, because she loves me' in Case 2 explains why Headstone proposes to her – 'I do not love him – I love you' – this is, indeed, what he does say in his proposal to her. But he then stalks Wrayburn under the reason, or pretext that Wrayburn knows where Lizzie is.

Modern erotomania is, of course, associated with stalking as in *Enduring Love*. In *The Psychology of Stalking*, Robert Lloyd-Goldstein writes,

> the relentless torments visited upon the victims, the psychological profiles of the stalkers, the grotesque dramas (including maimings and murders) that may ensue have become the subject of serious scholarly study. (1988, p. 193)

The words 'torments' and 'grotesque dramas' echo Headstone and Wrayburn's situation, as well as Miss Wade's. Headstone is another self tormentor: he proposes to Lizzie in order to be refused, but 'I hope I may never kill him' shows his desire to maintain a relationship with Wrayburn. (And 'each man kills the thing he loves', as Wilde writes in *The Ballad of Reading Gaol*.)

Headstone's 'jealousy and anger' (3.10, 534) could be due to class difference, but it could as well be explained by the homosexual wishful phantasy put forward by Freud. So Headstone's hatred could be his reaction to the desire for Wrayburn, a figure heterogeneous and yet fascinating to him, at both sex and class levels. Miss Wade admits in her autobiographical account to Arthur, that she 'soon began to like the society of your dear friend [Henry Gowan] better than any other. When I perceived (which I did, almost as soon) that jealousy was growing out of this, I liked this society still better' (II.21.681). Her (and Headstone's) 'jealousy' is not only sexual, but across class, and is also envy, since Headstone and Miss Wade are not in the position of having possession (Headstone shows *ressentiment*).

Following Freud, identity is never fixed, as not only the verb (love/hate), but also the object (him/her) and subject (I/not I) in the proposition 'I love him' are interchangeable. The notion of identity is, as Freud associates it with paranoia, decomposed. With this insight, we are ready to deal with jealousy in a relation which involves an imagined third party and a 'real' third party respectively. Both texts are written by Cervantes.

Chapter Three

Property: Cervantes' *El celoso extremeño*

This is one of two chapters on Cervantes: two jealous husbands will be discussed respectively, though their jealousies are different. In this chapter, I want to start discussion of jealousy in relation to possession, with Cervantes' *El celoso extremeño* [The Jealous Old Man from Extremadura], one of Cervantes' *Exemplary Stories* published in 1613.[1] This is a case of jealousy in its simplest and commonest form: a relationship between two persons in marriage. I will begin by giving a plot synopsis of *El celoso extremeño*.

The story opens: 'Not many years ago a gentleman born of noble parents set out from a village in Extremadura, and like a second Prodigal Son went off through various parts of Spain, Italy and Flanders, wasting his time and his substance' (J, p. 147). The protagonist's name is given by the end of the first page, in the second paragraph, Felipo Carrizales (or Filipo de Carrizales in J), who goes to the Indies as 'many ruined people of [Seville] are driven' to, and makes a fortune there (J, p. 147). After 20 years, when he is 68 years old, 'seeing himself rich and prosperous, and feeling the natural desire which everyone has to return to his native land' (J, p. 148), Seville, he returns to his home village. But the people living there are very poor and he becomes 'the target' of all their 'importunity' (J, p. 149). 'He wanted someone to whom he could leave his possessions at the end of his days, and with this wish in mind he looked into the state of his health, and it seemed to him that he was still fit enough to get married' (J, p. 149). Though he 'resolved at all costs not to marry' (J, p. 149) because 'by nature he was the most jealous man in the world' (J, p. 149), he decides to marry a beautiful girl, Leonora, whom he sees at a window. Driven by jealousy, he imprisons her after marriage in his newly built, heavily secured house with double doors to prevent her from being seen by any male. With an ageing black eunuch as the doorman, four white slaves with faces branded, two Negro slaves, a 'prudent and serious-looking' duenna as the governess and two young girls as companions, the 'young and innocent' Leonora is put into the prison-like (or convent-like) house in Seville. Driven by curiosity, a young bachelor Loaysa seduces the doorman 'Luis the Negro' by singing songs and promising to teach him to play music. It is interesting to note that the 'invader' uses music as the means of seduction, which echoes the problematic nature of sound, that which cannot be possessed, as discussed with *Gilda*. Sound, perhaps for this reason, is associated with the power of transgression.

Loaysa succeeds in entering the highly guarded fortress by suggesting Leonora steals the master keys from her husband by putting him into a deep sleep with a strong sleep-inducing ointment. The naive Leonora, convinced by her governess, agrees to sleep with Loaysa. However, she is able to repulse the 'ignoble advances of her cunning seducer' at the last moment and they both fall asleep because of the nightlong struggle. Having seen this heartbreaking spectacle, and thinking that his wife is unfaithful to him, Carrizales faints and dies after giving a speech which aims at an 'unusual revenge' (L, p. 182). He wills that she should marry a man, Loaysa, whom he has secretly named for her, and that her dowry should be doubled. After his death the slaves and the Negro are set free, Leonora is left 'widowed, tearful, and rich, [. . .] taking the veil in one of the most enclosed convents in the city' (L, p.182), not fulfilling the obligation written on the will. Loaysa goes to the Indies.[2]

The Crisis of Possession

Carrizales is jealous in marriage because of several 'causes': it could be due to (a) his status as a husband; (b) his old age; or (c) his identity as an Extremaduran. These 'causes' are interlocking and therefore should not be considered as separate. But nevertheless I will try to discuss the reactions toward the crisis of possession in terms of marriage and sex, the beloved being imprisoned, and the jealous husband's sense of self. We can see that the third party does not have to exist, he may be imagined. When Carrizales realizes that he has no friends and relatives left:

> He wanted to have someone to bequeath his riches to when he died, and with this desire in mind he examined the state of his health and came to the conclusion that he could still bear the burden of matrimony. As soon as this thought occurred to him, it gave him such a fright that it weakened and broke his resolve, like a wind dispelling a mist, because he was by nature the most jealous man in the world, even while he was still unmarried. For at the mere thought of the married state jealous thoughts began to disturb him, suspicions to torment him, and his imagination to alarm him so forcefully and so violently that he categorically gave up all intentions to marry. (L, p. 152)

Extremadura, Carrizales' home, is said to be the place best known in Spanish proverbs for producing jealous people (L, p. 311, n. 152). This might be because of the area's poverty; however, 'jealous thoughts' disturb Carrizales so much that he would rather give up intentions of marriage. Why is Carrizales so jealous? By giving a tautological reason, that a man is jealous because he came from a place where jealous people are produced, Cervantes does not provide the answer. It could mean that jealousy is so 'normal' that there is no need to provide the cause, or, which I think is more likely, Cervantes has the insight that jealousy is so problematic that all he can do is to provide a standard reason for its existence. 'The Jealous Old Man from Extremadura' is thus a *donné*, a 'given' name which is half allegorical, like calling a character 'Jealousy' or 'Old Age', as writers before the seventeenth century would do. But, by also giving reasons for Carrizales' jealousy (instead of accepting it as a given), the text shows something more 'modern'. It is the very thought that Carrizales could 'bear the burden of matrimony' that starts his jealous thoughts. Here 'the burden of matrimony' (L, p. 152) is ambiguous. Apart from the fear of being too old to have a wife (old age challenges his ability to consummate marriage), the ultimate burden of matrimony takes the form of jealous thoughts, which includes suspicions and a fearful imagination. Before Carrizales gets married he is already a jealous 'husband', and the desire for marriage is driven by the wish for having his wealth bequeathed: the wish to pass on his possession precedes the wish of getting married, which precedes the desire for a wife. Carrizales does get married at last, because he 'surrendered the weakness of his old age to the youthfulness of Leonora' (L, p. 152). He argues with himself that,

> This girl is beautiful, and judging by the appearance of this house, she can't be very rich: her tender age calms my suspicions. I must marry her; I will lock her up and mould her according to my desires, and this way she will have precisely the temperament I will teach her to have. (L, p. 152)

Leonora being 'not very rich' becomes one of the main reasons for Carrizales to marry her. He reasons in terms of capitalistic values, that is to say, the reason for marrying a certain girl is calculable; he is not driven by an irresistible desire. He 'buys' her from her parents for 20,000 *ducados* (J, p. 153). Carrizales is already thinking in terms of market value – whether a young girl may be possessed or not, and hence locked up, as part of his property. Here comes the problem: in order to own his wife as an object, Carrizales has to make her love him back. By locking her up, Carrizales dreams of moulding his wife according to his desire. What is involved here are three levels (or ways) of possession. First, to possess the other at a social level (marrying her); second, to possess the other at a physical level (imprisoning her); and finally, to possess the other at a mental level (moulding her). His suspicions will be calmed by her 'tender age': she has not grown up enough to desire what she might desire later. Carrizales' jealousy is temporarily suspended by his convincing himself that he could possess his wife completely, but none of these ways could truly possess a person. So Carrizales' jealousy is the anxiety of not being able to own properly. His jealousy is inseparable from the idea of possession: the 'burden' of marriage is the burden of ownership.

According to Paul Lewis-Smith:

> Carrizales' greatest passion, his jealousy, was clearly rooted in 'self-love' (what Spaniards call *amor propio*) and was the nastier side of deep-seated fear of being dispossessed of property, whose more acceptable side was his diligent care of his money. At the deepest level it was a manifestation of his possessiveness towards himself, of his stubborn will to control his own life. (2005, p. 200)[3]

In French literature, the equivalent idea of *amour propre* [self-love] is associated with the middle of the seventeenth century in such writers as Corneille, La Rochefoucauld and Molière, whose works play with the idea of *amour propre*, such as *Le Misanthrope* (1666). We can compare this with C. B. MacPherson's theory of 'possessive individualism' in *The Political Theory of Possessive Individualism* (1962). The book examines how this concept applies to the creation of property and the private person in the seventeenth century, and how it further contributes to the formation of modern man in the nineteenth century. Concepts such as freedom, rights, obligation and justice, argues MacPherson, are shaped by the assumption (and therefore ideology) that an individual has a 'natural' right to own. He writes:

> [The Individualism's] possessive quality is found in its conception of the individual as essentially the proprietor of his own person or capacities, owing nothing to society for them. The individual was seen neither as a moral whole, nor as part of a larger social whole, but as an owner of himself. The relation of ownership [...] was read back into the nature of the individual. The individual [...] is free inasmuch as he is proprietor of his person and capacities. (1963, p. 3)

The unquestioned assumption is that the individual is the owner of himself. MacPherson argues that the assumptions of possessive individualism and market society (and therefore capitalism) promote, protect and enhance each other. A modern concept like freedom is based on the idea that the individual is an owner of himself. Such a conception dates back to at least the seventeenth century, via the theories of property later developed and modified by Locke, Bentham and John Stuart Mill. If the conception of possession is only an ideological construct, Carrizales is, anticipatively, a representative of a man in the market society, whose 'jealous nature' is ideological, and is made normal. What is more disturbing is that the implication for Locke's theory of property rights (that 'all men are naturally equal in the sense that no one has natural jurisdiction over another' quoted in MacPherson 1963, p. 3) enables the jealous old man to imprison his wife. Perhaps that is why, apart from imprisoning her, Carrizales also wants to educate her according to his wishes, so that his wife could only 'desire' what he wants her to. It shows that ownership is problematic, because even for the rich Carrizales, possession can never be secured. The problem is not to do with the security of the house, but to do with the possibility of possession involved in jealousy. We can differentiate the concepts of ownership and possession. Ownership can be guaranteed by law, whereas possession is a concept much more problematic, which cannot be guaranteed by any form of legal contract. This is the basis of forming a single subject. Derrida draws attention to how this works out in grammatical constructions:

> We will see why that which lets itself be designated *différance* is neither simply active nor simple passive, announcing or rather recalling something like the middle voice, saying an operation that is not an operation, an operation that cannot be conceived either as passion or as the action of a subject on an object, or on the basis of the categories of agent or patient, neither on the basis of nor moving toward any of these *terms*. For the middle voice, a certain nontransitivity, may be what philosophy, at its outset, distributed into an active and a passive voice, thereby constituting itself by means of this repression. (1982c, p. 9)

Philosophy represses the ambiguity of the middle voice, forcing the subject to fall into either the active or passive voice, thus forming a subject who possesses, or is possessed. Philosophy is on the side of possession, it cannot tolerate a state which is neither centred on the 'own' self (as with the idea of 'self-love') nor where the self is possessed by another. Derrida writes, 'philosophy's unique thesis' is to keep 'the opposition of the proper and the nonproper' (1982c, p. 229). In that sense deconstruction is the attack on the proper, on what Derrida calls 'the history and system of the value of "properness"' (1982a, p. 246), which history it tries to write. If what is defined as the proper has a history, then it is produced by culture and is not absolute, or 'natural'. Nothing is inherently proper. Jealousy, which is based on the distinction of self and the other, and property in Carrizales' case, belongs to the history of the creation of 'properness': Derrida quotes Marx on the idea of the proper, propriety and property; obviously this includes *amour propre* (1982c, note 13).

In marriage, ownership of the spouse is guaranteed by law or by religion, but the feeling of possession is not. And the crisis of possession challenges the concept of ownership: a husband feels the crisis, and jealousy is the emotion which reacts to it. God announces himself to be 'a jealous God' in the second of the Ten Commandments, in which the making and worshipping of other carved images are prohibited:

> For thou shalt worship no other god: for the Lord, whose name is Jealous, is a jealous God. (*Ex.* 34:14)

One definition the *OED* offers for jealousy is 'anxiety for the preservation or well-being of something; vigilance in guarding a possession from loss or damage'. The words 'anxiety', 'vigilance' and 'guarding' are important in understanding what *Exodus* means by saying that God is jealous. Carrizales' dream of locking his wife up and moulding her according to his desire could be compared to God's prohibiting the making and worshipping of other gods. They are basically driven by the same anxiety and their symptom is vigilance in guarding one's possessions. Carrizales' jealousy is the same as God's in the sense that they cannot feel the proper ownership of the loved object unless they feel that they are the only one who is being loved. But from the cases of Carrizales and God, we know that ownership is difficult, if not impossible, to get and maintain. So jealousy is to do with 'vigilance' and is sometimes mixed with 'zealousy', (in *OED*, but said to be obsolete) as being 'zealous' usually signifies religious enthusiasm, and means being extreme: The *extremeño* [Extremaduran] in the Spanish title *El celoso extremeño* suggests *extremado* [extreme, extremely]. The jealous Extremaduran is the zealous Extremaduran. There is nothing more extreme than locking the innocent wife up to prevent the husband from feeling jealous. The jealousy of Carrizales is more to do with possession, with zealous (extreme) possession. What is at stake in jealousy is the idea of total possession, or property rights. Husbands are jealous (zealous) because they possess, or they feel the anxiety of losing possession. That is why Carrizales is jealous even while he is still unmarried.

One problem of jealousy is, as mentioned earlier, that it relies on the assumption that a human being is the proprietor of his own person. The word 'possess' already has implications from the realm of madness, because 'possession' means ownership, which is active, but it can be used in a passive sense, as in 'being possessed by a demon or spirit' or in its transferred sense, 'an idea or impulse that holds or affects one strongly; a dominating conviction, prepossession' (*OED*). Both the state of being controlled by a demon, and of being dominated by a certain idea (in other words, being held by an obsession or fascination) evokes a sense of losing control of one's own. Jealousy is a reaction to the fear of losing one's possession (ownership), and jealousy itself might be a kind of 'possession' (madness). The fear induced in jealousy involves the crisis of owning the other and also that of losing control of what is one's own.

Marriage, Sex and the Possessive Husband

Getting married is not enough for Carrizales to feel that he possesses his wife. The 'burden of matrimony' is related to his health (L, p. 152). In a mocking tone the narrator writes, '[Carrizales] began to enjoy the fruits of marriage, at least as well as he could' (L, p. 152).[4] He cannot be a proper husband as defined in the patriarchal system. He fails to 'own' his wife, not to mention to have his wealth bequeathed. The anxiety of not being able to have sex with his wife contributes to his jealousy, which drives him to imprison her, feeling that this is the only way to possess her.

The burden of matrimony for the aging Carrizales is a physical challenge from the patriarchal system, which is a challenge of 'the concern for the proper'. An old husband who marries a young wife is bound to be jealous, because they may not be able to have a sexually fulfilled marriage. Marriage, as a patriarchal and logocentric social construct, formulated in terms of property rights, drives the husband to be jealous.

The wish of keeping the possession, ironically enough, does not necessarily have to do with how much he loves her. In order to keep his possession, he was so jealous that he did not want 'to live with his wife until he had built a separate house for her' (L, p. 153). He would prefer feeling safe to spending a night with her.

The theme of an old man marrying a young wife appeared earlier in Chaucer's *Canterbury Tales*. For example in *The Miller's Tale*:

> This carpenter hadde wedded newe a wyf,
> Which that he lovede moore than his lyf;
> Of eighteteene yeer she was of age.
> Jealous he was, and heeld hire narwe in cage,
> For she was wylde and yong, and he was old
> And demed hymself been lik a cokewold. (*MilT* 3221–6)

The carpenter John is anxious about losing his wife, Alison, because he is old and therefore he keeps her caged, as the jealous old man Carrizales does. The Miller comments that:

> Men sholde wedden after hire estaat,
> For youthe and elde is often at debaat. (*MilT* 3229–30)

This is suggesting it is not 'natural' for an old man to marry a young wife, and the ending of the tale shows no punishment for the wife but only for the men, including the old carpenter. The young wife is left 'innocent' even after she has committed adultery. The Miller's mocking tone of the old carpenter is part of a response to the preceding storyteller's (the Knight) idealism.

The two lovers do not get together after the husband has died: a relationship is a structure of three. The ironic tone on commenting the attitude of the parents seems to suggest that jealousy is to do with wealth: Carrizales (and Leonora's parents) see Leonora in terms of what can be possessed, both financially and sexually. The narrative ends with a commentary made by the narrator, 'I', who appears only at the last paragraph of this 'exemplary' story:

> All I wanted was to get to the end of this affair, a memorable example which illustrates how little one should trust in keys, revolving doors and walls when the will remains free, and how much less one should trust youth and *inexperience* when confronted by the exhortation of these duennas in their black habits and their long, white head-dresses. The only thing that puzzles me is why Leonora did not make more effort to excuse herself and make her jealous husband realize how pure and *innocent* she was in that affair, but she was so confused that she was tongue-tied, and her husband died so soon that she could not find opportunity to explain herself. (J, p. 184, my italics)

The tone here seems moralistic. But perhaps innocence and experience do not form a binary opposite to each other as the narrator seems to think. Blake writes:

> *Unorganiz'd Innocence: An Impossibility.*
> Innocence dwells with Wisdom, but never with Ignorance. (1966, p. 380)[5]

Cervantes' text is commenting on itself, and of course the narrator may be acting as if he does not understand and is inviting the reader to read the text actively: innocence is not before experience, but comes after, as Blake suggests. In the earlier version (1604 or 1606) we have noted that the wife makes love to Loaysa, who dies in a gun accident, and perhaps this also contributes to the ambiguity of the ending of the story. Carrizales' position itself is one that he cannot read: as Lambert asks, 'who is more the cuckold, the man who thinks he has been cuckolded but has not, or the man who thinks he has not been cuckolded but has?' (1980, p.225).

The will rewritten before Carrizales dies instructs Leonora's dowry to be doubled and consents to her marriage with Loaysa. Carrizales sees this as an 'unusual revenge' (L, p. 182). He sees his will as revenge to the offence. It could be seen as the selling of his wife, just as Leonora's parents sell her to Carrizales. Perhaps the only way for Leonora to escape from Carrizales' 'revenge' is not to get married, and that is what she does at the end. To not marry is a way to get out of the patriarchal system which makes people jealous, because jealousy is possible only in a society where the idea of proper identity dominates. Carrizales tries to sell his wife to her lover, dreaming of repeating what he has done before he dies. Leonora ends up 'taking the veil in one of the most enclosed convents in the city' (L, p. 184):

Leonora was left to mourn [Carrizales], a wealthy widow; and when Loaysa hoped to see fulfilled what he knew her husband had ordered in his will, he found instead that within a week she went off to be a nun in one of the most enclosed convents in the city. The young man went off in despair, and indeed in shame, to the Indies. Leonora's parents were desperately sad, although they found consolation in what their son-in-law had left them in his will. (J, p. 180)

However, this surprising gesture seems to suggest that she repeats her state of being imprisoned as she was married; the only difference is that she is 'widowed, tearful, and rich' (L, p. 184). She becomes a proper widow, dutiful to the demands of the patriarchal society on a widow, but this can also be read as a gesture of not obeying Carrizales' 'will' – in every sense of the word. Carrizales' 'enemy' Loaysa, who goes off dishonoured, will return as a jealous old man years later. In this sense it suggests that jealousy works through the structure of patriarchy, which repeats itself, and seems likely to repeat itself in the future of the text.

Paranoia: Architecture and Identity

We can see jealousy as the realization of problems of possession – in this case, in marriage. The first 'outward indication' of Carrizales' jealous disposition is that he does not want any tailor to take his wife's measurements for the wedding dresses, and he solves the problem by hiring a woman with the same figure as his wife (L, p. 153). How does he possess his wife properly, if not by marrying her? What he could do is to prevent her from being seen or touched by the tailor. But why is the tailor afraid? Carrizales' 'jealous thoughts' take the form of 'suspicions and imagination' (L, p. 152) and therefore everyone could be a potential invader, depending on his viewpoint. Carrizales is so jealous that he is paranoid, in the sense summed up by what Hobbes describes as normative in the seventeenth century, 'during the time men live without a common Power to keep them all in awe, they are in that condition which is called Warre; and such a warre, as is of every man, against every man'(1985, p.185). Possessive individualism is the obvious result. But what happens when war is not just economic but in the sphere of gender, which economics has made also a matter of possessive individualism?

Because Carrizales is rich, he is currently under the threat of being 'a target of all the importunities that the poor are wont to impose on the rich man in their midst' in his homeland (L, p. 152). Both jealousy and paranoia take the form of 'extreme' suspicions and imagination, which is a way of perceiving reality. After his choice of a wife, 'the second indication that Felipo gave of his disposition was in not wanting to live with his wife until he had built a separate house for her', writes the narrator:

> He purchased a house for 12,000 *ducados* in a prestigious area of the city, with running water and a garden containing many orange trees. He blocked up all the windows which faced on to the street, replaced them with skylights, and then proceeded to do the same with all the other windows in the house. In the main entrance, which in Seville is called a *casapuerta*, he installed a stable big enough for one mule and on top of it a hay loft and accommodation for the man employed to take care of it, an ageing black eunuch. He raised the walls enclosing the roof terraces in such a way that anyone entering the house had to look directly to heaven because there was nothing else to see, and he linked the main entrance to the patio by means of a turnstile. He bought luxurious furnishings to decorate the house, which in its lavish tapestries, furniture, and canopies declared itself to be the property of a man of means. He also purchased four white slaves whose faces he branded and two other recently imported Negro slaves. He arranged for a caterer to deliver food, on condition that he neither slept in the house nor even set foot inside it except to hand whatever provisions he had brought through the turnstile. [...] He also had a master key made for the whole house, and locking up inside

it everything that it was usual to buy in bulk and in season, he stocked up
with provisions for the entire year. [...] [Leonora's parents] surrendered
her to him with considerable sorrow, because they felt as if they were
delivering her up to her grave. (L, p. 153–4)

The very action of building up something to protect oneself is a reaction to
the anxiety of being harmed or persecuted by the other. It is hard to say
whom the establishment is to protect: Leonora or Carrizales? Leonora is
confined in the highly secured, castle-like house with high walls and no
window. All the windows facing the street are blocked up. The entrance is
arranged so that nothing inside could be seen from the outside. Carrizales
is anxious about preventing the inside of the house to be seen from the
outside. The anxiety is so intense that after he has lived in the separate
house, 'His days he spent thinking, and at night he went without sleep, as
he patrolled and guarded his house like the Argus, of what he held dear'
(L, p. 156). Carrizales wants to look but not to be looked at. The house is
like a convent, a prison or a grave. Leonora is confined within the house's
doubled door, behind which is a garden with running water and orange
trees. This is Nature's plenteousness confined. What Carrizales guards
against are males: 'no man ever got beyond the door to the patio'; all persons
inside are all of the 'feminine gender' (L, p. 156). It is as if saying Carrizales
himself does not belong to the masculine gender, because even:

> the figures represented in the wall hangings which decorated [it] were all
> women, flowers, and woodland scenes. The entire house was redolent of
> chastity, seclusion, and restraint. (L, p. 156)

Building a 'separate house' is to draw a definite line separating Carrizales'
property and the outside world, which is also a function of architecture.
Derrida's deconstruction challenges the binary opposition of inside/outside.
The work of architecture, and, in Derrida's view, philosophy, is to keep
apart what is inside (proper) and outside (improper). (For example, the
title of Derrida's *Margins of Philosophy* in itself refers to the centre/margin
binary opposition.) In *The Architecture of Deconstruction*, applying Derrida's
notion of deconstruction to architecture, Mark Wigley suggests that:

> To exclude something by placing it 'outside' is actually to control it, to
> put it in its place, to enclose it. To exclude is to include. [...] To lock
> something up doesn't involve simply imprisoning it within four walls.
> [...] Each official prohibition marks the presence of a forbidden desire.
> (1993, p. 128)

The building is not only the protection of the jealous husband's possession but also his body (identity). Wigley writes, 'It is not simply that the subject is frightened. Rather, it is the constitution of the subject that is frightening' (ibid., p. 142). Freud says in 'The "Uncanny"' [*Das Unheimliche*],

> [T]his uncanny is in reality nothing new or alien, but something which is familiar and old-established in the mind and which has become alienated from it only through the process of repression. (1990e, pp. 363–4)

There is nothing new or alien for Carrizales, and to include his newly wedded wife Leonora is an act of concealing the fact that there is nothing new and alien. His fear is justified because boundaries between the 'inside' and 'outside' of an organism are always to be questioned, like the existence of the subject.

We should look in detail at the style of the architecture in relationship to the mode of family existing before and after Carrizales' time, taking a comparative example from England. Lawrence Stone, in a study of the changes of family mode in English society from the sixteenth to the early nineteenth century, describes three modes of family in England: The Open Lineage Family, the Restricted Patriarchal Nuclear Family, and The Closed Domesticated Nuclear Family. According to Stone:

> The early sixteenth-century home was neither a castle nor a womb. Lacking firm boundaries, it was open to support, advice, investigation, and interference from outside, from neighbours and from kin; and internal privacy was non-existent. (1977, p. 6)

He compares the Open Lineage Family to a bird's nest, in contrast to a castle or a womb, in which the jealous old man demands to live. This was the family mode before Carrizales' time. But a new mode, the Restricted Patriarchal Nuclear Family, replaced the first and became the dominant family mode around 1530–1640, contemporaneous with the period when Cervantes was writing. In the Restricted Patriarchal Nuclear Family:

> Both state and the church [...] actively reinforced the pre-existent patriarchy within the family, and there are signs that the power of the husband and father over the wife and the children was positively strengthened, making him a legalized petty tyrant within the home. (ibid., p. 7)

This is followed by the Closed Domesticated Nuclear Family, evolving from the late seventeenth century and predominant in the eighteenth.

The building of a house separating the inside and the outside world is a paranoid demand. The paranoiac could feel secure only when he is (never) sure that there is a definite boundary – 'a separate house' (L, p. 152) – between the inside and outside. Carrizales' jealousy is manifested through an old man's feeling of security only when he and his wife are locked up within four walls.

The dream of a jealous man is to draw the boundary between the inside and the outside, which coincides with the task of architecture which, according to Derrida, is also the dream of philosophy, the search for single truth, the concern of the proper. However, Carrizales shows that the very gesture of excluding is including, and for the 'outsider' the very existence of the four thick walls 'marks the presence of a forbidden desire'. For example, if the enclosed garden is the realm of feminine sexuality, it should not be separated from the outside.

The crisis involved in Carrizales' jealousy is a paranoid anxiety of boundaries being invaded – the confusion of limits, and the labour of architecture is to preserve the sense that the inside and outside could be separated. Windows are problematic in relation to the boundary of a building. They threaten the border because firstly they are the necessary openings on the walls (the literal boundaries) of a building which endanger the continuity of the walls, and secondly if the inside could be seen from the outside, what is kept inside is not secured, and windows invite the gaze from the outside. That is why the first order that Carrizales gives to his house is to 'block up all the windows which faced on to the street' (L, p. 153). The act could be a reaction to the realization of the impossibility of maintaining the border. Paradoxically Loaysa's 'urge to know' (L, p. 157) is aroused by the very fact that the windows were sealed.

The border for Carrizales is the border of his property, which is his house. Carrizales can be seen as an allegorical figure of Philip II (1527–98), who built and lived in El Escorial, the 'thrown-up' architecture in Spain as Wigley (2002) would call it, where he himself could be protected and the whole of Spain, metaphorically, overlooked. El Escorial was built after the defeat of France at the Battle of Saint Quentin (10 Aug 1557). It is located in Saint Lorenzo de El Escorial, 45 km northwest of Madrid. El Escorial was not only a palace for the Spanish kings, but also a museum and a library, with many paintings, including, originally, the works of Hieronymus Bosch ('The Garden of Earthly Delights' was appropriated by Philip II in spite of, or because of, his Puritanism). So El Escorial is also the place for keeping the possessions of the Spanish kings, although one motif for building it was to give Phillip II's father a 'worthy tomb'.[6]

Philip II thought in terms of severity and simplicity. Severity evokes a desire of setting up strict boundaries, and thus a demand which puns on 'severance', which means separating, cutting off from the outside. George Kubler points out that El Escorial is the major example of 'plain style' which is known as *estilo desornamentado*, which is common in Italy and Portugal, and was based on ancient Roman models and the writings of Vitruvius (1982, p. 17). He quotes Pevsner:

The Escorial ... is evidently a monument of the purest Mannerism, forbidding from outside and frigid and intricate in its interior decoration. (1982, p. 125)[7]

Arnold Hauser, in *Mannerism* (1965), suggests that El Escorial's severity and simplicity are

nothing but exhibitionist play with Puritanism and asceticism. The building displays its 'introversion' in a shrieking ostentatious manner. Besides being the residence of the most powerful monarch of his time, it includes a church and a monastery, yet in reality it is no more than the hideout of a lonely man withdrawn from the world, and the colossal proportions serve no practical purpose and are nothing but as a sham. Philip II lived in his palace like a monk in his cell; the Escorial combines grandeur with exaggerated simplicity in the same mannerist fashion as he did in his way of life. (1965, p. 283)

Hauser uses rhetoric for the mind ('introversion') to describe architecture. And he associates Philip II's state of mind ('lonely man') with the architectural style ('exaggerated simplicity'), as if saying that Philip II's interest (or obsession) in architecture reflects his state of mind and his 'way of life'.

We can see this architecture as an attempt to constitute identity. Lacan suggests that the child's identity is formed as a result of its identification with its own image seen in a mirror. Before the 'mirror stage' the child feels no sense of identity. If the child could think, his sense of his body would rather be in pieces, rather than as a single whole. In the mirror stage the child is fascinated with its own image and projects the sense of self onto its own body. The child's identity as a single being, possessing his own body, is thus formed:

The *mirror stage* is a drama whose internal thrust is precipitated from insufficiency to anticipation – and which manufactures for the subject, caught up in the lure of spatial identification, the succession of phantansies that extends from a fragmented body-image to a form of its totality that I shall call orthopaedic – and, lastly, to the assumption of the armour of an alienating identity, which will mark with its rigid structure the subject's entire mental development. (1989, p. 5)[8]

Lacan uses the phrase 'armour of an alienating identity' to describe the image of the body, which now seems ideal, yet once was fantasized as in pieces, which implies the anxiety induced in having a sense of a single self. Armour implies the sense of paranoia in keeping the sense of the subject. An alienating identity, which alienates from the child's sense of non-identity before the mirror stage, already implies a sense of the potential madness in thinking that there can be a single subject-state.

Concerning the motivation of the political behaviour of statesmen in the early modern period, Peter Pierson notes in *Philip II of Spain,*

when a man said 'Spain' or 'France' in regard to state policies, he was not thinking in terms of an abstraction, which summed up a congeries of objective interests and potentialities, but rather of the person of the king of Spain or the king of France. (1975, p. 131)

This implies that the state is part of the body of the king. In 'Géricault and "Masculinity"', Norman Bryson analyses the visual representation of soldiers by the artist Théodore Géricault (1791–1824), in the perspective of the cultural construction of masculinity:

The [military] body is no longer leased to the state, it *is* the state; the state emerges as a new kind of biopolitical entity, and by virtue of gender the male body belongs to the state, as state property. (1994, p. 247)

Bryson's idea of the body as the state and as state property is an application of Lacan's idea of the 'armour of an alienating identity'. Lacan compares the psychic structure of the subject with that of architecture:

The formation of the *I* is symbolized in dreams by a fortress, or a stadium – its inner arena and enclosure, surrounded by marshes and rubbish-tips, dividing it into two opposed fields of contest where the subject flounders in quest of the lofty, remote inner castle whose form [...] symbolizes the id in a quite startling way. Similarly, on the plane, we find realized the structures of fortified works, the metaphor of which arises spontaneously, as if issuing from the symptoms themselves, to designate the mechanisms of obsessional neurosis – inversion, isolation, reduplication, cancellation and displacement. (1989, pp. 5–6)

Two things happen: the body is symbolized as armour, and the self (the 'I') is represented as a secured building. Both use the rhetoric of architecture: fortress, stadium, enclosure, and castle. We can understand architecture as the extension of the body, which is imagined as a protective structure of the (inner) self. Architecture is used to protect the possession as well as the owner's body, his identity. The jealous man's anxiety is not just about losing his possession, but also about losing his identity, represented here as the bodily boundary. The house built by Carrizales may be the symbolized form of his psychic structure, a site for setting up a borderline, a paranoid architecture. Identity is to be secured within heavy armour or thick walls. We can take El Escorial as a typical fortress, aiming at protecting the inner castle, and take Carrizales' house and El Escorial as symbolizing the psychic structure of paranoia.

Hauser and Pevsner's comments imply that Philip II feels national paranoia, whereas for Carrizales, it is a jealous paranoia. Philip II began El Escorial in 1558, but major parts were not finished until 1584. Cervantes was born in 1547 and died in 1616. Though there is no question of direct 'influence', it may be possible to read Carrizales' house as part of the same 'structure of feeling' (Raymond Williams' habitual phrase) as that which generated El Escorial. Carrizales' house could be an allegorical representation of the palace. It could be a comment on Spain's national paranoia: an anxiety concerning the nation's purity and presented as the exclusion of the other. For example, the *moriscos* and Jews in Spain were expelled from 1492 onwards, during the end of the sixteenth and the beginning of the seventeenth century. There were more than eighty thousand *moriscos* in Granada relocated in the first forced dispersal in 1571, and in 1609 Philip III forced all *moriscos* to be expulsed from the Iberian peninsula (Pierson 1986, p. 142).

The boundaries of an architectural structure are also kept by doors, which are the potential breakthrough points of the boundaries. Shelley writes in *The Triumph of Life* (1822):

> The other long outlived both woes and wars,
> Throned in new thoughts of men, and still had kept
> The jealous keys of truth's eternal doors. (266–8)

Keys are jealous because they are used to open doors, which may be paranoid in character, as doors are the sanctioned openings of the architecture's boundaries. A key may be a metonym of jealousy. Carrizales' keys are also jealous, not only because he is jealous, but also because they are used to open the doors separating the inside and outside of his house. The jealous keys have to be kept, because he is paranoid, and also because he is possessive and is therefore possessed by the jealous keys. It is symbolic for Carrizales to keep the master key with him at night. Leonora has to 'slip her hand between the mattresses and remove the key' (L, p. 170).

We now move on to Francisco in *El*, as zealous and friendless as is Carrizales. The film is set in Mexico, whose colonial architecture imitates that of Europe, and the architecture in *El* is also a very important motif. Francisco lives in a house designed by his father, built when he returned from Paris in 1900. The house is odd, according to Raúl, who thinks it must be designed by somebody guided by 'sentiment, emotion, instinct, rather than reason'. Gloria's mother also agrees with Raúl, and thinks that Francisco's father was 'original and moody' as opposed to Francisco, who, in Father Velasco's words, is 'so normal and level-minded', and who, as is also agreed by Raúl, 'hasn't changed since we were boys together'. While they are talking, the camera shows the staircases from top to bottom, showing how 'odd' the house is. The staircases are in the middle of the living room, and lead to the upper floor, where Francisco sleeps. They divide the living room, showing a demand for order and partition. However, like the contradiction of the dusky room inside the orderly living room and behind the uniform door, the house is built from an 'odd' idea behind the heavy, stoned and normal façade of his house. And Francisco, when his jealousy is at its most extreme, walks on the staircases in a Z pattern. Architecture also tells lies.[9]

The architecture shows Francisco's megalomaniac psychic structure. The mixture of the chaotic and the orderly: the dusty room in which his servant Pablo tries to find a chair shows how chaotic his psychic structure is. Francisco's psychic structure, his seemingly 'normal' and 'level-minded' being (as commented by Father Velasco) is disturbed from within. His obsession of order is also shown by his demand for making straight, or level, a picture hung over a wall behind his bed. Outside the house is a garden, with trees planted by Francisco's grandfather. The garden is a place that Francisco associates with the sexual, and thus the realm of disorder, as opposed to his 'normal and level-minded' personality. He kisses Gloria, who still is the fiancée of his childhood friend Raúl, in the garden. He also 'judges' Gloria by the fact that she has been seen together with his lawyer in the garden. Also, he desires to put himself in photographs, with the architecture in his home town of Guanajuato as background. The obsession of architecture in *El* suggests the connection of jealousy and paranoia via the character of architecture: that is, to separate the outside from the inside. Architecture is the art of creating boundaries, and the jealous and paranoid man is anxious to keep the boundaries between what is proper and not proper, and thus, of keeping one's own property. Tambling, in *Lost in the American City*, writes that in the nineteenth-century 'architecture sides with *ressentiment*' (2001b, p. 56).[10] Nietzsche discusses *ressentiment* in *Genealogy of Morals*, defining it as bitterness, or 'rancour' towards the other:

> The slave revolt in morals begins by rancour turning creative and giving birth to values [...] Slave ethics [...] begins by saying no to an 'outside,' an 'other,' a non-self. (1956, p. 170)

The 'slave morality' needs an imagined hostile external world to respond to. If architecture sides with *ressentiment*, it carries a sense of a reaction to the outside. Architecture is anxious of keeping boundaries, as the art of rancour, paranoia, jealousy, and perhaps, envy.

Being Old: The Arrest of Death

Being old is a reminder of death, which could also be jealousy of life: life is afraid of the corruption by death. So, the elderly are more jealous, and more paranoid. That could be the case of the jealous old man. Being old is the fear of life being violated by death, which could be a form of adultery.

El celoso extremeño opens, 'Not so long ago a noble-born gentleman set out from somewhere in Extremadura and like a prodigal son, drifted through various parts of Spain, Italy, and Flanders, frittering away both the years and his fortune' (L, p. 150). The parable of the prodigal son, told as one of the stories told by Jesus in Luke 15:11–32, is about the return of a second son who wastes his possessions with wasteful living and returns home to be welcomed by his father. His son was 'dead and is alive again, and was lost and found' (Luke 15:32). But Carrizales does not manage to return home like the prodigal son being welcomed by his father, before his parents die. However it is not surprising he forgives Leonora and Loaysa before he dies, as he becomes the forgiving father in the parable of the prodigal son, while Loaysa, the seemingly Oedipal son in the triangulated relationship, is about to repeat Carrizales' journey to the Indies, now replacing his position as a prodigal son, but this time, being already forgiven by his 'father'.

An old man is jealous of life, because his right of possessing life is violated by death. He is afraid of his time being wasted. Carrizales' decrepitude seems to contribute to his jealousy, in the sense that jealousy is the anxiety about the border, both the border of property and the border of life and death. Jacques Derrida, when discussing Diderot and Seneca on borders with regard to death in his *Aporias*, argues that the concern for death involves 'a rhetoric of borders' (1993, p. 3). The property and the border of 'my life', and the identity of its 'master' would be at stake if we consider the difference between wasting time and giving time. 'To give one's life by sharing it' is something other than 'wasting one's time', writes Derrida:

> Wasting one's time would amount to wasting the only good of which one has the *right* to be avaricious and jealous, the unique and property itself, the unique property that 'one would take pride in guarding jealously.'[11] What is therefore in question is to think the very principle of jealousy as the primitive passion for property and as the concern for the proper, for the proper possibility, in question for everyone, of his existence. (ibid., p. 3)

If I could waste my own time I would have the right to be avaricious and jealous, 'self-jealous' as Blake (p. 770) says. But I am not the owner of myself; I cannot lay claim to 'possessive individualism': The border is in question. The border of what? Of death? It could be the border of the body and the border of the building enclosing the jealous body. It is as if I *could* first be (or not be) jealous of myself, but the fact is that time is not possessed by anybody and therefore to say I am self-jealous is as wrong as to say I am not jealous of myself. In the next chapter we will examine a jealousy which involves a real third party, and relate jealousy to curiosity in another narrative by Cervantes: *El curioso impertinente*.

Chapter Four

Curiosity: *El curioso impertinente*

Carrizales' jealousy in Cervantes' *El celoso extremeño* is the simplest form involving two parties: the jealous subject and the loved object. But the male-male relationships in Dickens' *Our Mutual Friend* discussed in Chapter Two involve relations with a third party as also here. And this chapter brings together another combination: jealousy and curiosity. I will explore the notion of curiosity as a kind of obsession (which might be another madness in addition to paranoia) which is to do with the desire to see, more than the desire to know, with reference to Freud's idea of scopophilia. Through proving jealousy as a reaction to the crisis of (non)-possession, and by tracing the changes in the meaning of curiosity in the history of modernity, I argue that curiosity takes up many different forms, including doubting, the desire to know and the desire to see.

El curioso impertinente is the third interpolated story in Cervantes' *Don Quixote* (Part I, chapters 33–5).[1] This framed story is written on eight sheets of manuscript papers 'in very fair character' (I.32; J, p. 275), or 'written in a very fine hand' (I.32; J, p. 278), kept together with three books in a locked 'little old cloak-bag' (I.32; J, p. 274), left behind at Juan Palomeque's inn. The manuscript is read aloud by a priest to a company including the innkeeper Juan, his wife, their daughter, their maid Maritornes, the barber Master Nicholas, the shepherd Cardenio, Andres (a boy Don Quixote 'helped' in the beginning of *Don Quixote* (I.4)), Dorothea and Sancho Panza, with Don Quixote sleeping next door.

Cardenio the shepherd is the mad 'Ragged Knight' Don Quixote meets again in I.23, who tells his story to Don Quixote and Sancho Panza in I.24, and to the priest in I.27. In Andalusia, Cardenio has been in love with the beautiful Lucinda since childhood, but before they get married he is requested to accompany Duke Ricardo's son, Don Fernando, who becomes a good friend. Don Fernando, although in love with a farmer's daughter, after reading a letter Lucinda writes to Cardenio, woos her for himself. After Cardenio receives Lucinda's letter asking him to stop her parents from marrying her to his friend Don Fernando, he rushes home, only to find out that Lucinda accepts the marriage, and then he goes mad.

Dorothea, who disguises herself as a man, tells her story independently in I.28, after Cardenio tells his. She is the daughter of a farmer in Andalusia. She is looking for a man who wooed her but abandoned her after she accepted the proposal. That man turns out to be Don Fernando. Cardenio and Dorothea's story resumes in I.36, when Don Fernando and Lucinda arrive in disguise at the Inn where the company is listening to *El curioso impertinente*. Don Fernando tells the company that he and his friend kidnapped Lucinda who had run away to a convent from the wedding. He and Dorothea embrace after he declares his love for her. Lucinda declares she is wife to Cardenio.[2]

The idea of the '*dos amigos*', discussed before, is repeated in *El curioso impertinente* and has both comic and tragic dimensions. Indeed, jealousy is the source of comedy (as with the jealous old man), as much as of tragedy. Peter Szondi writes,

> Unlike other passions, jealousy bears within itself the possibility of the tragic. [...] The essence of jealousy lies in the dialectic, which admittedly also allows it to turn into the comical. Jealousy is love that destroys by wanting to preserve. (2002, p. 71)

Szondi's idea about jealousy as dialectical, comic and sad and ruinous together, seems to describe this framed story here. The manuscript is chosen to be read because the priest, who does not take things tragically, says he does 'not dislike the title of this novel' (I.32; J, p. 278) and he reads for the company 'only for curiosity's sake' (I.32; R, p. 214) – reading being an act of curiosity.

To summarize the plot: The friendship of the two bachelors, Anselmo and Lothario, is so famous in Florence that they have come to be called *Los Dos Amigos* [The Two Friends]. Anselmo happens to fall in love with a beautiful lady, Camila, and after he gets consent from his friend, he marries her. Camila is so satisfied with the marriage that she feels she should give thanks to Lothario rather than to heaven because it was he who demanded Camila of her father and concluded the match. In this he compares with Don Fernando, who spoke to Lucinda's father. Lothario begins to come to Anselmo less after the celebration period, because,

> though true and real friendship neither can nor ought to be suspicious in anything, yet so nice is the honour of a married man, that it is thought it may suffer even by a brother, and how much (how) more by a friend? (I.33; J, p. 279)

Anselmo, upon noticing his friend's remissness, 'complain[s] bitterly' (I.33; R, p. 215) and tells Lotharío that he would never have got married if he had known his marriage would 'have the effect of diminishing their friendship' (I.33; R, p. 215). Anselmo 'beg[s]' him to come to his house as he used to, and assuring him that Camila has 'no other wish, no other desire, in any way different from his' (I.33; R, p. 215). But Lothario still tries to avoid going to Anselmo's house even if his friend keeps complaining.

Later, Anselmo tells Lothario that he is so obsessed with the idea that Camila should be seduced by his best friend Lothario to show her virtue, he says,

> I wonder if Camila, my wife, is really as good and perfect as I think she is, because I can't truly believe it unless I find some way to test her which will reveal just how good she actually is, the way we test gold by fire. (I.33; R, p. 217)

Lothario refuses at first and gives long speeches refusing Anselmo's request. Lothario says, 'you'll gain no happiness, no pride, you won't be any richer or more honoured than you are now, and if it goes badly you'll find yourself steeped in the greatest misery imaginable' (I.33; R, p. 219). He then illustrates it by comparing women with diamonds, and reasons that to test the wife is as foolish as to put a diamond between a hammer and anvil, as it will not increase the value of the diamond even if it passes the test. Having said that, Lothario continues:

> Remember, my friend, that women are imperfect creatures, and we ought not to put obstacles in their way, to make them stumble and fall, but rather remove obstacles and clear their paths for them, so that they can proceed without difficulty and achieve the perfection they lack, which consists of being virtuous. (I.33; R, p. 220)

Lothario then compares women with ermines, 'small animal[s] with gleaming white fur'. The trick to hunt the ermines is to smear their usual paths with mud, and then beat the bushes and make a great racket, so that they just stop there when their way is blocked by the dirty mud, because:

> the ermines let themselves be caught rather than walk through slime and thus stain, or even lose, their shining whiteness, which they value more than freedom or life itself. (I.33; R, p. 233)

Lothario argues that beautiful women are as pure as ermines, but the way to preserve their purity is 'quite unlike the ermine' – says Lothario:

The virtuous and modest woman is an ermine, and the virtue of chastity is whiter and cleaner than snow; and he who would not have her lost, but rather guard and preserve it, must take quite a different method from that which is used with the ermine: for he must not lay in her way the mire of courtship and assiduity of importunate lovers, since perhaps, and without a perhaps, she may not have virtue and natural strength enough to enable her, of herself, to trample down and get clear over those impediments; it is necessary, therefore, to remove such things out of her way, and set before her pure and unspotted virtue, and the charms of an unblemished reputation. (I.33; J, p. 319)

Women are then compared to 'a mirror of crystal' (I.33; J, p. 319), a holy relic that should 'be adored, but not handled' (I.33; J, pp. 319–20), and 'a fine garden full of roses and other flowers, the owner of which suffers nobody to walk among them, or touch anything, but only at a distance, and through iron rails, to enjoy its fragrance and beauty' (I.33, J, p. 320) (as in Carrizales' garden). They are also called 'glass' (I.33; J, p. 320) in the verse Lothario composes, because they are beautiful but should be kept away from any danger of being touched. But the second half of the quoted passage creates a possibility of women's lack of 'natural strength' to resist 'the mire of courtship', which subtly agrees with Anselmo's curiosity. Women's 'virtue of chastity is whiter and cleaner than snow', evoking the coldness of a glass body, which also associates with a dead body, as Desdemona's body is described by Othello as being 'as smooth as monumental alabaster' (V.ii.5) (to be discussed in Chapter 5). The rhetorical power of the speech that turns Camila into a dead, clean, untouchable statue may contribute to the possibility of Anselmo's marriage not being consummated. (Not in the way Carrizales fails, nor Othello.) Being turned into glass is the motif of Cervantes' *El licenciado Vidriera* [The Glass Graduate] (1613) (one of his *Novelas ejemplares*), in which a young man has a delusion that he has a glass body. Lothario ends his long speech by quoting the section in which God creates Eve from Adam's rib in Genesis (2:23–4):

when Adam woke and saw her he said: 'For this is flesh of my flesh and bone of my bone.' And God said: 'And for her a man must leave his father and his mother, and they shall be as two in one flesh.' [...] And so it happens that, the wife's flesh being the same as the husband's, anything that stains her, any imperfections for which she strives, fall equally on her husband's flesh, even though, as I've said, he'd done nothing to bring them into being. (I.33; R, p. 222)

Anselmo persuades Lotario by confessing that he has suffered from a woman's disease, as he is 'fleeing from what is good and running toward what is evil', says Anselmo:

> You must realize that what I'm suffering from, now, is the same disease that often afflicts women when they have a longing to eat dirt, or plaster, or charcoal, or still worse things, nauseating even to look at, but worse to swallow. (I.33; R, p. 223)

Anselmo argues that his desire to eat dirt or the like cannot be cured if his wife's virtue is not tested. Lotario agrees to 'put the experiment in practice', in order to 'avoid a greater evil' (I.33; J, p. 291) because Anselmo claims that he will ask other people to do it if Lotario refuses. Anselmo tells Lotario that 'Camila was just as resistant to bribes and pledges as she was to words' (I.33; R, p. 225) but in fact he just sits there without wooing her. Desiring to be an 'eye-witness' to his wife's virtue, Anselmo hides in a wardrobe in order to see how Lotario seduces her. (It echoes in Cardenio's narrative in telling his tale, that rather than intervene, he watches the wedding of Lucinda and Don Fernando in secret, and he 'thrust[s] out [his] head and neck through the partings of the tapestry, and with the utmost attention and distraction of soul, set [himself] to listen to what Lucinda answered' (I.27; R, p. 251) in her and Don Fernando's marriage: he could have stopped the marriage if he wanted to. The tapestry and the wardrobe serve as a '*jalousie* window'.)

After Lotario's lies are discovered (that he has not done anything), he promises to seduce Camila. He begins to woo Camila after he falls in love with her as 'the combination of Camila's beauty and her goodness, and the opportunity which her stupid husband had himself placed in their hands, [steals] away Lotario's loyalty to his friend' (I.33; R, p. 227). Camila sends a letter to her husband complaining about Lotario's wooing but Anselmo tells her to stay. Finally, Lotario '[overthrows] all Camila's reserve, and at last triumph[s] over what he least expected, and most desired' (I.34; J, p. 297).

Lotario sees a man leaving at dawn, and not knowing that it is the lover of Leonela, Camila's maid, believes it to be another lover of Camila. Feeling jealous, and aiming to take revenge, Lotario tells Anselmo that Camila 'is ready to do whatever [he] want[s] her to' (I.34; R, p. 233), and plans to let Anselmo hide in the wardrobe so that he could 'see with [his] own eyes' (I.34; R, p. 234) his pretended seduction. Only when Camila tells Lotario the fellow was Leonela's lover does Lotario know that he was wrong.

But Camila tells him not to worry and do what he planned. The next day, with Anselmo witnessing through a key hole, Camila acts in a way so well that Anselmo is delighted and convinced, as she pretends to kill Lothario with a dagger, and pretends to commit suicide after Lothario's defence. His eye is tricked by the 'drama' within a manuscript, which is itself within a larger literary text, *Don Quixote*. The deceptiveness of seeing makes the text self-reflexive.

They all are happy, with Anselmo the only one being deceived, for several months, until Anselmo discovers a man hiding in Leonela's room. Being threatened with being killed, Leonela promises to tell him a secret the next day but she runs away at night. Without expecting to hear anything concerning his wife, he tells Camila that Leonela will tell him something very important. Terrified, Camila takes all her jewels and money to see Lothario and begs him to go away with her. Instead of doing what Camila desires, Lothario takes her to a convent and leaves Florence. At the end Anselmo dies in another friend's house, and a paper is found in his hands:

> A stubborn, stupid wish has taken my life. Should Camila happen to hear of my death, let her know that I forgive her, because there was no need for her to perform miracles, nor should I have wanted her to, and since I myself fashioned my own dishonour, there's no reason why … (I.35; R, p. 247)

or, to compare Jarvis' translation:

> A foolish and *impertinent* desire has deprived me of life. If the news of my death reaches Camila's ears, let her know I forgive her; for she was not obliged to do miracles, nor was I under a necessity of desiring she should: and, since I was the contriver of my own dishonour, there is no reason why − (I.35; J, p. 321, my emphasis)

The word dishonour (*deshonra*) appears in both translations. Spanish culture was, of course, fascinated with a sense of honour as the dominant quality.[3] Anselmo's paper thus ends unfinished − 'it could be seen that it was at exactly this moment, without being able to finish his explanation, that his life had ended' (I.35; R, p. 247). Camila will not leave the convent, but does not become a nun, although she is now a widow. After hearing that Lothario was killed at the battle of Cerinola, fought in the kingdom of Naples by Monsieur de Lautrec and the great Captain Hernández of Córdoba, she takes the veil and dies soon, out of melancholy. The narrator of *El curioso impertinente* ends the story by commenting 'So this was what happened to each of them, united in their deaths by such a wildly wilful beginning' (I.35; R, p. 247). The curiosity is associated with being 'wilful', a fascination with a self-punishing element. The priest, who reads the story to the company, ends *El curioso impertinente* by commenting that:

> This strikes me as a very good story, but I can't convince myself that it's really true, and if it's invented, then the author has made a serious mistake, because I can't believe there's truly a husband who could be as foolish as Anselmo and want to risk anything that could cost him so much. Had this been told as something that happened between a lover and his lady, I could be persuaded, but between husband and wife it smacks too much of the impossible. But as far as style is concerned, I have nothing to criticize. (I.35; R, p. 247)

The narrative then goes on to Dorothea's story in the next chapter.

The Curious Narrative

There are several translations of the title *El curioso impertinente*:

1. The Novel of the Curious Impertinent (Jarvis)
2. The Tale of Foolish Curiosity (Cohen)
3. The Story of the Man Who Couldn't Keep from Prying (Raffel)
4. The Novel of 'The Man who was Recklessly Curious' (Grossman)
5. The Story of the One who was too Curious for his own Good (Cascardi 1986, p. 244)
6. The Tale of Inappropriate Curiosity (Rutherford)

The narrator foretells 'his impertinent curiosity will cost poor Anselmo his life' (I.34; J, p. 313); the narrative (written on a manuscript read aloud by a priest) ends with the death of Anselmo, so the curious impertinent now is proved to be foolish, the title has done its work, yet this title misses out many aspects in the narrative. For example, it leaves out the fact that Lothario dies in a battle, and it also lacks any account of Camila before her life is taken by 'the rigorous hands of grief and melancholy' (I.36; J, p. 321), and of the affair of Camila's maid, Leonela. In this sense, every title is in a sense inadequate. The narrative *El curioso impertinente* is not self-contained and is invaded by other narratives. The reading is disturbed in the middle (at the beginning of I.35) immediately after Anselmo's death is foretold, by Sancho because Don Quixote has been having a nightmare, in which he is,

according to Sancho, fighting with a giant in order to save the princess
Micomicona (I.35; R, p. 349). Also, the battle Lothario fights in the kingdom of Naples between Monsieur de Lautrec and the Great Captain Gonzalo Hernández of Córdoba was historical. The battle is usually referred to
as that of Cerignola, when France invaded Naples in 1503 (J, p. 955). The
captain appears as a protagonist and in the title of a book called *la Historia del
Gran Capitan Gonzalo Hernández de Córdoba* [The History of the Grand Captain
Gonzalo Hernández of Córdoba], which is found in a cloak-bag together
with two other large books and the manuscript of *El curioso impertinente*
(I.32). *La Historia del Gran Capitan Gonzalo Hernández de Córdoba* is commented
on by the priest as 'a true story', while for *El curioso impertinente* the priest,
we recall, 'cannot persuade [himself] it is a true story: and if it is a fiction,
the author has erred against probability: for it cannot be imagined' (I.35;
J, p. 321). Perhaps it is because *El curioso impertinente* is a text which cannot
be stabilized into a single subject, which involves difference, and provides a
possibility for the appearance of something 'other'. Or perhaps because *The
History of the Grand Captain Gonzalo Hernández of Córdoba* is a printed book, and
thus comparatively more 'proper', whereas *El curioso impertinente* is a manuscript, a handwritten text which has more possibilities of heterogeneity,
since it involves the chance of there being missing letters, misspelling, variation of styles and formats, and therefore, misreading. Anselmo's final paper
stops at the middle and he is unable to give a reason: 'there is no reason
why −' (I.35; J, p. 321), which is a moment suggestive of the appearance of
otherness. Perhaps the priest is not convinced by the story, because he does
not understand the power of curiosity, which is also the power of obsession.
In short, both titles, *El curioso impertinente* and the friends' label of *Los dos
amigos*, lack something which is also in the text in latent form. If a title is
a proper name, the title is always not proper, as a title always misnames
the novel. Even the word *impertinente* means 'irrelevant', which implies the
improper, the excluded, the other.[4]

The heterogeneity of the 'novel' and of the curiosity becomes the source
of horror and the object of curiosity − a word with its meaning just at the
point of changing: from a blameable sense, as with doubting Thomas, to a
natural or good sense in the early seventeenth century. Anselmo could be
a case study of the development of the symptom of modern curiosity.

The Two Amigos

The inadequacy of the story's title points to an alternative title which
appears three times in the story (the first two times appear soon after the

opening (I.33; R, p. 214 and I.33; R, p. 215), the second near the end (I.35; R, p. 246)): *Los dos amigos* which is also the name Anselmo and Lothario acquired.[5] The structure of 'the two friends' is important throughout, as in *Gilda* (Mundson and Farrell).

In contrast, why do neither Francisco in *El* and Carrizales have a friend? (Francisco's servant Pablo, Father Velasco, or Raúl could hardly be his friend, and as for Carrizales, he has 'few friends left' (I.35; J, p. 147) before setting off to the Indies and he 'look[ed] up his friends, found them all dead' (I.35; J, p. 148) after getting rich in his sixties). Perhaps the structure of the 'two friends' involves a homoerotic desire which motivates jealousy in different senses, although this would not apply in Carrizales' case, since his jealousy is more an issue about possession, which reduces the other into an object, and sees that other as enemy, whereas in 'the two friends' cases, relationships are motivated by desire, rather than anxiety. However, *Los dos amigos* as the title framing the text, is also not sufficient, since it misses out the woman who is important to the narrative.

When Lothario is trying to convince Anselmo to give up his desire of testing his wife, Lothario makes the point that husband and wife 'shall be one flesh' by quoting the Holy Scriptures (I.33; J, p. 289). If Anselmo has accepted the notion about the body of husband and wife, his obsession of testing Camila with Lothario might be a desire of looking at himself making love with his friend. If Anselmo's obsession is associated with a repressed homosexual desire, his curiosity is driven more by the desire of sex with his friend Lothario, than to test his wife's virtue. He has no sign of jealousy like the jealous old man from Extremadura. He is rather trying to create jealousy, or to invite jealousy. Girard comments on *El curioso impertinente* in his 'Triangular Desire':

The hero seems to offer the beloved wife freely to the mediator, as a believer would offer a sacrifice to his god. But the believer offers the object in order that the god might enjoy it, whereas the hero of internal mediation offers his sacrifice to the god in order that he might not enjoy it. He pushes the loved woman into the mediator's arms in order to arouse his desire and then triumph over the rival desire. He does not desire *in* his mediator but rather *against* him. The hero only desires the object which will frustrate his mediator. Ultimately all that interests him is a decisive victory over his insolent mediator. (1976, pp. 50–1)

Girard sees the erotic triangle as Anselmo – Lothario – Camila, in which Lothario is the mediator, and Anselmo desires to frustrate Lothario, so that Lothario could have 'a decisive victory over his insolent mediator.'

However, if we reverse the role of the lover and the mediator, Girard's notion of 'triangular desire' might be true as well for the later love of Lothario towards Anselmo's wife, as Anselmo could be his 'rival' in the erotic triangle. Anselmo's fascination for Camila is her being desired by Lothario. His obsession is both the desire to know (whether Camila is faithful or not) as well as the desire to see (Camila to be seduced by Lothario). By marriage, Anselmo is identifying with Camila: in a desire of phantasizing the sexual encounter of him as his own wife with his friend Lothario. But this implies that his fascination is more a desire to phantasize than to know. Here, jealousy takes the form of curiosity and of seeing his wife making love with his friend: Anselmo is not jealous until he does find out that Camila is not faithful. But this is also problematic, for if jealousy is the anxiety of losing the loved Camila, by the time he is jealous he has already lost her.

Hans Blumenberg, in *The Legitimacy of the Modern Age*, examines the legitimacy of the concept of progress as the characteristic of modernity. He points out that the secular knowledge which legitimates curiosity is only a pretext. On 'gossip curiosity', he writes:

> man's supposed 'interest' in other men is directed especially at hidden wickedness, which it seeks to bring to light and publicize through 'gossip.' This gossipy curiosity is directed at the intimate sphere of one's fellow man and penetrates the secrecy [...] of human wickedness. It puts into words, and into the circulation of talk, the unspeakable things that pertain to others, so that, in an extreme comparison, adultery can be described as a sort of curiosity about someone else's carnal pleasure. (1991, p. 298)

Anselmo's desire to test his wife's faithfulness is of the same level. His curiosity could be the desire to know his wife's carnal pleasure, using the disguise of Camila's virtue – 'I wonder if Camila, my wife, is really as good and perfect as I think she is' (I.33; R, p. 217). Anselmo almost forces Lothario to seduce Camila.

Nicolás Wey-Gómez points out that Anselmo's belief in his theory of feminine eating disorder expresses 'his desire to occupy the place of the beloved Camila he wishes both to exalt and to defile, and to perpetrate "unspeakable abominations" with Lothario' (1999, p. 177). Concerning Anselmo's theory about an eating disorder, Armas Wilson argues that

> Anselmo explicitly metaphorizes his disorder as a longing for female longings. Even as twisted signs or signifiers, Anselmo's cravings for what he

believes to be female fare are a part of the curious dynamic of his sex/
gender relationships: Anselmo's desires to test, taste, and even swallow
the other (Camila) can be fulfilled only through 'the instrument' of the
same (Lothario). (1987, p. 21)

She sees Anselmo's desire to test his wife as motivated by a repressed desire
towards the 'same'. As a tool for facilitating the communication 'between
men', Camila acts as the third party. Sexual difference becomes crucial.

Eating dirt evokes a sense of disgust, which is the subject of Julia Kristeva,
whose *Powers of Horror* (1982) argues that in 'abjection' the subject's bodily
boundary is called into question, and that the subject has the fear of
being contaminated when is confounded with the 'disgusting' thing. The
bodily boundary is confused by the abject object, and the abject state.
She mentions food loathing:

> Food loathing is perhaps the most elementary and most archaic form of
> abjection. When the eyes see or the lips touch that skin on the surface
> of milk – harmless, thin as a sheet of cigarette paper, pitiful as a nail
> paring – I experience a gagging sensation and, still farther down,
> spasms in the stomach, the belly; and all the organs shrivel up the body,
> provoke tears and bile, increase heartbeat, cause forehead and hands to
> perspire. Along with sight-clouding dizziness, *nausea* makes me balk at
> that milk cream, separates me from the mother and father who proffer it.
> [...] But since the food is not an 'other' for 'me,' who am only in their
> desire, I expel *myself*, I spit *myself* out, I abject *myself* within the same
> motion through which 'I' claim to establish *myself*. (1982, pp. 2–3)

The abjection of the self is the moment when the subject realizes that the skin
as a bodily boundary of 'myself' is problematic. The abject puts the self:

> On the edge of non-existence and hallucination, of a reality that, if I
> acknowledge it, annihilates me. (ibid., p. 2)

What are the 'powers of horror'?

> For abjection, when all is said and done, is the other facet of religious,
> moral, and ideological codes on which rest the sleep of individuals and
> the breathing spells of societies. Such codes are abjection's purification
> and repression. But the return of their repressed make up our 'apoca-
> lypse', and that is why we cannot escape the dramatic convulsions of reli-
> gious crises. (ibid., p. 209)

The 'powers of horror' are those which unveil (the 'apocalypse' means 'the unveiling') the fact that there is something unclassifiable, something escaping any binary order, namely the way in which we codify the world. The subject/object distinction is formed by the suppression of that which cannot be classified. Kristeva uses 'abjection' to describe the state of disgust and melancholy when a person is facing that which endangers or threatens his bodily boundary. She also talks of the corpse as the ultimate source of abjection:

> There, I am at the border of my condition as a living being. My body extricates itself, as being alive, from that border. (ibid., p. 3)

The dead body threatens the idea of the boundary between life and death, subject and object, inside and outside, the owner and the owned. Kristeva thinks of the 'abjection of the self' (ibid., p. 5) as the moment of such realization, to realize that one's bodily boundary is not that definite. This is also the moment of the crisis in architecture, philosophy, and in any nation state where the ruler is anxious about the nation's purity. The horror is that to discover that what is alien is in fact part of him.[6] Anselmo's 'eating disorder' can be a sign of the abject – the anxiety of identity. Curiosity is ambivalent, an attraction to what is called disgust. It is a desire for the apocalypse, for the powers of horror.

The History of Curiosity

The *OED* defines curiosity in two opposite senses: as blameable and as good (or neutral). Curiosity, in the blameable sense, means 'the disposition to inquire too minutely into anything; the undue or inquisitive desire to know or learn', which dates back to 1380. This sole blameable sense of 'curiosity' continues until the beginning of the seventeenth century, when it began to possess a good or neutral signification: 'the desire or inclination to know or learn about anything, especially what is novel or strange; a feeling of interest leading one to inquire about anything'. For example, the *OED* quotes James Hayward's translation of Cavalier Giovanni Francesco Biondi's *Eromena, or Love and Revenge* (1632), 'A noble and solid curiosity of knowing things in their beginnings'. To know things in their beginnings is the desire of finding the 'origin', perhaps out of a belief in a linear time. The *OED* also quotes Sir Thomas Herbert's *Relation of Some Yeares Travaile* (1638), 'In curiosity I put some of the wood into my mouth and chewed it.' Although these examples are supposed to show the good sense that curiosity began to signify, they could be taken in a blameable sense. The very title, *Eromena, or*

Love and Revenge, is already in the realm of 'blameable' curiosity: to taste something uneatable (wood) out of curiosity echoes the disgust in Anselmo's eating disorder.

Near the end of the sixteenth century and the beginning of the seventeenth century, curiosity started having a positive sense. The blameable sense of curiosity fits the negative emotions discussed so far: paranoia, jealousy and envy. The *OED* cites Thomas Brooks's *Golden Key* (1675), 'Curiosity is the spiritual adultery of the soul. Curiosity is spiritual drunkenness.' The desire to know is as transgressive as committing adultery. In Anselmo's case, ironically enough, curiosity is not only the 'spiritual adultery of the soul', but also the direct cause of his wife's adultery.

'Curioso' means 'in the seventeenth [century], usually one who is curious in matters of science and art', and 'later, an admirer or collector of curiosities; a connoisseur, virtuoso' (*OED*), which makes good sense. Anselmo's curiosity echoes Brooks' negative sense of curiosity. Barbara M. Benedict, in *Curiosity*, argues that:

> Lothario equates Anselmo's 'domestic jealousy' with an enveloping attitude of resistance to authority – specifically with the distrust of religious and social authorities, notably the arguments of speculative or metaphysical thinkers. [...] Curious men [...] demand a private showing of eternal truths. Their intellectual passion is at once arrogant and irrational. (2001, p. 124)

If jealousy in the form of paranoia was a symptom of believing in possession, then curiosity, the will to knowledge, would be another symptom. Donald R. Howard, in *The Three Temptations* (1966), points out that the three temptations for medieval men are the lust of the flesh, the lust of the eyes and the pride of life. Howard highlights what St Augustine says on the three temptations in *Confessions* as follows: 'Lust of the flesh comprizes gluttony, greed, self-indulgence, drunkenness, sexual pleasure, the love of shapes, colours, art objects, clothes, or vessels (X.xxx–xxxix), in Augustine's words, "the lust inheres in the delight given by all pleasures of the senses" (X.xxxv). The phrase "the lust of the eyes" is quoted from the Bible (John 2:16), and is the will to know. The third one, pride of life, is "envy and the pursuit of riches, vainglory, praise, and honour" (X.xxxvi–xxxx)' (1966, p. 46). Lust of the eyes, according to Howard's reading, includes a part of the lust of the flesh, since 'Seeing is the property of our eyes', argues St Augustine:

> 'But we also use this word in other senses, when we apply the power of vision to knowledge generally. We do not say 'Hear how that flashes,'

or 'Smell how bright that is,' or 'Taste how that shines' or 'Touch how that gleams.' Of all these things we say 'see.' But we say not only 'See how that light shines,' which not only the eyes can perceive but also 'See how that sounds, see what smells, see what tastes, see how hard that is. So the general experience of the senses is the lust [...] of the eyes, because seeing is a function in which eyes hold the first place but other senses claim the word for themselves by analogy when they are exploring any department of knowledge. (*Confessions* X.xxxv)

For St Augustine the lust of the eyes is almost equal to the lust for knowledge. He almost arrives at the conclusion of what Martin Jay argues, that modern western culture is dominated by what he calls 'ocularcentric' culture (1994). Howard (1966, p. 46) quotes Augustine's *Fathers of the Church*, 'From this craving, comes the tendency to examine closely the hidden things of nature outside of us, although knowledge of them is of no value, men crave for nothing but to know them.' To know the hidden things of nature outside is a temptation to the eyes.

One aspect of curiosity is the desire to know, which relates to understanding: the expression 'I see' means 'I understand.' Also, the 'bystander' and 'onlooker' also evoke a sense of seeing and looking or even voyeurism.

Lothario goes in agreement with Chaucer and Thomas Brooks, because when he tries to convince (or condemn) Anselmo due to his desire to test Camila's virtue, he starts by comparing Anselmo's curiosity to the Moors' insistence to believe only in things that can be seen:

you are at this time in the same disposition that the Moors are always in, whom you cannot convince of the error of their sect, by citations from Holy Scripture, nor by arguments drawn from reason, or founded upon articles of faith [...]. And, when they do not comprehend this in words, [...] you must show it to them with your hands, and set it before their very eyes. (I.33; J, p. 284)

Lothario is insightful because he foresees that Anselmo's desire to know can only be satisfied when the lust of his eye is satisfied. If we understand curiosity as the lust of the eye, curiosity would be the desire to satisfy the eye, even more than the desire to know, to understand.

Perhaps the first case in human history concerning 'impertinent curiosity' (I.34; R, p. 348) is described in Genesis where Eve has to test on the cost of her life whether or not she will die if she eats the forbidden fruit. Benedict (2001, p. 123) claims that 'jealous curiosity' brings death (or the fall, in biblical terms) to both man and love. Why does Eve eat the forbidden fruit? Because of deadly curiosity (the desire to know whether one will die or not if one eats it)? Because of hunger (the tree is good for food)? Because of gluttony? Or because of the desire for wisdom: one's eye will be opened, and after 'like God, knowing good and evil' (Gen. 3:5). Howard comments that the fruit suggests 'gluttony', the lust of the flesh; 'vainglory', the lust to be like god, the pride of life; and 'curiosity', the lust of the eyes (1996, p. 54). He notices that the order of these three sins are not consistent in the Bible, when he compares Christ's temptations as narrated in John, Matthew, and Luke. He admits that these temptations are 'tangible' (ibid.), and concludes that:

> The lust of the flesh was the clearest: it was gluttony or fleshly desire, and sometimes fornication, lechery, and pleasure. Its objects were food and drink, sexual pleasure, excessive sleep, and other fleshly indulgences. The lust of the eyes was avarice or curiosity but, not always distinguished from pride of life, was also called vainglory or boasting. Its objects were money, gold, silver, gems, and other worldly attractions such as honour, high position, glory, and rich garments – Augustine mentions spectacles, theatres, sacraments of the devil, magic arts, and misdeeds in general as the objects of curiosity, and Bede adds seeking out and carping on the vices of neighbors. The pride of life, not everywhere distinct from the concupiscence of the eyes, was called worldly ambition, pride, or vainglory, and occasionally boasting. The objects of this *superbia vitae* were kingdoms, power, worldly honor, and dignity, but it was also associated with riches, human praise, large households, pomp, false doctrines, and knowledge. (ibid., p. 54)

The lust of the eyes could be any of these temptations. It could be avarice. It could also be curiosity, whose objects could be spectacles, theatres, sacraments of the devil, and magic arts. The objects for the lust of the eyes and for the lust of the flesh could also be those of the pride of life. In short, curiosity is always associated with the eyes, which are in turn related to knowledge. So the curious impertinent is the one who is desirous of seeing or knowing. But to see what?

I will take an example from the Prologue to Chaucer's *The Miller's Tale* as an example to illustrate the relationship between seeing, knowing and curiosity. The Miller comments:

> An housbonde shal nat been inquisityf
> Of Goddes pryvetee, nor of his wyf.

> So he may fynde Goddes foyson there,
> Of the remenant nedeth nat enquere. (*MilP* 3163–6)

This condemns curiosity: a husband 'shal nat been inquisityf' and it equates
God's 'secret' ('Goddes pryvetee', the 'mysteries of providence' (1996,
p. 284, n. 3164)) with the wife's, which puns on the lovers' pryvetee, or the
wife's fidelity. It evokes the sense of curiosity as blameable. The word 'pryvetee' puns on several things: God's secrets (religious), the wife's secrets
(private); the lovers' privacy, privy parts and fidelity. 'God's secret' could
even be read as God's private parts (1996, p. 284, n. 3164).[7] So, the husband
should not become too inquisitive about his wife's secrets, provided that she
gives him all he wants: it is better not to question what else happens to the
wife's private parts. The other possible meaning is that the God-given joys of
life should be welcome, rather than spoiling life by being curious. Curiosity,
and being jealous at old age are both mocked. Like Carrizales, John is jealous, old and possessive. He marries the young and attractive Alison, who is
seduced by the scholar Nicholas. The carpenter is portrayed as a supersti-
tious person who is 'inquisityf' and is punished.

But to compare 'Goddes pryvetee' with 'his wyf's [pryvetee]' is to make
God feminine, as Madame Edwarda associates her private parts with God in
Bataille's novella, *Madame Edwarda* (written 1941, published 1956):

> [Madame Edwarda] was seated, she held one leg stuck up in the air, to
> open her crack yet wider she used fingers to draw the folds of skin apart.
> And so Madame Edwarda's 'old rag and ruin' loured at me, hairy and
> pink, just as full of life as some loathsome squid. 'Why,' I stammered in a
> subdued tone, 'why are you doing that?' 'You can see for yourself,' she
> said, 'I am GOD.' (1995, p. 150)

Madame Edwarda's genitalia are described as 'full of life'. God, woman's
private parts, and life's enjoyments are brought together. In Caravaggio's
(1571–1610) painting *The Incredulity of St Thomas* (1601–02) (or *Doubting
Thomas*) St Thomas' curiosity is associated with doubt, which is the absence
of faith. After Jesus' crucifixion, Thomas declares that 'Except I shall see in
his hands the print of the nails, and put my finger into the print of the nails,
and thrust my hand into his side, I will not believe' (*John* 20:25), namely
that Jesus came back to life. Jesus 'Then saith he to Thomas, Reach hither
thy finger, and behold my hands; and reach hither thy hand, and put it into
my side: and be not faithless, but believing' (*John* 20:27).[8] *Doubting Thomas*
portrays the imaginary moment when St Thomas puts the finger into Jesus'
wound (which he never did in *John*): on the left stands Jesus in white clothes,

half naked, and on the right Thomas appears in the foreground, stooping, his right hand is guided by Jesus' right hand, 'thrusting' into his body. There are two disciples standing on the right behind Thomas, also looking attentively, or curiously, at Jesus' wound. Caravaggio's version of Doubting Thomas transgresses what is portrayed in Bible, whereas in the instance of *Madame Edwarda*, Bataille is quoting from Caravaggio's picture, and suggests a further transgression: putting the finger into Jesus' body is an erotic act (perhaps homoerotic), while the act in Madame Edwarda is feminine, autoerotic. Both works deal with 'the abject' and disgust, working as transgression of the abject. Curiosity is the fascination with disgust, not with 'clean' or ideal knowledge. Interestingly, Thomas' demand of 'thrusting' his hands into Jesus' wound makes Jesus feminine (passive, subject to examination, being penetrated). Nietzsche makes the gender of truth feminine in *The Gay Science*:

> One should have more respect for the bashfulness with which nature has hidden behind riddles and iridescent uncertainties. Perhaps truth is a woman who has reasons for not letting us see her reasons? Perhaps her name is – to speak Greek – *Baubô*? (1974, p. 38)

So if truth is a woman and her name is Baubô, a primitive and obscene female demon, then God, truth, and life's enjoyment are feminine.[9]

Like Carrizales, John may not be able to consummate his marriage. Whittock writes:

> The carpenter's jealousy springs not from suspicions founded on Alison's character but from envy of her youth and obsession with his own age: the expression '*lik* a cokewold' [*MilT* 3226] suggests not that he thought she had betrayed him but that he is being cheated of something she can enjoy. (1968, p. 80)

John is envious of his wife's youth and is obsessed with his old age. Curiosity is on the opposite side of enjoying (or letting the young wife enjoy) the joys of life, God's secret. In *The Miller's Prologue*:

> An housbonde shal nat been inquisityf
> Of Goddes pryvetee, nor of his wyf. (*MilP* 3163–4)

is echoed in *The Miller's Tale*:

> Men sholde not knowe of Goddes pryvetee. (*MilT* 3454)

The Miller condemns curiosity and jealousy at the same time by saying two things at once: one should not be suspicious of 'Goddes pryvetee', which means: one should neither be suspicious (as some questions could not be answered) nor be jealous (as the God-given joy of life should not be wasted).

To return to Augustine: his examples of the object of curiosity include spectacles, theatres, sacraments of the devil and the magic arts. These are all in the realm of Lacan's notion of the 'evil eye' as discussed in *The Four Fundamental Concepts of Psychoanalysis*, 'there is no trace anywhere of a good eye, of an eye that blesses' (1998b, p. 116). The eye is always conceptualized as evil. He then quotes Augustine's *Confessions* – Augustine as a child who is envious of his younger brother at his mother's breast. Differences between jealousy and envy will be dealt with in the next chapter, in which envy is defined as 'a longing for the advantages enjoyed by another person' (*OED*). Earlier, we saw that Ayala Malach Pines argues that envy involves two people, whereas jealousy includes three. Lionel Kreeger has a similar view, except that envy also involves a destructive impulse and jealousy not.[10] Lacan adds that:

> everyone knows that envy is usually aroused by the possession of goods which would be of no use to the person who is envious of them. (1998b, p. 116)

So the evil eye which has the power of drying the milk is also a fascinating eye. The gaze of the jealous/envious Augustine is bitter and evil, possessing the power of destroying the good breast, of drying up the milk, although he no longer needs it. Lacan argues that the true character of the organ of the eye is to be filled with voracity, the evil eye, which fits the meanings the *OED* offers for envy: 'Malignant or hostile feeling', or the 'active evil, harm, mischief'. Augustine's case is an exemplary *invidia*, the Latin for envy, which comes from *videre*, 'to look'. So the lust of the eyes could also be the temptation of destroying.

The evil eye is no less a negative view of the gaze than Freud's notion of the scopophilic instincts, or voyeurism (the desire to look). Freud argues that the desire to look (i.e. voyeuristic desire) and the desire to know (i.e. curiosity) are closely related. The desire to look could be disguised in the desire to know. He argues, in 'Three Essays on the Theory of Sexuality' (1905) that 'the instinct for knowledge in children is attracted [...] to sexual problems and is in fact first aroused by them' and that the instinct for knowledge makes use of the energy of scopophilia (1991f, p. 113). Scopophilia, voyeuristic desire, is driven by the source of energy which precedes the instinct for knowledge. So curiosity could be said to be the token of satisfying the energy of scopophilia. The scopophilic drive for the curious

Anselmo is so great that he desires to watch his wife's sexual encounter with Lothario at the cost of losing his wife. He has to turn himself into a voyeur before he can be jealous. He is in this way the direct opposite to the jealous old man Carrizales, who is jealous before he gets married. Anselmo is jealous after his curiosity is satisfied, at the same time he discovers his wife has already gone.

On seeing, Heidegger takes up a similar view, though he does not openly link the desire to see to the sexual. He writes:

> When curiosity has become free, however, it concerns itself with seeing, not in order to understand what is seen [...] but *just* in order to see. It seeks novelty only in order to leap from it anew to another novelty. (1982, p. 216)

So seeing is for seeing's sake. He continues:

> Therefore curiosity is characterized by a specific way of *not tarrying* alongside what is closest. Consequently it does not seek the leisure of tarrying observantly, but rather seeks restlessness and excitement of continual novelty and changing encounters. In not tarrying, curiosity is concerned with the constant possibility of *distraction*. (ibid., p. 216)

What curiosity concerns, for Heidegger, is neither to understand nor to satisfy the desire to see, but 'the constant possibility of *distraction*', the desire to get the self to be distracted.

Chapter Five

Envy: *Othello*

In previous chapters we have examined paranoia and curiosity as qualities which are related to possession, and are part of jealousy. We have also dealt with the idea that the desire for knowledge is a disguise of curiosity, which always works in the sphere of sexuality and may be a form of voyeurism. This chapter starts with how identity is structured in a patriarchal society like seventeenth-century Venice: the subject is Othello's jealousy. We will differentiate between jealousy and envy, as embodied by Iago. (It should be noted that there are altogether 21 references to 'jealous' or 'jealousy' in *Othello*, while there is no single reference to envy.) Moving from discussion of obsession with the ocular, this chapter finishes with an attempt at exploring how language creates the jealous subject. The chapter concludes with examining how male jealousy acts as a substitute for the absence of identity, whose existence can only be in the fetishized form of the lost handkerchief.

Whether the play should be called *Iago* instead of *Othello* is an issue which rises out of the work of A.C. Bradley. For example, the psychoanalyst André Green writes, 'Othello and Iago are two sides of a single character' (1979, p. 119). But Wilson Knight writes that, 'we see the Iago-spirit gnawing at the root of all the Othello values, the Othello beauties; he eats into the core and heart of this romantic world, worms his way into its solidity, rotting it, poisoning it' (1978, p. 119). He sees Iago as a figure of 'pure cynicism', who is opposed to Othello's sentimentalism. Iago is undefined, devisualized, inhuman, colourless, and ugly (ibid., p. 119). In this way Knight plays down the role of Iago.[1] Bradley in *Shakespearean Tragedy*[2] (1904) had argued most famously that Iago is the central figure who is responsible for Othello's jealousy. He writes, 'the tragedy of Othello is in a sense [Iago's] tragedy too' (ibid., p. 218), and he says that:

> Iago has been represented as an incarnation of envy, as a man who, being determined to get on in the world, regards everyone else with enmity as his rival. (ibid., p. 232)

F. R. Leavis, in 'Diabolic Intellect and the Noble Hero: or The Sentimentalist's Othello' (1972), argued against Bradley, asserting that:

Iago's power [. . .] in the temptation-scene is that he represents something that is in Othello. (ibid., pp. 140–1)

Whereas Bradley argues that Othello's jealousy is imposed by Iago and is conventional in kind, mere convention, Leavis implies that Othello would be jealous even if there was no Iago, so the play should indeed be called *Othello*.

If we follow Bradley that Iago is a figure of envy, it might be useful to start with the differentiation that Othello is jealous and Iago envious: Othello is in the position of possessing, whereas Iago of wanting. André Green points out that Iago is speaking the language of envy, and his language is also the language of megalomania. Envy and megalomania seem contradictory to each other, except that both are a reaction to an anxiety about the completeness and homogeneity of the self, which is also the case in jealousy. In this sense jealousy and envy would both be symptoms of a crisis in masculinity.[3] If we take Leavis' points, that there is something in Othello which characterizes him as a jealous figure, it is worth starting with his foreignness.

Jealousy and Violence on the Body

Carrizales in Cervantes' *El celoso extremeño* is a direct contrast to Othello, in being the jealous old man from Extremadura. He goes back where he belongs. As the Moor of Venice, Othello is an outsider, a split subject. Ferial J. Ghazoul, in 'The Arabization of Othello', an article discussing the translation of *Othello* and its criticism in the Arab world, points out that Othello:

is the product of an acculturation involving a double circulation of the Other and a complex intertwining that combines the effect of an African/Arab (i.e. Othello and his background) on European imagination. (1998, p. 1)

Venice was a world capital in the early seventeenth century. The 'Moor of Venice' is the combination of contradictions:

1. In racial terms, because Othello is a black man in a white-dominant country.
2. In political terms, because Othello is an outsider (the Moor) fighting against another outsider (the Turks) in relation to Venice (the European).
3. In religious terms, Othello belongs to Christianity, the dominant religion in Venice.

The first reason that comes to Othello's mind when he reflects on the possible reasons for his wife's potential infidelity is his race, his skin colour (i.e. his otherness) – 'Haply for I am black' (III.iii.266). Julia Reinhard Lupton, however, argues in '*Othello* Circumcised' that 'in *Othello* religious difference is more powerfully felt than racial difference' (1997, p. 74), which is a minority view, in relation to current debates about Othello and race. For example, Michael Neill emphasizes the racial importance of Othello's blackness, 'Capitalizing on the ancient prejudices associating blackness with evil and death, Iago sets out to demonstrate that the tokens of malign otherness inscribed on the Moor's "visage" correspond to the inward exposed by his anatomical method' (1997, p. 145). But that Othello is a split subject driven by the state (Venice) is dramatized in his speech before his suicide:

> Soft you, a word or two before you go.
> I have done the state some service, and they know't:
> No more of that. I pray you, in your letters,
> When you shall these unlucky deeds relate,
> Speak of me as I am. Nothing extrenuate,
> Nor set down aught in malice. Then must you speak
> Of one that loved not wisely, but too well;
> Of one not easily jealous, but, being wrought,
> Perplexed in the extreme; of one whose hand,
> Like the base Indian, threw a pearl away
> Richer than all his tribe; of one whose subdued eyes,
> Albeit unused to the melting mood,
> Drops tears as fast as the Arabian trees
> Their medicinable gum. Set you down this,
> And say besides that in Aleppo once,
> Where a malignant and a turbaned Turk
> Beat a Venetian and traduced the state,
> I took by th' throat the circumcised dog
> And smote him – thus!

(V.ii.337–55)

We should note about this that the desire to narrate ('to relate') and to comment are central in the play. The play opens with a reference to telling:

> Tush, never tell me, I take it much unkindly.

(I.i.1)

which stresses the importance of story-telling. Iago achieves his 'revenge' by making up stories, or by telling lies. The play ends with the noble Venetian Lodovico saying:

> Myself will straight aboard, and to the state
> This heavy act with heavy heart relate.
>
> (V.ii.368–9)

The very last word of the play is 'relate'. Stephen Greenblatt, in *Renaissance Self-fashioning* (1980), argues, 'at the heart of this tale [he means *Othello*] is the telling of tales' (p. 237). He pinpoints the nature of putting oneself into narrative (such as how Othello wins his wife, how Iago takes revenge or how Desdemona leaves her father) as characteristically improvisatory:

> Iago knows that an identity that has been fashioned as a story can be refashioned, inscribed anew in a different narrative: it is the fate of stories to be consumed [. . .] or interpreted. (ibid., p. 238)

Othello demands that his story is told 'as I am' (V.ii.340). Leavis argues, inspired by T. S. Eliot's essay 'Shakespeare and the Stoicism of Seneca' (1951), that Othello 'does tend to sentimentalise' (1972, p. 151).[4] He is 'the stoic-captain whose few words know their full sufficiency', but soon 'the emotion works itself up' (ibid.). So, Othello's last speech is a demand for self-justification, a confession, in the sense that his speech is trying to evoke emotion and identification, but is not necessarily objective. He does tell his life once:

> Then must you speak
> Of one that lived not wisely, but too well;
> Of one not easily jealous, but, being wrought,
> Perplexed in the extreme.
>
> (V.ii.344)

But the 'confession' Othello makes creates himself as the subject of the patriarchal ideology of Venice. Jeremy Tambling (1990a), quoting Green – 'Othello seek(s) confession rather than truth' (1979, p. 198) – argues that what Othello wants, when he calls out for 'confession' (IV.i.36) is for subjection to himself; to confess to someone puts you in the position where you have to crawl to them. Othello wants the full display of a narrative of confession which will put the confessant into a weak position, but which will also humiliate him, destroy his identity, because of the content of the confession, which will affect his own estimate of himself.[5] Hence Othello's own confession is all the more devastating, even castrating. Killing himself, Othello desires an Oedipal acceptance by the state as a patriarchal power. So he must insert himself in the narrative as the despised other:

> . . . in Aleppo once,
>
> Where a malignant and a turbaned Turk
> Beat a Venetian and traduced the state,
> I took by th' throat the circumcised dog
> And smote him – thus.

(V.ii.351–4)

As a general in the Venetian army, he had a duty to kill the Turk, who was not his personal enemy but Venice's. The state creates the structure of inclusion and exclusion, which is the very basis of jealousy. And yet he has to turn himself from being the Moor of Venice (the Christian), to a Turk in order to kill himself. He is caught between Venice (the Christian nation which invents him) and the Turk (the pagan other of Venice). He is the punisher and the punished at the same time. The image of the 'circumcised dog' is heavily loaded with symbolism, because Muslims (and Jews) practise circumcision whereas Christians do not. On circumcision, Freud writes:

> those who do not practise [circumcision] look on it as very strange and are a little horrified by it, but those who have adopted circumcision are proud of it. They feel exalted by it, ennobled, as it were, and look down with contempt on the others, whom they regard as unclean. Even to this day a Turk will abuse a Christian as an 'uncircumcised dog'. (1985, p. 268)

Freud is punning on Othello's speech here. By referring to a 'circumcised dog' Othello speaks the language of the Venetian. But he is doubly marginalized and whichever side he takes is doomed to be an alienated position: after affirming his hatred of the circumcised dog, he then identifies with it/him by killing himself as though he was the Christian Iago killing the Turk. For Lupton, suicide is 'a cut that (re)circumcises Othello' (1997, p. 84). His words make him Venetian, and his action, in stabbing, is a quasi-circumcision which makes him pagan. This act of conformity to the Venetian state shows the 'reconversion of the Moor to Christianity'(ibid., p. 84). Othello's suicide, argues Lupton:

> functions as a martyrological baptism in blood, an act that completes and terminates the era of the law. [. . . The suicide] effects a circumcision according to the Judeo-Islamic rather than the Pauline-internal paradigm, constituting a self-validating signature that separates out Islam as a historico-theological position distinct from paganism, a regime defined by the singular imprint of circumcision as the persistent 'seal and symbol' of the law. (ibid., p. 84)

Only suicide allows Othello to be acceptable to the patriarchal Venice; it is more than just revenge on himself for having killed Desdemona, but an outworking of what it means to have been the split subject: both the Moor and the Venetian.

Jealousy, as self-protection, in this sense, is the fear of not being able to keep oneself together as a single subject. 'With this ritual gesture', that is to say, committing suicide by stabbing himself, Lupton continues:

> Othello signs his final autobiography, exacerbating and inflaming as much as redeeming that ancient scar in the Pauline discourse of nations. (1997, p. 84)

And in concluding his autobiography, Othello has turned to make himself the obedient subject of the Venetian patriarchy. Patriarchal ideology creates jealousy (and conceals itself as a structure of jealousy in its nontolerance of the other), and is monotheistic, believing in one and only one god, who is jealous in nature (discussed in Chapter 3). Yet the text shows that the world of the 'circumcised dog' and the Christian are not dissimilar: Iago is referred to by Lodovico as a 'Spartan dog' (V.ii.360), as if showing an equivalence between the two.

The means that Othello thinks of for killing Desdemona are worth discussing: he kills himself by stabbing himself, while Desdemona is killed by being smothered. However, this is not Othello's first design. His first reaction is to murder by cutting Desdemona in pieces – 'I will chop her into messes! Cuckold me!' (IV.i.196) (as if wanting to devour her), so echoing his earlier claim, 'I'll tear her all to pieces!' (III.iii.434) after he hears and credits Iago's report of the erotic dream Cassio has had. The desire of doing violence to the body is actualized in Othello's suicide in the final scene (his stabbing himself is a parallel to a circumcision), while there is no visible violence to Desdemona's body. After Iago's comment, Othello changes the method of killing from poisoning – 'get me some poison' (IV.i.197), an order which is also turned down by Iago, who tells him to 'strangle her in her bed, even the bed she hath contaminated' (IV.i.200–1). To poison someone is to keep a distance from them, but to strangle in bed is associated with the sexual: a sexual image is created by Iago's suggestion, which is voyeuristic. This is more subtly suggestive than the sexual implication in eating Desdemona, as smothering in bed implies consummation, that she is being 'tupped' – Iago's word (I.i.89 and III.iii.398).

Othello kisses the 'contaminated' Desdemona a few times before he kills her. He sees Desdemona having a body as 'smooth as monumental alabaster' (V.ii.5), associating her with being 'cold, cold' (V.ii.274), which evokes a sense of keeping a distance from the body. It resembles the repression of the Glass Graduate (Cervantes' *El licenciado Vidriera*), who thinks of his body as glass, or recalls how women are associated with glass in Lothario's speech (discussed in Chapter 4). Othello kisses Desdemona as if she has been turned into a stone, a body which cannot be contaminated, so resisting what we have seen Kristeva call 'abjection', a reaction or attraction towards the body, keeping himself from being 'contaminated' (to use Iago's word), by its warmth and otherness. He will not 'shed her blood' (V.ii.3) as, perhaps, he has never shed her blood in sexual terms: she remains pure within the wedding sheets, whose absent stains are therefore unable to testify to her purity. (This may assume that the wedding has never been consummated. Othello cannot possess his wife sexually, as suggested by Nelson and Haines in 'Othello's Unconsummated Marriage' (1983); so that Othello's jealousy is due to his failure of consummation.[6]) Anthony J. Cascardi comments that neither Othello nor Anselmo understand their wives, and that they may neither consummate their marriage, 'Anselmo is unable to see that Camila was unfaithful, whereas Othello is unable to see that Desdemona was not' (1986, p. 245).[7] He writes, 'Othello's search for "ocular proof", for evidence and convincing argument, could then be said to conceal his reluctance to recognize the limitations of his powers and the human conditions of knowledge' (ibid., pp. 242–3). Othello and Anselmo desire to know their wives' characters when they are absent. Hence Othello demands 'ocular proof' from Iago to prove Desdemona's infidelity – 'give me the ocular proof' (III.iii.362).

Othello can only deal with Desdemona as reduced to a stone, with an absolute, chaste body, as shown also in what he says about his heart being turned into stone, made emotionless, when he confronts Desdemona about the handkerchief (V.ii.64). Perhaps this is also the reason for not tearing her in pieces, but smothering her, so that her body is kept clean, like the 'chaste stars' (V.ii.2). And, in addition, to strangle Desdemona could also be an act of unconscious identification with her, since she is believed to have slept with Cassio: in this case the desire of Othello may be for Cassio, rather than Desdemona. Othello finally does not strangle her, but smothers her by forcing a pillow on her face, which implies repression: he does not see her face (the face of the other, as Levinas would say) or her reaction as he would in strangling.

The way Othello puts himself into his last narrative: the fragmented body parts, hand (V.ii.345), eyes (347), head (turbaned) (352), throat (354), the reference to circumcision (354), once again remind us of what Lacan calls 'the disjointed limbs', or 'the 'fragmented body', which are in dreams the symptom of hysteria, as the 'aggressive disintegration in the individual' (1989, p. 5). The violence Othello expresses in wanting to 'tear her all to pieces' (III.iii.432), may be approached through what Lacan calls 'aggressivity', thinking of a boy who hits the other and yet claims that he himself is being beaten (1989, pp. 8–29). Lacan, in 'Aggressivity in Psychoanalysis' in the *Ecrits* writes:

> one will record the emotional reactions and the articulated evidences of a normal transitivism. The child who strikes another says that he has been struck; the child who sees another fall, cries. Similarly, it is by means of an identification with the other tha[t] he sees the whole gamut of reactions of bearing and display, whose structural ambivalence is clearly revealed in his behaviour, the slave being identified with the despot, the actor with the spectator, the seduced with the seducer. (ibid., p. 19)

The 'structural ambivalence' Lacan describes is not only the emotion, love and hate, for instance, but also inherent in the identity of the person in question. If we follow Lacan, Othello is at the same time 'the slave being identified with the despot, the actor with the spectator, the seduced with the seducer'. It is almost like restating Freud's view of the alcoholic husband who himself desires the other man, and yet is jealous of the wife: the jealous man is the being who is fearing seduction, identified with the seducer (see above, p. 30). The identities of Othello as supervisor/spectator, Cassio as lieutenant/object of desire, and Iago the storyteller, are not fixed. The 'hatred' of Iago towards Othello and Cassio, that of Othello towards Desdemona is not necessarily 'pure' hatred but a component of attraction, if we follow Lacan.

Iago and Nihilism

Othello: Speak of me as I am.

(V.ii.341)

The play is not just about how a jealous husband reacts to his wife's imagined adultery, but also about the revenge an envious man takes by inventing narrative: Iago is envious of Cassio, because he has not been made Othello's lieutenant (I.i.7–32), but that is not the only reason: he is afraid of Cassio sleeping with Camila – 'For I fear Cassio with my nightcap too' (II.ii.298), and he says that Cassio 'hath a daily beauty in his life / That makes me ugly (V.i.18–19). His envy seems to be comprehensive and to need rationalizing. He wants something the other (Cassio) possesses. This is the simplest form of envy. Iago says that people came:

> In personal suit to make me his lieutenant,
> Off-capped to him; and, by the faith of man,
> I know my price, I am worth no worse a place.
> But he – as loving his own pride and purposes –
> Evades them with a bombast circumstance,
>
>   (I.i.8–12)

Iago shows a high self esteem. However, later he declares:

> Were I the Moor, I would not be Iago.
> In following him I follow but myself.
> Heaven is my judge, not for love and duty,
> But seeming so for my peculiar end;
> For when my outward action doth demonstrate
> The native act and figure of my heart
> In compliment extern, 'tis not long after
> But I will wear my heart upon my sleeve
> For daws to peck at: I am not what I am.
> (I.i.56–7)

The lines are ambiguous; they could mean that his wish to be Othello's ancient are private and selfish reasons. For he is only 'seeming' to follow for 'love and duty'. If it were only the post of lieutenant Iago is envious of, it would be foolish for him to make Othello kill Desdemona: this would not necessarily get him the lieutenantship. And even if Iago gets the lieutenantship, he will remain only the substitute, the placeholder (the meaning of lieutenant).

The line 'Were I the Moor, I would not be Iago' might mean that Iago sees himself as nothing, as a self which does not exist. The line implies several things: a) if I was the Moor, I would not exist as Iago, I would have no identity. b) But at the same time, I would *not* be the Moor, because I am only Iago. c) Or, if I was the Moor, 'Iago' would lose identity. d) Or, if I was the Moor, that would make the Moor nothing, because he would really be Iago. The plus in the Moor would be negatived by Iago as the minus sign. The first three senses here delete Iago, the fourth also deletes Othello.

In that sense, the line leads into 'I am not what I am', which negates identity altogether. Language (as excess) becomes a way of affirming nothingness, but according to Lacan, 'I am not what I am' is what everyone must say in front of the mirror, it is the experience of the 'mirror stage'. All my identity comes from the other. (Iago's nihilistic sense of emptiness is constructed by the 'mirror stage', which is ideological in character.) Iago's claim to be nothing is a version of what Lacan puts forward in *The Four Fundamental Concepts of Psychoanalysis* that the 'I', or the 'seer' is not inside the body of the subject, because:

> one sees [. . .] the emergence of something like the search for an unnamed substance from which I, the seer, extract myself. From the toils (*rets*), or rays (*rais*), [. . .] of an iridescence of which I am at first a part, I emerge as eye, assuming, [. . .] emergence from what I would like to call the function of *seeingness* (*voyure*). (1998b, p. 82)

Lacan quotes Paul Valery's phrase, 'I see myself seeing myself' to illustrate the idea that the 'I' is the absent hole within the subject, like the blind spot on the retina, if the 'I' is the seer, at the very centre of the subject there is an empty hole, and the *object a* is the reminder of it. Iago's self is nothingness.

In response to Othello's consent of promoting him to be the lieutenant, Iago replies:

> I am your own for ever.
>
> (III.iii.482)

This line can mean that Iago shows his loyalty to Othello, that Iago is owned by Othello forever. It can also mean that Iago's desire to be Othello's lieutenant is intertwined with the desire to be possessed by Othello. But it also matters that the 'I' (Iago) am your (Othello) 'own', echoes 'I am not what I am'. Both selves (one empty Othello/Iago, one negative Othello/Iago) are occupying each other. Honigmann, the editor of the New Arden Shakespeare Third Series edition, suggests that it also implies the opposite, that 'you [Othello] belong to me through all eternity' (1997, p. 240, note to III.iii.482). See also Neill's note, that ' "for ever" hints at the Mephistophelian bargain by which Iago has ensnared Othello's soul' (2006, p. 312, note to III.iii.479). This opposite sense is not noted by other editors, such as Ridley, Alvin Kernan and R.T. Jones. Michael Black argues that 'at this moment they have reversed roles: Othello is *his* lieutenant, and in a real sense his, Iago's, own for ever: for Othello has embraced the true self Iago has liberated in him' (1975, p. 23). This seems absolutely right, even without endorsing Black's idea that there is a 'true self' in Othello.

In James Joyce's *Ulysses*, Stephen comments on *Othello* and *Hamlet*:

> The boy of act one is the mature man of act five. All in all, in *Cymbeline*, in *Othello* he is bawd and cuckold. He acts and is acted on. Lover of an ideal or a perversion, like José he kills the real Carmen. His unremitting

intellect is the hornmad Iago ceaselessly willing that the moor in him shall suffer. (1993, p. 174)

Stephen thinks that a sadistic Iago who wants to be cuckolded contains the moor Othello in him. If there is an Othello inside the self of Iago, or an Iago inside Othello, then Iago's desire to destroy Othello is motivated by a structure of the negative other in himself.

'Who do You Identify With?'

There is a structure of desire involving Othello, Cassio, Iago and possibly Desdemona. For example, Iago suspects that Othello and Cassio have both slept with his wife. In this scenario he is jealous. But the route Iago takes to vengeance is extraordinary. He tries to make Othello jealous of Cassio, so that he can eliminate both men. Iago has said about Othello:

> I follow him to serve my turn upon him.
>
> (I.i.41)

The word 'turn' is also suggestive, as it can mean several things: Michael Neill notes that it is Iago's pun on 'serve' as military service and serving a master (2006, pp. 198–9, note to I.i.41). And together with 'my turn', it implies 'to play a trick' (ibid., p. 199), 'to do a bad turn' (*OED*), or do a 'detour'.[8] Lacan uses the expression '*la pulsion en fait le tour*' to explain how the drive which pursues the *objet petit a* is tricked:

> *Tour* is to be understood here with the ambiguity it possessed in French, both *turn*, the limit around which one turns, and *trick*. (1998b, p. 168)

So, the turn is also the turn in language, the trope Iago uses in order to make Othello jealous is a kind of linguistic 'turn', which is also a trick.

In the erotic dream fantasized by Iago to Othello, there is one example of Iago's 'turn':

> I lay with Cassio lately;
> And, being troubled with a raging tooth,
> I could not sleep. There are a kind of men
> So loose of soul that in their sleeps will mutter
> Their affairs – one of this kind is Cassio:
> In sleep I heard him say 'Sweet Desdemona,

Let us be wary, let us hide our loves';
And then, sir, would he gripe and wring my hand,
Cry 'O, sweet creature!', and then kiss me hard,
As if he plucked up kisses by the roots
That grew upon my lips, then laid his leg
Over my thigh, and sighed, and kissed, and then
Cried 'Cursèd fate that gave thee to the Moor!'

(III.iii.415–27)

The report Iago gives Othello could be a story made up by Iago, in which the imaginary erotic relationship between Cassio and Desdemona is envisioned. And at the same time, a curious homoerotic triangle between Othello, Iago and Cassio is formed, with Desdemona as the token of heterosexuality, because Othello can choose among Desdemona, Cassio or the narrator Iago to identify with.

Consider the erotic triangle: Othello – Cassio – Desdemona. Cassio is the third party in Othello's marriage, not only because he is suspected to have committed adultery with Othello's wife, and perhaps Iago's, but also because he woos Desdemona for Othello (III.iii.94–103). The triangle is complicated by the stories told by Iago and therefore could be revised as: Othello – Cassio (through the story told by Iago) – Desdemona. Using Freud's model, Cassio might be the one who is desired by Othello. But it is Iago who provides the wish-fulfilling 'dream' to Othello, in which more than three parties are involved: Iago; Othello; Cassio; Desdemona. Who does Iago, the storyteller, identify with? As the supervisor and the audience to Iago's story, who does Othello identify with? With Iago? With Cassio? Or with Desdemona?[9] If he identifies with either Iago or Desdemona, that would be the satisfaction of a homosexual wishful phantasy.

If Othello identifies with Desdemona, he puts himself in the position of being the lover of Cassio. Othello stands in the position of his wife and imagines himself as the lover of Cassio. This erotic triangle, Othello – Cassio – Desdemona, is the classic Girardian triangle, with Cassio as the mediator. Cassio represents Othello both sexually as a wooer and militarily as a lieutenant. If we employ the Girardian triangle to think about the relationship between Othello, Cassio and Desdemona, it seems from the account given of the wooing that there is a *dos amigos* relationship between Othello and Cassio, and the homoerotic implications of this are exploited by Iago, who also is part of a triangular relationship: Othello – Cassio – Iago. Freud's Schreber Case (1990c) argues that the alcoholic delusions of jealousy as a category of paranoia are due to the reaction against a homosexual phantasy towards a man. The sentence 'I (a man) *love* him (a man)', in this case, is contradicted in the subject to produce 'It is not *I* who loves the man – *she* loves him' (see above, p. 30). So jealousy is displaced onto the wife, from the husband. This structure is like that of the *dos amigos* in Cervantes' *El curioso impertinente*. If there was a homoerotic attraction between Anselmo and Lotario, Anselmo could unconsciously imagine that he and Lotario are in an erotic relationship with each other through the mediation of his wife. Iago exploits or abuses the potentialities of the *dos amigos* tradition in initially questioning Othello about Cassio's role in the wooing (III.iii.94–103). The language that Iago speaks in the reported dream (or that which speaks him) creates for Othello's unconsciousness, the phantasy that it is actually the other man whom the jealous man desires, not hates. Only by identifying with a woman can Othello complete the phantasy.

If Othello identifies with Cassio, it is not his desire towards Desdemona being satisfied, but Iago's, if what Iago wants is the love of Othello. Iago is kissed by Cassio (and therefore, perhaps, Othello) in the dream. In the process of identification, Othello puts himself in the position of Cassio: We should not forget that Cassio is Othello's lieutenant. So Cassio both replaces and displaces Othello in the dream (and this is also Othello's fear in reality), and yet Othello, in listening to Iago, replaces his own lieutenant. The erotic triangle set up between the three men involved in the play: Iago – Othello – Cassio is intertwined into the realm of storytelling. Iago creates in Othello a desire towards Cassio, and Iago tells a story to satisfy Othello's desire on the one hand, and fulfils Iago's own desire of Othello on the other, echoing the power of 'my turn' in language.

If Othello identifies with Iago, he is identifying with both Desdemona as protagonist in Iago's narrative and also with Iago the storyteller. Othello's desire (if there is any) towards Cassio could be aroused as well, assisted by the change in tense for the actions, starting from the address to Othello, which becomes the imperfect (a repeated action): 'And then, sir, would he gripe and wring my hand' (III.iii.422), 'then kiss me hard' (423), 'then lay his leg / Over my thigh' (425–6). It should be noted that Honigman (1997) corrects the Quarto and Folio reading to 'lay'; Neill (2006) follows the Quarto and Folio with 'laid'. If the present tense is adopted, it becomes even more intense and gives the actor more opportunity to dramatize the actions, suggesting that Iago invites Othello to identify with him, so that Othello could imagine himself to be kissed by Cassio. But the past tense is almost as rich in opportunities for drama.

Iago's address to Othello, 'And then, sir', draws his attention in, and at the same time acts to him what happened in the dream. Iago, as if acting both parts, might actually 'wring' Othello's hand and make Othello identify with Desdemona (as in the dream), in which case Iago is in the place of

Cassio. The erotic encounter of Cassio and Desdemona is transformed into the encounter of Iago and Othello, the storyteller and the audience. The change in this transformation involves both gender and power relationships, because Othello is changed into a woman (Desdemona) submitting to sexual intercourse, like Schreber in his phantasy. Also, Othello's (and perhaps Iago's) voyeuristic desire could also be satisfied by envisioning the scene. The reported dream is followed by the actual replacement of the post of lieutenancy of Cassio with Iago: 'Now art thou my lieutenant' (III.iii.478). However, there is no place for a lieutenant in the presence of the supervisor. Julia Genster notes in 'Lieutenancy, Standing in and *Othello*'[10] that lieutenancy seems:

> the ideal place for a man who is not what he is, whose identity is, like lieutenancy, a locus for substitution, impersonation, displacement. (1990, p. 797)

As Genster argues, lieutenant literally means 'place holding'. Lieutenancy, 'is a position that marks an emptying out rather than a presence' (ibid., p. 796). In the same way, the name 'Othello' starts and ends with an 'O', evoking a sense of absence at the level of the signifier, and yet Othello is the supervisor, which gives the sense that he has the crisis of being replaced, or to pun, that his place is held by, or stood in for by, the lieutenant. In 'The Sound of *O* in *Othello*: The Real of the Tragedy of Desire' (1991, p. 152) Joel Fineman argues that the sound of *O* in Othello is the reminder of the 'subjectivity effect' Lacan discusses in *Television* (1990). The sound of *O* is the reminder of the hollowness, the void at the very centre of the Lacanian subject. Fineman argues that the sound *O*, which appears in the play repeatedly, including the names *O*thell*o*, Iag*o*, Cassi*o*, Desdem*o*na, Brabanti*o*, L*o*dovic*o*, Gratian*o*, M*o*ntan*o*, and so on, act 'both to occasion and to objectify in language Othello's hollow self' (1990, p. 151). For example:

> **Othello**: O, Desdemona dead, Desdemona. Dead! O, O!
>
> (V.ii.281)

And:

> **Iago**: O treacherous villains!
> What are you there? Come in and give some help.
> **Roderigo**: O help me there!
> **Cassio**: That's one of them.
> **Iago**: O murderous slave! O villain! [*Stabs Roderigo.*]
> **Roderigo**: O damned Iago! O inhuman dog!
>
> (V.i.58–62)

And:

> **Bianca**: What is the matter, ho? who is't that cried?
> **Iago**: Who is't that cried?
> **Bianca**: O my dear Cassio!
>   My sweet Cassio! O Cassio, Cassio, Cassio!
>
> (V.i.74–6)

And, after Emilia challenges Othello, he roars, 'O! O! O!' (V.ii.195), and after he falls on the bed he says, 'O, she was foul' (V.ii.198). Fineman argues that the sound *O* could be associated with the Lacanian *objet a*.

The sound *O*, therefore, because it suggests awareness of absence, and also absence itself, could be a reminder of the missed encounter with the real which will always come back upon itself; it is also a symbol of the lack of representation of the structure of desire. The sound of *O* in Anselmo and Lothario in Cervantes' *El curioso impertinente* might also be in the same realm. Why do the names for the other three female characters, Desdemona, Emila and Bianca (and Camila in *El curioso impertinente*) have no *O* but 'a'? Maybe the last 'a' is also a reminder of the *object a*, something which tricks the drive to detour and turn.

If the name Othello is derived from the Greek verb *ethelõ*, which means 'desire', 'will', or 'want', as pointed out by Fineman (1991, pp. 145–6), the play is about desire, which for Lacan is by definition a need which cannot be satisfied, that which is always pointing to something else, like the structure of lieutenancy, which always defers fulfilment, because it always evokes the place one rank below the desiring subject. Iago asks Othello:

> And may – but how? how satisfied, my lord?
> Would you, the supervisor, grossly gape on?
> Behold her tupped?
>
> (III.iii.397–399)[11]

The supervisor is to look over, and the look is a jealous one, because he must look after his possession. Two sequences in Buñuel's *El* are relevant for comparison: when Francisco first discovers Gloria's fiancée is Raúl, his childhood friend, Francisco is watching Raúl and Gloria (still his fiancée) having dinner, Francisco's back is shown first, then his face is seen in profile. Raúl and Gloria are framed by a window, and are under Francisco's gaze. This is envy, or the evil eye working. Later, Francisco looks over (from his house) on Gloria and Raúl when she is stepping out from Raúl's car, after Francisco's failed attempt to murder her on the top of a bell tower. The jealous man looks over, while the envious man watches with an evil eye. Othello has to ask Iago, his would-be lieutenant, to look for him, to stand in his place, so as to satisfy himself. But Othello's green eyes could not be satisfied with seeing nothing. Iago is the expert who knows the relationship between eye and satisfaction. The words 'tupped', and 'satisfied' are sexually loaded. Being 'tupped' means having intercourse (like animals). To 'behold' Desdemona having sexual intercourse is an invitation to Othello's voyeuristic desire. His eyes could only be satisfied with seeing something, even if it is made up. And the identity of the supervisor is given to the lieutenant. Genster writes:

> For the lieutenancy exposes a curious paradox at the centre of the structure: on the one hand the chain argues that each occupant must be uniquely suited, by temperament and training, to the office he occupies – each office has its peculiar requirements and each officer should manifest them rightly; on the other it insists that each officer is replaceable by a subordinate who can, if necessary, assume the command which devolves on him. Though not a knave in office and a dog out of it, the lieutenant is a cipher in his captain's presence, a power in his absence. (1990, p. 796)

A 'cipher' is a zero, it is also 'a person who fills a place, but is of no importance or worth, a nonentity, a 'mere nothing' (*OED*). If the lieutenant is a cipher in comparison to the supervisor, the supervisor is marked by absence, and lieutenant being 'the power' in the supervisor's absence. Genster continues:

> The lieutenant himself is keenly aware of the jealousy from above, and of danger that he himself may be replaced from below. (ibid., p. 797)

We could say the supervisor is dominated by jealousy and the lieutenant by envy. So Iago's envy is doubled, since lieutenancy is itself a post of envy. To prove Desdemona's infidelity, Othello has to give place to Iago not as the lieutenant in a military sense, but as the place-holder, or as a stand-in. Othello urges Iago to:

> Be sure thou prove my love a whore,
> Be sure of it, give me the ocular proof.

(III.iii.362–3)

The ocular proof is the proof that can be seen. Lothario discusses the moors' insistence on believing only in things that are 'palpable, straightforward, easy to understand, demonstrable, indisputable' (*El curioso impertinente* I.33; R, p. 300). To convince the moors, argues Lothario, one has to 'have it [the proof] placed in front of their eyes', in other words, to give them ocular proof. Jealousy only works by not having ocular proof, because it is not possible to have it. References to the eye and the look are extraordinarily frequent. For example:

> **Othello**: Good Michael, look you to the guard tonight.
> Let's teach ourselves that honourable stop
> Not to outsport discretion.
> **Cassio**: Iago hath direction what to do,
> But notwithstanding with my personal eye
> Will I look to't.
>
> (II.iii.1–6)

The references to eye and satisfaction are exceptionally close in the scene when Iago is inducing Othello's suspicion – one meaning for jealousy is suspicion, as was discussed in Chapter 3. The following quotation shows how Iago makes Othello jealous, in both senses of the word, by addressing his desire to see:

> **Othello**: By the world,
> I think my wife be honest, and think she is not,
> I think that thou art just, and think thou art not.
> I'll have some proof. Her name, that was as fresh
> As Dian's visage, is now begrimed and black
> As mine own face. If there be cords or knives,
> Poison, or fire, or suffocating streams,
> I'll not endure it. Would I were *satisfied*!
> **Iago**: I see, sir, you are eaten up with passion.
> I do repent me that I put it to you.
> You would be *satisfied*?
> **Othello**: Would? nay, and I will!
> **Iago**: And may – but how? how *satisfied*, my lord?
> Would you, the *supervisor*, grossly gape on?
> Behold her topped?
> **Othello**: Death and damnation! O!
> **Iago**: It were a tedious difficulty, I think,
> To bring them to that prospect. Damn them then
> If ever mortal *eyes* do *see* them bolster

More than their own. What then? how then?
What shall I say? where's *satisfaction*?
It's impossible you should *see* this
Were they as prime as goats, as hot as monkeys,
As salt as wolves in pride, and fools as gross
As ignorance made drunk. But yet, I say,
If imputation and strong circumstances
Which lead directly to the door of truth
Will give you *satisfaction*, you may have't.
Othello: Give me a living reason she's disloyal.

(III.iii.385–411, my emphasis)

The desire to prove Desdemona's *in*fidelity, for Othello, is great, but involves a contradiction: while having identity is to know, in order to know, the supervisor has to give away his identity to the person he uses to produce the proof. That reminds us that voyeuristic (or scopophilic) desire precedes curiosity.

But for Othello the unknown is unbearable. Othello urges Iago to give him the 'ocular proof' (III.iii.363) or else wants to see the proof himself. But it is not possible to prove someone's faithfulness, as Anselmo discovers. You have to test it repeatedly, as your curiosity will not be 'satisfied'. Othello urges Iago to prove 'my love a whore' (III.iii.361). He prefers to prove his wife unfaithful rather to bear the uncertainty that she may not be innocent. Death will be less unbearable than to be in doubt, and the only way to satisfy his curiosity is to satisfy 'the lust of the eyes'. Iago is the first one who refers to the eyes in the first scene in the first act:

> And I, of whom his eyes had seen the proof
> At Rhodes

(I.i.27–8)

Iago not only refers to the eyes, but also stresses their relationship with 'proof', a very important notion related to the handkerchief (to be discussed below). He promotes the importance of vision, though he knows, and says, it is impossible to see the lovers together; he is therefore making Othello visualize the affair in his mind, which will have the effect of magnifying the sense of horror. The repeated and circular *O*, instanced by Othello's gaping mouth mentioned by Iago – 'would you, the supervisor, grossly gape on' (III.iii.398), shows the bodily reaction of Othello: both the eye and the mouth (and perhaps the ear as well) are 'tricked' and being 'turned'.

Iago: Turning and Being Turned

In an all-important scene (III.iii), Iago 'warns' Othello:

> O beware, my lord, of jealousy!
> It is the green-eyed monster, which doth mock
> The meat it feeds on.

(III.iii.167–9)

This is the second time in this scene that Iago has spoken of jealousy: the first time was as if he was speaking of something in himself already, 'my nature's plague' (III.iii.149) and 'my jealousy' (III.iii.151). That leads into a third reference:

> Good God, the souls of all my tribe defend
> From jealousy.

(III.iii.178–9)

To be in a tribe or to acknowledge tribalism, is already to be structured by jealousy, as it involves division and the right to declare possession. In his speech before committing suicide (V.ii.352) Othello realizes he belongs to a 'tribe' and therefore has been in a sect promoting possession and structuring jealousy. Although Iago *is* jealous (he has fears of his wife), and is trying to bring out jealousy in Othello, he is also, and more significantly, envious and his declaration of what the character of jealousy is involves a misrecognition. Here, I will turn the stress from the ocular to the auricular, as there seems to be four ways in which language, whose importance is stressed throughout, does not quite encapsulate his meaning, where Iago cannot see how his words construct himself.

First, Iago thinks in terms of jealousy and never mentions envy, but because the word is not used, it could be seen as that absent cause which constructs everything in the play. Envy is the desire to have something that one's self does not have and which it intuits to exist in others: such as in Cassio or Desdemona, the beauty that makes Iago ugly (V.i.18–20). Second, the colour of jealousy, according to Don Cameron Allen (1936), is traditionally yellow, not green, which is associated with youth and joy.[12] Green may be a displacement of the yellow colour of jealousy. Third, Iago draws attention to the eyes, and Othello demands ocular proof, which, as with the moment when the handkerchief is visible, proves nothing. When Othello says 'Now do I see 'tis true' (III.iii.445), he sees nothing. But it seems that envy works through the power of verbal poison being poured into the ears of Othello – his power 'to abuse Othello's ear' (I.iii.385), appears in the way language is swapped between the two:

> **Othello**: What dost thou think?
> **Iago**: Think, my lord?
> **Othello**: 'Think, my lord'? By heaven, thou echo'st me,
>   As if there were some monster in thy thought
>   Too hideous to be shown.
>
> (III.iii.107–11)

He 'echoes' Othello who later 'echoes' Iago's word 'jealousy' – 'Think'st thou I'd make a life of jealousy' (III.iii.180). It is the language of Iago which Othello internalizes: 'the Moor already changes with my poison' (III.iii.327). Othello, self-conscious in language (with the 'Othello music') wishes to hear more, and to enlarge it, as Desdemona had asked him 'that I would all my pilgrimage dilate' (I.iii.153). He thinks that Iago's hints are 'close dilations' (III.iii.127): that much more could be said by Iago.[13] The desire for words appears as his demand for 'confession' – IV.i.32–40, in a speech where 'confession' and its cognates appear four times. We return to the question, why confession is so important. Jeremy Tambling comments on Othello in *Confession: Sexuality, Sin, the Subject,*

> [Othello] must know the surety of Desdemona's conduct – the demand for proof – but his demand for confession (from Cassio, from Desdemona) is separate from this: it is the desire for power and the truth that is produced from it seems merely instrumental and self-confirming of the confessor's status. (1990a, p. 197)

What the confessor wants is the 'self-confirming' of identity. The desire is to be a confessor and to have a confession made, rather than to know the truth, even though Tambling argues that Othello commits himself to a belief in 'unitary truth' (ibid., p. 197). In 'Logic of Lacan's object (a) and Freudian Theory', André Green comments that, 'Othello, like all those who are jealous, seeks confession more than truth' (1983, p. 184). This comment is also applicable to such jealous men as Francisco and Proust's Swann. Francisco wants to be Gloria's confessor after they get married, in the train heading to Francisco's hometown – Francisco's first jealous act comes when he suspects Gloria is thinking of Raúl when they kiss. What Francisco wants is surprisingly explicit: the 'self-confirming of the confessor's status'.

Finally, we should note that what is monstrous cannot be shown – it is 'too hideous to be shown', as Othello says (III.iii.111). The green-eyed monster can only look from a place of invisibility. And its power is invisible: since it is the power of words to construct proof. The monster mocks the food it feeds on. In the case of Othello, there will be no mockery of anything; he even feels that if Desdemona is unfaithful, 'then heaven mocks itself' (III.iii.282), which would be the supreme impossibility. There is no irony in Othello, as perhaps there cannot be in jealousy. Iago, however, works by mockery, as a supreme form of irony, because of his own nothingness. Envy works by mockery, and Othello has a sense that he is mocked by Iago: as when he comes out of his epilepsy – 'Dost thou mock me?' (IV.i.56), for Iago is mocking the food that he himself feeds on and which is necessary to him (he needs to destroy Othello: part of the destructiveness of envy).

The four displacements do not seem to be what Iago is aware of when he speaks. What he says to Othello about jealousy characterizes himself in terms of displacement: Iago is not wholly in charge of his language. Language speaks the subject and constructs the identity (as being envious) of the speaking subject.

The Handkerchief as Signifier

The handkerchief Othello gave Desdemona is referred to ten times in this play. Othello sees its loss by Desdemona as a sign of her adultery. He is afraid of Desdemona's passing his handkerchief to others, as it is the 'recognizance [i.e. token] and pledge of love' (V.ii.212). It is also the recognition of Desdemona's love towards him. In a sense Othello cannot love Desdemona without the handkerchief: it works like a fetish. And two origins of this handkerchief are mentioned by Othello. First, he warns Desdemona that it was given to his mother by an Egyptian 'charmer':

> that handkerchief
> Did an Egyptian to my mother give,
> She was a charmer and could almost read
> The thoughts of people. She told her, while she kept it
> 'Twould make her amiable and subdue my father
> Entirely to her love; but if she lost it
> Or made a gift of it, my father's eye
> Should hold her loathed and his spirits should hunt
> After new fancies. She dying gave it me
> And bid me, when my fate would have me wived,
> To give it her. I did so; and, take heed on't,
> Make it a darling like your precious eye:

To lose't or give't away were such perdition
As nothing else could match.

[...]

A sybil, that had numbered in the world
The sun to course two hundred compasses,
In her prophetic fury sewed the work;
The worms were hallowed that did breed the silk,
And it was dyed in mummy, which [with – Quarto] the skilful
Conserved [Conserves – Quarto] of maidens' hearts.

(III.iv.54–64)

The first origin of the handkerchief suggests the power of the feminine: to 'subdue' and 'hold' the father, so that he will not go astray: it is anti-patriarchal in its subversive power. Otherwise, the 'eye' of the father will hold her despised. Othello's mother has passed on the handkerchief to Othello, and he draws out its feminine power: produced by a Sybil, dyed in the juice from mummies (perhaps with an additional thought of 'mothers' here), and, if we follow the Quarto, it has added to it conserves (mixtures that would preserve) which come from virginal blood. The handkerchief, which looks as if it is covered with strawberries, then resembles wedding-sheets after the bride has been deflowered, and it contrasts with the desire of Othello, already quoted, not to shed Desdemona's blood on the wedding-sheets. The stained wedding sheet (supposed to be displayed to show the husband's honour), which shows patriarchal power over women, is a token of love. When the husband says 'Make it a darling like your precious eye', we may note how the eye is referred to as an image or metonym for the woman, but its necessity to be shown unveils a jealous patriarchy at work, a spirit ready to loathe the woman – as with Brabantio, who is marked out by 'spite' (I.ii.17), and a normative jealousy which amounts to paranoia as when he comments after his daughter has left him – 'This accident is not unlike my dream' (I.i.141), as if he was always in a state of fear over his daughter. Brabantio's spite shows when he tells Othello before he goes to Cyprus,

> Look to her, Moor, if thou hast eyes to see:
> She has deceiv'd her father, and may thee.

(I.iii.293–4)

The handkerchief, then, is an apotropaic against jealousy. Women keep men from being jealous by the power of this fetish, which has some magic within it.

This first origin is contrasted with another: when Othello answers Gratiano about the handkerchief:

> It was a handkerchief, an antique token
> My father gave my mother.

(V.ii.214–15)

Here, another origin is proposed: the handkerchief is made utterly patriarchal in character, and Othello shows his Oedipal inferiority to his father in that his wife has given it away. At that point he learns of Brabantio's death, killed by 'grief' over the loss of his daughter. Patriarchy cannot survive: its jealous structure kills Brabantio, while Othello fails in patriarchal potential in comparison to his father. Brabantio's spite proves an unsuccessful revenge: it kills him and Desdemona and Othello. Iago picks up the spite when he quotes Brabantio, 'She did deceive her father, marrying you' (III.iii.209).

The handkerchief given by the mother to the father acts as a cover for female castration; hence its fetish value. Its progress through the play to Bianca suggests the idea of the mother as the 'whore', and also suggests that male jealousy has to do with the attempt to maintain stability in the face of the mother: the loss of it implies femininity, castration, and hence necessitates the jealous character of patriarchy. The handkerchief, as fetish, covers up the repression caused by jealousy. Hence, André Green (1979, p. 125) argues that 'the handkerchief is a signifier of desire whose signification is apprehended only when it is missing' (ibid., p. 125).

The dual origin of the handkerchief points to the delusional nature of the signifier: that which has no origin, since, as here, if the origin is dual, there is no origin. Talking of Othello's jealousy, Desdemona says to Emilia, 'I never gave him cause' (III.iv.153), and Emilia replies:

> But jealous souls will not be answered so.
> They are not ever jealous for the cause,
> But jealous for they're jealous. It is a monster
> Begot upon itself, born on itself.

(III.iv.154–7)

Jealousy has no 'cause': jealous people are 'jealous for they're jealous'. The chronological order which jealousy desires to follow is not applied to jealousy itself. The idea of 'the cause', or of 'natural' origin for character, is challenged by Emilia. We have seen that there is no cause for jealousy: in the last scene Othello says 'It is the cause, it is the cause, my soul' (V.ii.1).

What is the cause? For Lacan, the 'cause' would be *la chose*, the thing, and 'the thing' is that which is always lost, but which haunts the subject as the lost object (1992, p. 52) a suggestion of the lost mother.

The working of language, wordplay, which in this play includes a chain of puns and quibbles, displacements and replacements of signifier and 'place', as Neill notes, in his introduction to the Oxford edition (2006, pp. 147–58), when he discusses 'Place, Office and Occupation', is instanced in the working of the handkerchief, which accrues a sacred origin when it has lost its unique 'place'. The significance of the handkerchief works, as a sign, when it is 'missing', or 'purloined', as in the case of Desdemona. What Othello needs is not just an 'ocular proof', but an absent sign, like the handkerchief, which then accrues other meanings. When it is in the hand of a 'whore', Bianca, it represents infidelity. Green argues that Othello does not know what to see, because what he wants to see is the absence of faithfulness. Three absences converge. There is the absent O of Othello (the absent identity) which rushes in to give meaning to the absent handkerchief (which, when present is only the fetish) and the absence of signs of faithfulness. Male jealousy substitutes within this space of absence.

Chapter Six

Disappointment: Proust's *Un Amour de Swann*

Anecdotically, Shakespeare and Proust are the two writers who are said to thematize love the most. But where there is love, there is jealousy, and with this in mind, I turn to Marcel Proust (1871–1922). In this chapter, I will concentrate on the heterosexual relationship between Charles Swann and Odette de Crécy. Their love affairs are mainly portrayed in the novel-length narrative *Un Amour de Swann* [Swann in Love] interspersed into *Du côté de chez Swann* [Swann's Way] (1913), the first of the seven volumes of Proust's *À la recherche du temps perdu* [In Search of Lost Time/Remembrance of Things Past].[1] The next volume appeared in 1918: *A l'ombre des jeunes filles en fleurs* [Within a Budding Grove, or, as the new Penguin translates it, In the Shadow of Young Girls in Flower], and in 1920, *Le Côté de Guermantes* [The Guermantes Way]. *Sodome et Gomorrhe* [Sodom and Gomorrah] and *La Prisonnière* [The Captive] appeared posthumously in 1922, after Proust's death on 18 November. *Albertine disparue* [The Fugitive] appeared in 1925, and *Le Temps retrouvé* [Time Regained] in 1927.

The first book, *Du côté de chez Swann*, includes three parts: 'Combray', 'Swann in love', and 'Place-Names: The Name'. *À la recherche du temps perdu* opens, 'For a long time I would go to bed early' (*SW*, p. 1), said about a time when the narrator was, perhaps, in a sanatorium, an experience which started sometime before 1914, and during and after the First World War. The narrator (who is referred to as 'Marcel' only twice) tells the story from a first person point of view throughout the entire work, except in *Un Amour de Swann*, where he is deliberately giving a different kind of narration more like a realist novel, in the third person. So in a way *Un Amour de Swann* is an interpolated novel in terms of the change in point of view, like the interpolated narratives in *Don Quixote*. But it is not an interpolated story, because its protagonists appear in other parts of the work.

'M. Swann' first appears in 'Combray' as 'almost the only person who ever came to the house at Combray, sometime to a neighbourly dinner (but less frequently since his unfortunate marriage, as my family did not care to receive his wife) and sometimes after dinner, uninvited' (*SW*, p. 16). His love affair, which culminates in his marriage to Odette, a 'kept woman', is a story the narrator heard later, towards the end of 'Combray':

> Thus would I often lie until morning, dreaming of the old days at Combray, of my melancholy and wakeful evenings there, of other days besides, the memory of which had been more recently restored to me by the taste – by what would have been called at Combray the 'perfume' – of a cup of tea, and, by an association of memories, of a story which, many years after I had left the little place, had been told me of a love affair in which Swann had been involved before I was born, with a precision of detail which it is often easier to obtain for the lives of people who have been dead for centuries than for those of our own most intimate friends, an accuracy which it seems as impossible to attain as it seemed impossible to speak from one town to another, before we knew of the contrivance by which that impossibility has been overcome. (*SW*, p. 226)

So *Un Amour de Swann* is the 'love affair in which Swann had been involved before I was born', which is told because of 'an association of memories' ('restored to me by taste') as a story he heard many years after he left Combray, where he first met Swann. The 'faithfulness' (to use the word appearing in the opening paragraph of *Un Amour de Swann*) of *À la recherche du temps perdu* is put into question, not to mention *Un Amour de Swann* itself because of the problems of narrative and of memory which are basic to the work. (And the narrator of *Un Amour de Swann* is not necessarily 'Marcel', the narrator of the whole work.) Combray is a fictional town outside Paris where the narrator as a child used to spend his summer with his family, and the much older narrator 'remembers' this. Charles Swann's father befriended the narrator's grandfather, and they also have a house in Combray, hence 'Swann's Way' (the title of Volume 1), through which the family used to take a walk; the other route is 'The Guermantes Way' (the title of Volume 3), associated with aristocracy, and more realized when the narrator's family lives in Paris.

Swann is associated with intellectualism, with high taste and art criticism, and is one of the influences on the literary tastes of the narrator. Respectable, high-bourgeois and Jewish, Swann is obsessed with Odette, the prostitute, and is slightly marginalized for his Jewish origins. After he marries her, the class difference between him and Odette makes him not as popular as he had been previously. Odette is 'ordinary' if 'enigmatic' (Shattuck 1974, p. 52), and Swann's jealousy grows with his obsession with her possibility of telling lies. He first met her in the 'little nucleus' of middle-class socialites at the Verdurins.

We can begin with an incident which is called a 'misadventure' (*SW*, p. 391), which involves Swann knocking on a wrong window behind which he thinks Odette is waiting for another man. Before that, in front of the members of the 'faithful', Odette had told Swann not to visit her too late, which showed the members of Mme Verdurin's social circle that they were seeing each other regularly every evening. This night, Swann arrives at Odette's house late, partly to keep an appointment with Odette, and therefore he knows that she is expecting no one else; and partly because of the rain. Odette tells Swann to leave a little while after because she is tired. She asks him to put out the light before he goes. But exactly because of this Swann suspects that:

> perhaps Odette was expecting someone else that evening, that she had merely pretended to be tired, so that she had asked him to put the light out only so that he should suppose that she was going to sleep, that the moment he had left the house she had put it on again and had opened her door to the man who was to spend the night with her. (*SW*, pp. 386–7)

Tormented by this jealous and curious thought, and perhaps also by the refusal of having 'a nice little cattleya' (that is, making love with Odette), Swann comes back to spy on Odette's window (*SW*, p. 386). A cattelya is 'an epiphytal plant belonging to the orchidaceous genus *Cattleya*, native to Central America and Brazil, bearing handsome violet, rose-coloured, or yellow flowers' (*OED*). It suggests the male sexual organ, because of its relation to the orchid; it is a symbolic sign between Swann and Odette. He sees one and only one light 'amid the glimmering blackness of the row of windows in which the lights had long since been put out' (*SW*, p. 387). He knocks on the window which he thinks Odette will open, but it turns out to be her neighbour's. Before he knocks on the window, he sees the light (actually the wrong light) which would mean Odette is waiting for him, but now, with a different situation, it would mean, if it was indeed her light that she was expecting someone else:

> Swann saw one, and only one, from which percolated – between the slats of its shutter, closed like a wine-press over its mysterious golden juice the light that filled the room within, a light which on so many other evenings, as soon as he saw it from afar as he turned into the street, had rejoiced his heart with its message: 'She is there – expecting you' and which now tortured him, saying 'She is there with the man she was expecting.' (*SW*, p. 387)

He chooses to interpret the light on as a sign, but there is no reason for him to take it as a sign at all. He was led, wrongly, by the light not lit in Odette's apartment, but one flat beyond hers. This is the first example of the nature of the sign: it may be misleading, not even a sign at all. The light could mean many things: assuming it is indeed from her apartment, it can mean that Odette is not sleeping, but it does not necessarily imply that she is waiting for somebody. If it is not from her apartment, Swann does not interpret the absence of light as the opposite (that she is sleeping); he thinks its absence should be accompanied by the absence of all the lights in the neighbours' (or at least the two flanking hers). The presence of light in the neighbour's window 'misleads' him, and he interprets it in the way he wants to (that Odette is lying). Later, he does not tell Odette, because:

> [Swann was] glad that the satisfaction of his curiosity had preserved their love intact, and that, having feigned for so long a sort of indifference towards Odette, he had not now, by his jealousy, given her the proof that he loved her too much, which, between a pair of lovers, for ever dispenses the recipient from the obligation to love enough. (*SW*, p. 391)

After knocking on the wrong shutter, Swann feels glad that 'the satisfaction of his curiosity' has preserved love. It is because he can then assume that Odette is not seeing somebody and therefore she has not lied to him. It does not turn out that his curiosity is satisfied at the cost of proving Odette unfaithful. The cases of Anselmo in *El curioso impertinente* and Othello fall in the same categories, but there is the opposite outcome in Swann. His knocking at the window is a sign of love, and he is driven by curiosity and jealousy: they are brought into one here, as if saying that one is the synonym of the other. If Odette knows that it is Swann who knocks, it implies that his pretended indifference was only a disguise for his love/jealousy/curiosity to her. But now because Swann knocks on the wrong window, this sign of excessive love cannot be interpreted by Odette. Since jealousy/curiosity is the 'proof' of love in excess, it seems that Swann would be afraid to let Odette know that his indifference is only pretence, and that he is really jealous, because if so Odette will not need to show her love to him so much as she does.

The Swann–Odette disappointment in love is a pattern repeated in others, as Adele King notes, Swann's love towards Odette is 'the mixture of jealousy and fascination inspired by the unknown life of the beloved' (1968, p. 19), and so is the narrator's love for Albertine, and the narrator's friend Saint-Loup for Rachel (whom the narrator had met in a brothel, but who is also an actress), and Charlus for Morel. To analyse the affairs of the narrator, Saint-Loup and Charlus requires a new dimension which is different from that of Swann, that is, the relationship of homosexuality to jealousy. These affairs will be discussed in the next chapter.

Curiosity and Fidelity: Suspicion versus Love

In the following passage, jealousy, curiosity, desire for truth, intellectual pleasure and the thirst for knowledge are intertwined in a single paragraph. It is taken from the moment before when Swann is about to knock on the wrong window which he misrecognizes as the window of Odette's apartment:

> And perhaps the almost pleasurable sensation he felt at that moment was something more than the assuagement of a doubt, and of a pain: it was an *intellectual* pleasure. If, since he [Swann] had fallen in love, things had recovered a little of the delightful interest that they had had for him long ago though only in so far as they were illuminated by the thought or the memory of Odette now it was another of the faculties of his studious youth that his *jealousy* revived, the *passion for truth*, but for a *truth* which, too, was interposed between himself and his mistress, receiving its light from her alone, a private and personal truth the sole object of which (an infinitely precious object, and one almost disinterested in its beauty) was Odette's life, her actions, her environment, her plans, her past. At every other period in his life, the little everyday activities of another person had always seemed meaningless to Swann; if gossip about such things was repeated to him, he would dismiss it as insignificant, and while he listened it was only the lowest, the most commonplace part of his mind that was engaged; these were the moments when he felt at his most inglorious. But in this strange phase of love the personality of another person becomes so enlarged, so deepened, that the *curiosity* which he now felt stirring inside him with regard to the smallest details of a woman's daily life, was the same *thirst for knowledge* with which he had once studied history. And all manner of actions from which hitherto he would have recoiled in shame, such as spying, tonight, outside a window, tomorrow perhaps, for all he knew, putting adroitly provocative questions to casual witnesses, bribing servants, listening at doors, seemed to him now to be precisely on a level with the deciphering of manuscripts, the weighting of evidence, the *interpretation* of old monuments – so many different methods of scientific investigation with a genuine intellectual value and legitimately employable in the *search for truth*. (*SW*, pp. 388–9, my emphasis).

The curiosity for knowledge of Odette's private life, not just her affairs with others, but the smallest details of her daily life, is compared to Swann's 'thirst for knowledge' in the study of history. So curiosity 'stirring inside him with regard to the smallest details of a woman's daily life' is compared to abstract study, and the means to fulfil this is to interpret the other's private life. Curiosity and thirst for knowledge are understood as the same drive. The realms of the sexual (curiosity) and non-sexual (study of history) collapse (there is no desire for knowledge which is not cathected by the sexual (Freud) or by power (Foucault)). The passion aroused by the stirring curiosity and the thirst for knowledge cannot be separated from the passion called love, and jealousy is its sign.

Such a desire appears as a will to knowledge, which comes together with jealousy. It is for Swann 'an intellectual pleasure' like studying history. The comparison is insightful because the need to fulfil this will to knowledge assumes belief in cause and effect (to which David Hume objects), and in 'fact' and 'truth'. Nietzsche, in 'On the Utility and Liability of History for Life' (1874), writes, 'We need history; but our need for it is different from that of the pampered idler in the garden of knowledge – regardless of the noble condescension with which he might look upon our crude and inelegant needs and affliction' (p. 85). Nietzsche thinks of the study of history as propelled by an aesthetic indulgence: the historian as the 'pampered idler' (or 'spoiled loafer', as the translator of Benjamin's 'Theses on the Philosophy of History' puts it (1973a)). Here, the study of history and the pursuit of Odette's past are similar forms of curiosity which promote the idea that all forms of knowledge are necessary and valid because of their emphasis on being objective. (Anselmo's curiosity took the form of trying to create a 'scientific' experiment.) Jealousy produces its own demand for knowledge, or, we can say that history becomes a form of jealousy (as when its effort tries to protect the national culture, finding its pure origins, by digging into the national heritage).[2] Hence Swann sees his knocking on the shutter (like a *jalousie* window) as an 'intellectual pleasure', even though an 'error'. The 'pleasurable sensation' is compared to the relieving of pain and doubt.

Again, in a later incident, to be discussed later in the chapter, his curiosity is satisfied when he reads a letter which he thought was a love letter but turns out not to be one. His jealousy;

> rejoiced at the discovery, as though that jealousy had an independent existence, fiercely egotistical, gluttonous of everything that would feed its vitality, even at the expense of Swann himself. (*SW*, p. 402)

When he is jealous, he desires to know what happened, but when he knows, his jealousy is still unsatisfied, he is 'gluttonous of everything that would feed its vitality'. When he does know the truth, he is suspicious of something else. He is searching for something which he can be jealous of in the desire to know. Jealousy feeds itself even at his own expense. The words 'satisfy' and 'feeding itself' are the language of *Othello*. Also, jealousy is almost like a death drive aiming at the death of the man himself. But Swann's jealousy is not quite a Freudian death drive. Swann the jealous lover is certainly not the master of his jealousy but is mastered by its 'independent existence'. Swann's supreme pleasure is to be guaranteed, having 'immunity, for so long as his love should last and he remain vulnerable, from the assaults of jealousy' (*SW*, p. 385). It seems as if the reason why he desires Odette is to get rid of the possibility of jealousy, but, to eliminate that, his curiosity must be satisfied, which is of course saying that jealousy can only be removed by jealousy:

> The life of Swann's love, the fidelity of his jealousy, were formed of the death, the infidelity, of innumerable desires, innumerable doubts, all of which had Odette for their object. If he had remained for any length of time without seeing her, those that died would not have been replaced by others. But the presence of Odette continued to sow in Swann's heart alternate seeds of love and suspicion. (*SW*, p. 529)

Fidelity is commonly used to describe the sexual relationship between lovers. But in the phrase 'the fidelity of his jealousy', it means something like the persistency of one form of jealousy without changing into another. One of the anxieties (or shall I say the only anxiety) for Swann is that he can never be sure whether Odette is lying or not. Odette is not only unpossessable but unknowable. Roland Barthes says that it is not true that the more you love the better you understand. He says that the only wisdom in love is that 'the other is not to be known' (1999, p. 135). Knowledge is a means to possess the other, as Said argues in *Orientalism* (1978). Another meaning of fidelity the *OED* offers is 'strict conformity to truth or fact' which can be both 'of persons' or 'of a description [or] translation'. So, jealousy keeps Swann faithful.

The seeds of love and suspicion in the lover's heart come together. In one example of suspicion and its relationship with love, Swann happens to have a chance to read secretly, without Odette's knowledge, a letter to Forcheville which he is supposed to post for her. It reveals that not long ago it was Forcheville who was deceived by Odette because of the unexpected arrival of Swann. Forcheville was told and is assured in the letter that the visitor was her uncle. Swann is happy because he can think:

From which it followed that he, Swann, was the man to whom she attached importance and for whose sake she had sent the other away. (*SW*, p. 402)

But then he is puzzled:

And yet, if there was nothing between Odette and Forcheville, why not have opened the door at once [. . .] If she was doing nothing wrong at that moment, how could Forcheville possibly have accounted for her not opening the door? For some time Swann stood there, disconsolate, bewildered and yet happy, gazing at this envelope which Odette had handed to him without a qualm, so absolute was her trust in his honour, but through the transparent screen of which had been disclosed to him, together with the secret history of an incident which he had despaired of ever being able to learn, a fragment of Odette's life, like a luminous section cut out of the unknown. (*SW*, p. 402)

There is something about Odette which is always unknown to Swann, who would be happy if he could learn the 'fragment of Odette's life' whose whole (the adding up of fragments) is not known. The simile 'like a luminous section cut out from the unknown' appears to show how valuable the fragment of the unknown is to Swann. But the paradox is: if the section is cut out from the unknown, the fragment of Odette can only be unknown as well. One can only learn the whole truth or nothing at all, because if the 'whole' Odette is kept unknown, what is luminous is only an illusion of a token to deceive Swann that she is knowable. But there is no such thing as the 'whole' Odette.[3]

Odette does not lie. To conceal her doings from Swann is only logical to her, but he does not understand that. The desire of 'recapturing' the charm which has already gone keeps his passion. His love towards Odette is driven by the will to 'capture' her secret or the Odette which has gone. Malcolm Bowie, in *Freud, Proust and Lacan: Theory as Fiction* (1987), writes,

Jealousy [. . .] is the quest for knowledge in a terrifying pure form: a quest for knowledge untrammeled and unsupported by things actually known. It is a continuous journey towards a receding goal, an itinerary with no stopping-places and no landmarks; it is an appetite for knowledge, but knows nothing. (p. 58)

For Bowie the 'journey' towards knowledge (or 'reality') is possible, but it is not driven by jealousy. It is not possible to have 'pure' and absolute knowledge, not because there are 'persistent obstacles to knowledge' (ibid., p. 58), but because the idea of achieving absolute knowledge is only an illusion. Derrida discusses Hegelian *savoir absolu* (absolute knowledge) throughout *Glas* (1986). But there is no absolute knowledge. Jealousy is the reaction to this realization, though it might not be conscious to the jealous man. Bowie writes:

> Jealousy is an alertness of eye and ear and intellect; it is an experience of manifold potentiality; it is a stimulus to the making of fictions; it is a comprehensive way of inhabiting space and time. When these things are produced by pain and absence they may be called jealousy. But the same thing, rediscovered in joy, and by joy transformed, may as fittingly be called *knowledge*. (ibid., p. 64)

Bowie points out that, though indirectly, jealousy and knowledge might be interchangeable, and he might want to say that love falls into the same category as jealousy and knowledge, because love could be 'the same thing rediscovered' in, say, hatred. But he misses the point that joy and pain are always inseparable, as are jealousy, knowledge and love. One remaining problem is: does the absence of knowledge induce jealousy, and thus love? If so, it implies that love and jealousy are on the same side, that is, love and jealousy prove each other; both of them are on the other side of knowledge, that is, love and jealousy are guaranteed by the lack of knowledge of the beloved.

The difference between thirst for knowledge and curiosity is perhaps not as distinguishable as in Cervantes' and Shakespeare's time, because the critical sense of curiosity has been replaced by a positive sense, probably because of the growth of colonialism in the early modern period, and the advance in technology in the modern. For example, Proust is the contemporary of Einstein, and the Western world is dominated by the spirit of exploration, which requires curiosity. One famous maxim from Albert Einstein is: 'I have no special gift; I am only passionately curious', which shows that curiosity is not, for Einstein, negative.

Jealousy and Signs

The state of being in love is to be sensitive to the 'signs' emitted from the beloved. The jealous lover readily interprets the signs of the beloved. A classic example of this paranoid-critical interpretation of signs is Francisco in *El*. Luis Buñuel was associated with Dalí; (*Un chien andalou* [An Andalusian Dog] (1929), was co-written with Dalí), who discusses what he calls the 'paranoid-critical' method. Everything is to be interpreted paranoid-critically, as everything for the paranoiac is meaningful. The signs for the jealous lover, Francisco for instance, are interpreted paranoid-critically.[4] He interprets others' signs; for example, in a restaurant the laughter of a young man whom his wife Gloria knows is interpreted by him as laughing at him, and talking behind his back. Francisco's later illusion is the result of that kind of interpretation: only in terms of its extent can it be classified as paranoia. However, Umberto Eco argues that all signs can be lies. He writes in *A Theory of Semiotics*:

> Semiotics is concerned with everything that can be taken as a sign. A sign is everything which can be taken as significantly substituting for something else. This something else does not necessarily have to exist or to actually be somewhere at the moment in which a sign stands in for it. Thus semiotics is in principle the discipline studying everything which can be used in order to lie. (1979, p. 7)

So to understand jealousy is to understand signs and the reading of them, that is, semiotics – the study of signs, or following Eco's argument, the study of what may be lies. Concerning lies, Lacan, in *The Psychoses* (1993), discusses a joke quoted by Freud in 'Jokes and their Relationship to the Unconscious' (1905): the 'Jewish joke', where one man thinks he is being lied to by the other. The joke goes as follows:

> Two Jews met in a railway station carriage at a station in Galicia. 'Where are you going?' asked one. 'To Cracow,' was the answer. 'What a liar you are!' broke out the other. 'If you say you're going to Cracow, you want me to believe you are going to Lemberg. But I know that in fact you're going to Cracow. So why are you lying to me?' (Lacan 1993, p. 161)

Lacan writes:

> What the subject tells me is always fundamentally related to a possible feint, in which he sends me, and I receive, the message in an inverted form. (1993, p. 37)

So there is always a possibility of receiving a message 'in an inverted form'. Jealousy is the anxiety about this possibility, which points only to the mobility of signs. Leo Bersani writes in 'The Culture of Redemption':

> Jealousy of the other is the paranoid interpretation of desire's mobility. (1986, p. 415)

However, to say 'desire is mobile' is not just to say desire is the need which cannot be satisfied. It also means that to love someone is not to love the beloved as such. To love is a process of idealization. Hence, as Freud says, 'Where they [men] love they do not desire and where they desire they cannot love' (1991d, p. 250). He would agree that desire is mobile, in the sense that all the objects of desire are only substitutions for something which has already been lost. Also, Lacan applies Saussure's notion of arbitrary relationships between the signifier and signified and argues that the beloved is always displaced in the Symbolic Order.[5] The mobility of signs constitutes the mobility of desire. For example, the narrator realizes that his love for Albertine is maintained by 'painful anxiety':

> Love, in the pain of anxiety as in the bliss of desire, is a demand for a whole. It is born, and it survives, only if some part remains for it to conquer. We love only what we do not wholly possess. (*LP*, p. 133)

For Bersani, jealousy is the reaction to the fluidity of desire. Not just interpretation, but 'paranoid interpretation', (the phrase derived from Dalí) must deal with the burden of the realization of desire's mobility. Why is this interpretation paranoid? It is because to come up with one interpretation of the mobile sign is to fix the meaning of the sign. But to have a fixed meaning of the sign is to suppress the other possible meanings, and the return of the repressed makes the interpretation paranoid. Jealousy is the attempt to deal with the lying character of signs and the means is the violence done to the mind to achieve knowledge.

In *History and Ideology in Proust*, alluding to Bowie and Bersani, Michael Sprinker writes:

> Jealousy is the condition or structure produced by the mobility of desire, by desire's incapacity to rest or to be confined to a single object. (1994, p. 129)

We may add that jealousy is also the reaction to the (fear of the) mobility of desire. 'In the language of signs', writes Deleuze in one of the pioneer books on Proust, *Proust and Signs*:

> There is no truth except in what is done in order to deceive, in the meanders of what conceals the truth, in the fragments of a deception and a disaster; there is no truth except a betrayed truth, which is both surrendered by the enemy and revealed by oblique views or by fragments. (2000, p. 112)

Truth is supposed to be absolute and universal. What is betrayed is truth in the sense that any truth is 'the result of a violence in thought' (ibid., p. 16), and therefore arbitrary and unjust, and certainly incomplete. The language of signs is the language of lies, that is, any absolute meaning interpreted from it is arbitrary. Plurality is betrayed to produce a single and homogeneous 'truth'. The 'truth' interpreted from the signs of love is both betraying and concealing. The jealous lover fails to see that what he thinks is truth is only 'done in order to deceive'.

Consider what Deleuze says of love and jealousy:

If the signs of love and of jealousy carry their own alteration, it is for a simple reason: love unceasingly prepares its own disappearance, acts out its dissolution. The same is true of love as of death, when we imagine we will still be alive enough to see the faces of those who will have lost us. In the same way we imagine that we will still be enough in love to enjoy the regrets of the person we shall have stopped loving. It is quite true that we repeat our past loves; but it is also true that our present love, in all its vivacity, 'repeats' the moment of dissolution or anticipates its own end. Such is the meaning of what we call a scene of jealousy. This repetition oriented to the future, this repetition of the outcome, is what we find in Swann's love of Odette, in the hero's love of Gilberte, of Albertine. (2000, p. 19)

What Deleuze means by the 'scene of jealousy' is that love 'repeats' the moment of dissolution of its own end. The very structure of love is already in the process of disappearing. The nature of love and of jealousy is that they 'carry their own alteration', opposite to the assertions made in Shakespeare's 'Sonnet 116', also obsessed with love and time:

> Let me not to the marriage of true minds
> Admit impediments. Love is not love
> Which alters when it alteration finds,
> Or bends with the remover to remove:
> O no! it is an ever-fixed mark
> That looks on tempests and is never shaken;
> It is the star to every wand'ring bark,
> Whose worth's unknown, although his height be taken.
> Love's not time's fool, though rosy lips and cheeks
> Within his bending sickle's compass come.
> Love alters not with his brief hours and weeks;
> But bears it out ev'n to the edge of doom.

> If this be error and upon me proved,
> I never writ, nor no man ever loved. (1977, p. 100)

With the love described in Sonnet 116, 'Love is not love' if it 'alters'. At the end, there is a kind of anxiety, 'If this be error' then 'I never writ, nor no man ever loved'. But for the love described in Proust, the structure of love is like death, which involves an impossibility: the jealous lover imagines and longs for the 'regrets of the person we shall have stopped loving', as we imagine the mourning face of 'those who have lost us' (Deleuze 2000, p. 19). The mourning faces in reaction to our death are what we long for, and we think we 'will still be alive enough' to enjoy them; just as the regret of the person in reaction to our ceasing love is what one desires, and we think that we 'will still be enough in love' to enjoy them (ibid.). There is a secret narcissism involved in both cases: the mourning faces and the lover who regards are all imagined fulfilling the jealous lover's narcissism. But when we die, we can no longer see the mourning faces, just as, when we cease to love, we care not for those we did not love. (And death is the ultimate adulterer, as Romeo knows in *Romeo and Juliet* (V.iii.102–8)). We cannot stop loving the other, nor can we stop being jealous even if the beloved is dead. Only when the jealous lover himself dies could jealousy stop.

Although Swann has married Odette, his jealousy has nothing to do with his status of being a husband. *Un Amour de Swann* finishes with Swann exclaiming to himself:

> To think that I've wasted years of my life, that I've longed to die, that I've experienced my greatest love, for a woman who didn't appeal to me, who wasn't even my type! (*SW*, p. 543)

To experience 'great love' has nothing to do with whether or not the beloved is appealing, but whether or not the lover is jealous of the beloved. Odette is 'not even [Swann's] type'. Swann's love grows with his obsession with Odette's affairs with other men. And by saying this, Swann's anger is mixed with pride. The structure in this sentence is balanced: life and death contrast with each other, and the three 'that'-phrases are metonymic sequences. Does Swann mean that it is not the woman's quality of arousing love but of arousing jealousy that guarantees his experience of great love? It implies that love (and jealousy) involves a certain degree of oddness. For example, the narrator uses words like the 'morbid feeling' that Swann cherished for Odette (*SW*, p. 536). To be in love guarantees jealousy. How about the reverse? Does jealousy guarantee love? Swann is jealous of Odette, but he does not love her. Or, as Deleuze says, the signs of love and jealousy currently 'carry their own alterations', so that we can no longer separate love and jealousy.

In *A Lover's Discourse* Barthes writes, 'jealousy is ugly, is bourgeois' (1999, p. 146). This is another way of saying that jealousy presupposes the culture of possessive individualism, that is, the distinction made between the owning subject and the beloved object, as discussed in Chapter 3. In view of this, bourgeois marriage is on the side of jealousy. Denis de Rougemont, in *Love in the Western World* (1983), argues that it is not the beloved whom we love, but the state of being in love that we love. We could feel that we are in love the most when the beloved is not there. De Rougemont writes:

> What they [the lovers] need is not one another's presence, but one another's absence. (ibid., p. 42)

It is because what the lover needs is not the beloved, but the feeling that they are in love. De Rougemont calls this 'the love of love'. He then argues that the love of love is only a disguise for a more unavowable passion: 'the desire for death' (1983, p. 42). When Swann exclaims to himself, he feels that 'he was no longer unhappy', because he thinks that:

> the suffering through which he had passed that evening, and the plea-sures, as yet unsuspected, [...] were linked by a sort of concatenation of necessity. (*SW*, pp. 542–3)

So when he is no longer suffering, he thinks that he will not be happy. Suffering and happiness become the necessary condition for each other, paradoxically, and Swann feels that they must be linked. If signs are only used to tell lies, suffering and pleasure are not necessarily separable. For de Rougemont:

> Passion means suffering, something undergone, the mastery of fate over a free and responsible person. To love love more than the object of love, to love passion for its own sake, has been to love to suffer and to court suffering all the way from Augustine's *amabam amare* down to modern romanticism. Passionate love, the longing for what sears us and annihilates us in its triumph – there is the secret which Europe has never allowed to be given away; a secret it has always repressed – and preserved! (1983, p. 50)

Swann's suffering (passion and passivity) is also a sign of love for Odette. But Odette is only the 'object of love', from whom the 'text' contain-ing the signs (love signs or jealous signs) are read and interpreted by the paranoid-critical, and therefore jealous, lover. It is the love of love (*amabam amare*),[6] the love of passion, or the love of death that the lover seeks, not the beloved 'itself'.

Swann's jealousy, which forces him to interpret it, results from what Lacan calls 'paranoid knowledge' in *The Psychoses*:

> All human knowledge stems from the dialectic of jealousy, which is a primordial manifestation of communication. It's a matter of an observable generic notion, behavioristically observable. What takes place between two young children involves this fundamental transitivism expressed by the fact that one child who has beaten another can say – *The other beat me.* It's not that he is lying – he *is* the other, literally. (1993, p. 39)

The dialectic of jealousy is like the Socratic dialectic, which puts words into the other's mouth and makes the other no longer heterogeneous. So for the jealous man the other's desire must be the same as his, and thus arouses paranoia and anxiety. In *Lacan and Language*, Muller and Richardson provide a reading of Lacan:

> Human knowledge is paranoiac because imaginary ego-properties are projected onto things; things become conceived as distorted, fixed, rigid entities; and things have salience for man insofar as they are desirable to other. (1982, p. 34)

Only those things that are desired by the other are important for jealous men, and that becomes 'primordial jealousy'. It is because things that are valuable are bound to have the risk of being taken away by the other. This is a logical consequence of the formation of the 'I' in the 'mirror stage', when the subject misidentifies the image and misidentifies the other as the reflection.

Human knowledge is the result of the violence involved in turning the difference of the other into the same. 'The dialectic always carries the possibility that I may be called upon to annul the other', writes Lacan:

> The beginning of this dialectic being my alienation in the other, there is a moment at which I can be put into the position of being annulled myself because the other doesn't agree. (1993, p. 40)

My alienation in the other threatens my subjectivity. The dialectic of jealousy aims at annulling the heterogeneity of the other. Buñuel's *El* ends with Francisco saying, 'time has proven my point', when he learns that Gloria, his ex-wife, has married and given birth to a son by her ex-fiancé

Raúl (to whom she was engaged before Francisco). What really concerns Francisco is to 'prove' his point, not the fidelity of his wife.

Swann is more afraid of Odette's untruthfulness than her unfaithfulness (*SW*, p. 516), and feels that:

> her very admissions [. . .] of faults which she supposed him to have discovered, served Swann as a starting-point for new doubts rather than putting an end to the old. For her admissions never exactly coincided with his doubts. In vain might Odette expurgate her confession of all its essentials, there would remain in the accessories something which Swann had never yet imagined, which crushed him anew, and would enable him to alter the terms of the problem of his jealousy. (*SW*, p. 526)

Confessions induce more doubts, which force the jealous man to demand more confessions.

A jealous man is concerned with the infidelity of the beloved, not the fidelity. As the title of Anthony Trollope's novel suggests, *He Knew He was Right* (1869), what a jealous man needs is to prove that he was right. But unknowability is everywhere:

> Like many other men, Swann had a naturally lazy mind and lacked imagination. He knew perfectly well as a general truth that human life is full of contrasts, but in the case of each individual human being he imagined all that part of his or her life with which he was not familiar as being identical with the part with which he was. He imagined what was kept secret from him in the light of what was revealed. (*SW*, p. 510)

Swann disavows the fact that Odette may not be the same in her private life. Jealous men lack imagination and yet delude themselves in their phantasies. The gender difference – 'like many other men' – is suggestive. The 'unitary truth' that jealous men believe also involves the reaction to the crisis of masculinity. The cure for jealousy may be imagination, but too much imagination may only drive one jealous.

Jealousies and their Vicissitudes

Swann is disturbed at being deceived by Odette. When she confesses a lie to Swann, that she had not been to Maison Dorée on the day he looks for her at Prévost's because Forcheville had paid her a visit, Swann is even more jealous because it implies that Odette might have lied to him many times on any occasion imagined:

> [Swann] could feel the insinuation of a possible undercurrent of falsehood which rendered ignoble all that had remained most precious to him [...] everywhere disseminating something of the shadowy horror that had gripped him when he had heard her admission with regard to the Maison Dorée, and [...] shattering stone by stone the whole edifice of his past. (*SW*, p. 529)

Architectural rhetoric appears in 'edifice of the past'. In *El*, Francisco's house is an architectural site which constructs jealousy. Swann's past is like a large building, stone by stone, falling apart. Jealousy is also the anxiety of the collapse of the 'edifice of the past'. The name 'Maison Dorée' first disturbs Swann in the beginning, but

> Then it happened with the Maison Dorée as it had happened with the Island in the Bois, that gradually its name ceased to trouble him. For what we suppose to be our love or our jealousy is never a single, continuous and indivisible passion. It is composed of an infinity of successive loves, of different jealousies, each of which is ephemeral, although by their uninterrupted multiplicity they give us the impression of continuity, the illusion of unity. (*SW*, p. 529)

What we call jealousy is a name given to a collection of passions. With this in mind, the English title of *El*, 'This Strange Passion' (discussed in the Introduction) could be called 'This Strange Passion which is not One', alluding to Luce Irigaray's *This Sex Which is Not One* (1985). Jealousy is the name given to an unnameable emotion because passions cannot be reduced to a single unity. Or, jealousy is the anxiety created by ephemeral jealousies, so that the dream of the jealous man is to reduce love to one single jealousy.

If the emotion we call jealousy contains different jealousies, which might include such similar emotions as envy, which is more primary, envy or jealousy? For Melanie Klein, envy, rather than jealousy or gratitude, is the primary emotion of an infant. Klein, in 'Envy and Gratitude' (1957), points out that primary envy would project badness onto the feeding breast, which is the first object one can be envious of and which makes it to be spoiled and destroyed. She writes:

> the very ease with which the milk comes – although the infant feels gratified by it – also gives rise to envy because this gift seems something so unattainable. (Klein, 1997, p. 183)

In contrast, for the Proustian narrator, these different jealousies include envy and therefore envy is 'part of' jealousy.

Although jealousy is plural, the narrator puts love and jealousy together, as if saying love and jealousy cannot be distinguished. Now in his theory of plural jealousy, one particular form of jealousy 'dies' easily. So if Odette (the object of desire and doubts) is not seen for a while, Swann's love and jealousy will not persist. The persistency of jealousy parallels the life of love. What we call jealousy may be in fact love and what we call love, may be jealousy. The narrator equates love automatically with jealousy. But he has not proved directly why they are equated. Is it because 'jealousy' is the name given to a collection of different jealousies, and is sometimes mixed up with love? Or is it because love is also a discontinuous and indivisible passion, and among the uninterrupted multiplicity love and jealousy coincide? If jealousy and love are multiple or plural, there may be a passion which is thought to be love but is 'in fact' jealousy, or vice versa. Swann may not be in love, but in jealousy. To see whether one is jealous or not is the sign of being in love, if love is a passion which is always unknown. If love and jealousy are different and both plural, discontinuous, and incompatible, we cannot tell whether we are in love or jealous. Perhaps when Swann is jealous he is only jealous – it has nothing to do with falling in love or not. Or jealousy is not the necessary condition for love: it may be Swann is jealous and he misrecognizes it as love, but he nevertheless thinks that he is in love. In this sense jealousy has a more positive sense, because if there was no jealousy as the cure to the illusion of love, there would be no love.

These ephemeral jealousies have the nature of uninterrupted multiplicity which gives us the impression of continuity and the illusion of unity. Actually they are unrelated to each other. Perhaps some of these jealousies are what we call jealousy and some, envy. If these jealousies are different kinds of jealousies (perhaps envy is one of them), and love is also included in the collection of jealousies, it provides an explanation for Johnny and Gilda's 'curious love-hate pattern' in *Gilda*: it is the 'impression of continuity' and the 'illusion of unity' which deceives them, making them think that love is the other side of hatred. But in fact love and hatred are not necessarily opposite.

I will close this chapter by a reminder of Derrida's *Glas* (1986):

The mother fascinates from the absolute of an *already*. Fascination produces an excess of zeal. In other words, jealousy. Jealousy is always excessive because it is busy with a past that will never have been present and so can never be presented nor allow any hope for presentation, the presently presenting. One is never jealous in front of a present scene – even the worse imaginable – nor a future one, at least insofar as it would be big with a possible theater.

So one is only jealous of the mother or of death. Never of a man or a woman as such. (p. 134)

Jealousy is excessive not only because it is a passion which cannot be controlled, not in the way we normally think that it is, but also because it is 'busy with a past that will never have been present'. The 'zeal' produced by fascination with the mother is jealousy, but because it is produced by fascination, that which relates to the evil eye, it is envy. We can see the birth of jealousy out of the spirit of envy. The fascination is with the idea of the complete sexual satisfaction of the mother, from which it is utterly cut off, and which it can have no access to: it will never have been present both because that satisfaction never took place as fantasized, and because it cannot be made present. (The narrator's desire to have his mother stay the night with him in his room, recalled in Part One of 'Combray', evokes that envy.) 'In Search of Lost Time' was earlier translated as 'Remembrance of Things Past'. Nietzsche argues in 'On the Utility and Liability of History for Life' (1995) that history is the past being interpreted, and 'only from the highest power of the present can you interpret the past' (p. 129). To quote Tambling's interpretation of Nietzsche:

> A narrowed and alienated present cuts off the ability to read the past, or leads to its overvaluation or to its idealisation; or perhaps the construction of *ressentiment* as the dominant within bourgeois modernity means that the past cannot be read, except in kitsch or parodic form, so depriving the present of the uses of history. (2001a, p. 100)

What we understand as the past is the result of a representation made in the present, and the past is in danger of being devalued or idealized in that interpretation. For Nietzsche, the past can only be thought of by somebody who is not possessed by *ressentiment* (ibid.).

The other woman to be jealous of lies in the future: it is death: Derrida is recalling Freud's 'The Theme of the Three Caskets' (1990d). (The second woman, the woman in the middle, also a source of jealousy, for Swann, at least, is Odette.) Jealousy has no present tense: you are either jealous (envious) of the past (the mother), or jealous of the future (death, the other absolute, about which nothing can be said). The cure for jealousy might be not psychology but a certain form of psychoanalysis as its task is to provide another representation of the past for the patient who is fixated in the past (not what psychology gives: 'an unalterable notion of "identity" '). It is less important whether the representation is 'faithful' or not. The cure of jealousy, or the cure performed by jealousy might be the disavowal of the fact that there is no past or present. Why is jealousy at stake? Perhaps because belief in single, knowable causes and effects are at stake if jealousy is the dream of fixing the mobility of signs, desire, and identity.

This chapter makes jealousy the reaction to the mobility of desire, and jealousy as plural: many jealousies. Jealousy as the sign of love, and the lying characteristic of signs have also been discussed. We have focused on Swann's love, whose love towards Odette is primarily heterosexual; in the next chapter we will move on to the discussion of homosexuality, and it will be motivated by modernist theories of allegory.

Chapter Seven

Belatedness: À la recherche du temps perdu

> Plus tard, j'ai compris.
> [Later, I understood.]
> Marcel Proust[1]

We have dealt with Swann's love, or rather, Swann's jealousy in reaction to the signs read from Odette. Jealousy is the reaction to the mobility of signs emitted from the beloved as a text, or rather, jealousy seeks out and reads such signs. And we have discussed the lying that may be characteristic of any sign, which is Eco's theme. In this chapter, other more 'queer' forms of jealousy will be dealt with. We will consider being jealous of oneself and, jealousy which is evoked by the possibility of the beloved's homosexuality, which produces a realization of the allegorical nature of sexuality. In terms of jealousy, I will concentrate on the narrator, his friend Marquis Robert de Saint-Loup, and Saint-Loup's uncle, Baron de Charlus.

We begin by looking at a conversation between the narrator and Swann, narrated in *Sodome et Gomorrhe*, at a party when the narrator is about to take leave of Mme de Surgis and Charlus, because he does not want to be too late for meeting Albertine. Albertine is the narrator's third lover, described in *À la recherche du temps perdu*. (His first love was with Swann's daughter Gilberte, and second was his fascination for Mme Guermantes.) Swann is asked a question about something he might or might not have said, and he replies that he has been slandered, and that:

> 'People are very inquisitive. I've never been inquisitive, except when I was in love, and when I was jealous. And a lot I ever learnt! Are you jealous? I told Swann that I had never experienced jealousy, that I did not even know what it was. 'Well, you can count yourself lucky. A little jealousy is not too unpleasant, for two reasons. In the first place, it enables people who are not inquisitive to take an interest in the lives of others, or of one other at any rate. And then it makes one feel the pleasure of possession, of getting into a carriage with a woman, of not allowing her to go about by herself. But that's only in the very first stages of the disease, or when the cure is almost complete. In between, it's the most agonising torment.

However, I must confess that I haven't had much experience even of the two pleasures I've mentioned – the first because of my own nature, which is incapable of sustained reflexion; the second because of circumstances, because of the woman, I should say the women, of whom I've been jealous. But that makes no difference. Even when one is no longer attached to things, it's still something to have been attached to them; because it was always for reasons which other people didn't grasp. The memory of those feelings is something that's to be found only in ourselves; we must go back into ourselves to look at it. [. . .]' (*SG*, p. 139)

Swann compares jealousy to disease, and says that it is not too unpleasant at the beginning and when the cure comes, though it is tormenting in the middle. In the beginning, jealousy 'enables people who are not inquisitive to take an interest in the lives of others'; and secondly, jealousy 'makes one feel the pleasure of possession', which includes 'not allowing a woman to go about by herself'. Swann could enjoy those pleasures only briefly. The narrator suffers much more torment, than Swann says he ever did, since his jealousy (or suspicion) grows before and after he holds Albertine captive in Paris. The narrator claims that he has never experienced jealousy, and does not even know what jealousy is, but whether this is true may be questioned, since he had an infant desire to keep the mother in his room, in opposition to his father, as recorded at the beginning of 'Combray'. Swann describes jealousy in wholly general terms, and without reference to Odette, so contradicting the thesis of *Un Amour de Swann*, and making implicitly any realist narrative problematic in terms of what it can or cannot say in representing reality. Unless we assume that he has repressed his past, his '*temps perdu*'.

In the following two volumes, *La prisonnière* and *Albertine disparue*, the narrator tells of his affair with Albertine; placing his jealousy at the heart of the books. But what complicates the issue from Swann's relationship to Odette, is that the dimension of homosexuality, or rather lesbianism in Albertine, is introduced in the narrator's love affair with her, as it was not with Odette in any significant way.

Further, the question of love and jealousy is more problematic in the narrator's relationship with Albertine, than Swann with Odette, because Swann's sexuality is not as ambiguous as that of the narrator's. Barthes, in the entry 'jealousy' in *A Lover's Discourse*, writes:

The Proustian narrator has little relation to Werther. Is he even a lover? He is merely jealous; in him, nothing 'lunar' [*lunaire*] – except when he loves, in the fashion of a lover, the Mother (his grandmother). (1999, p. 144)

For Barthes, the narrator is 'merely jealous', and not even a lover. But is it possible to be jealous but not in love? Swann believes that he loves Odette especially (or even, only) when he is jealous. For Barthes, jealousy is contrasted with being '*lunaire*' (mad, as in Schoenberg's *Pierrot lunaire*). So, being jealous and being mad are opposites, because the jealous person knows he is right, and wants to be in control, whereas madness takes away subjectivity. The idea that the lover is mad suggests, of course, Breton's modernist novel *L'Amour fou* [Mad Love, 1937].

The narrator has commented on Swann's jealousy (and curiosity) in relationship to love. He says to himself:

'If I could have known such and such witnesses!' – from whom, if I had known them, I should probably have been unable to extract anything more than from Andrée, herself the custodian of a secret which she refused to surrender. Differing in this respect also from Swann who, when he was no longer jealous, ceased to feel any curiosity as to what Odette might have done with Forcheville, I found that, even after my jealousy had subsided, the thought of making the acquaintance of Albertine's laundry-girl, of people in her neighborhood, of reconstructing her life in it, her intrigues, alone had any charm for me. (*AD*, p. 743)

This is the second example of when the narrator compares himself with Swann. Swann's curiosity ceases together with his jealousy, whereas the narrator's curiosity is sustained even when his jealousy 'subsides'. But the narrator's jealousy has never subsided, not even after Albertine has died:

Thus one acquires the habit of having as the object of one's musings an absent person, and one who, even if she remains absent for a few hours only, during those hours is no more than a memory. Hence death does not make any great difference. (*AD*, p. 706)

The death of the beloved does not make any difference because she is no more than a memory (which is also the effect of death) even if she is absent for a few hours. So the death of the beloved does not cure jealousy.

Memory and the Jealous Historian

In the passage in *Sodome et Gomorrhe*, when the narrator revisits Balbec, one year after his grandmother has died: 'Upheaval of my entire being', he writes as he has bent down to take off his boots:

But scarcely had I touched the topmost button than my chest swelled, filled with an unknown, a divine presence, I was shaken with sobs, tears streamed from my eyes. The being who had come to my rescue, saving me from barrenness of spirit, was the same who, years before, in a moment of identical distress and loneliness, in a moment when I had nothing left of myself, had come in and had restored me to myself, for that being was myself and something more than me (the container that is greater than the contained and was bringing it to me). (*SG*, p. 210)

The narrator realizes that the influence of 'involuntary memory' is much greater than 'voluntary memory'. There are events 'stored' in memory which come involuntarily and, so sudden and intense that they overthrow the narrator's subjectivity – they are 'something more than me'. It is his body (touching 'the topmost button'), rather than his mind (which can only access the voluntary memory), which 'remembers' his grandmother. But the touching of the topmost button is contingent and unplanned, and cannot be repeated to yield the same memory twice. The narrator calls that intruding memory, which is more 'real', a 'complete and involuntary recollection' (*mémoire involontaire*) (*SG*, p. 210):

This reality does not exist for us so long as it has not been re-created by our thought [...]; and thus, in my wild desire to fling myself into her arms, it was only at that moment – more than a year after her burial, because of the anachronism which so often prevents the calendar of facts from corresponding to the calendar of feelings – that I became conscious that she was dead. (*SG*, p. 211)

That his grandmother was dead only overwhelms his being a year later, in a 'belated' and 'anachronistic' manner. Walter Benjamin, who translated Proust into German, writes in 'On Some Motifs in Baudelaire':

One afternoon the taste of a kind of pastry called *madeleine* [...] transported him [the narrator] back to the past, whereas before then he had been limited to the promptings of a memory which obeyed the call of attentiveness. This he calls the the *mémoire volontaire* [voluntary memory] and it is its characteristic that the information which it gives about the past retains no trace of it. [...] According to Proust, it is a matter of chance whether an individual forms an image of himself, whether he can take hold of experience. (1973b, p. 155)

Benjamin then discusses *mémoire involontaire* by making use of what Freud discussed in relation to trauma and shock in 'Beyond the Pleasure Principle'

(1920). Benjamin argues that memory fragments are most enduring when they do not enter consciousness. The more important the memory to the individual, the more powerful the protective shell, and thus the more untraceable the memory. So, voluntary memory cannot access the experience which is important for us. Benjamin writes:

> the replacement of the older narration by information [e.g. journalism], of information by sensation, reflects the increasing atrophy of experience. (ibid., p. 155)

(Linear) narrative (journalistic) information, and sensation are decreasing in power of representing experience. Experience cannot enter consciousness, not because it is not worth remembering, but because it is too intense to afford remembrance. The 'older narration' is what the jealous historian wants, as he desires to tell stories in a linear narrative. But when experience becomes too much of a shock, it is 'stored' beyond consciousness and can only be accessed by involuntary memory, that is to say, by chance, by the awakening of the bodily memory which the narrator experiences. Involuntary memory is heterogeneous for the jealous person; it overthrows being. However, Malcolm Bowie, in *Freud, Proust and Lacan* (1990), argues that jealousy is an 'alertness of eye and ear and intellect', and 'a stimulus to the making of fictions' (p. 64). In that sense, jealousy induces narrative. However, I would also suggest that jealousy and voluntary memory are on the same side, as both are working for the establishment of a single subjectivity. The otherness of heterogeneity comes not from the outside, but from within. The very struggle of dealing with that heterogeneity, which induces the other potential within the subject's sexuality, constitutes jealousy as the fear of the unknown other.

In the following, the narrator contemplates the life of his beloved:

> One pays no attention to anything that one does not connect with the real life of the woman one loves; one forgets immediately what she has said to one about such and such an incident or such and such people one does not know and her expression while she was saying it. And so when, in due course, one's jealousy is aroused by these same people, and seeks to ascertain whether or not it is mistaken, whether it is indeed they who are responsible for one's mistress's impatience to go out, and her annoyance when one has prevented her from doing so by returning earlier than usual, one's jealousy, ransacking the past in search of a clue, can find nothing; always retrospective, it is like a historian who has to write the history of a period for which he has no documents; always belated, it dashes like an

enraged bull to the spot where it will not find the dazzling, arrogant creature who is tormenting it and whom the crowd admire for his splendour
and cunning.

[...]

One does not know, and one will never know; one searches desperately
among the unsubstantial fragments of a dream, and all the time one's life
with one's mistress goes on, a life that is oblivious of what may well be of
importance to one, and attentive to what is perhaps of none, a life hagrid-
den by people who have no real connexion with one, full of lapses of
memory, gaps, vain anxieties, a life as illusory as a dream. (*LP*, p. 189)

Jealousy is always belated because the signs that the jealous man interprets
are always showing the wrong message – the beloved was unfaithful long
before the scene which the jealous man sees. The narrator's jealousy is retro-
active. The jealous man is compared to a historian who 'has to write the
history of a period for which he has no documents'. But even if he has got
the documents he can never write a history because what is important is
in the involuntary memory which cannot be recorded in documents, not to
mention the very notion of history as problematic if jealousy aims to restore
the life of the beloved only with incidents, 'full of lapses of memory, gaps,
vain anxieties, a life as illusory as a dream'. Deleuze suggests the idea that
jealousy is always belated in *Proust and Signs*:

The jealous man's memory tries to retain everything because the slightest
detail may turn out to be a sign or a symptom of deception, so that the
intelligence will have the material requisite to its forthcoming interpretations. [...] But it comes too late, for it cannot distinguish within the
moment that phrase that should be retained, that gesture that it could
not yet know would assume a certain meaning. (2000, p. 52)

The jealous man 'tries to retain everything' and tries to interpret every sign
he can read from the beloved. He sees every detail as 'symptoms of decep-
tions' but he does not understand that jealousy always comes too late. Sprinker (1994, p. 152) writes: 'The lover is like a historian, one who excavates
materials from the past and recovers their meaning.' The dream of the jealous historian is to have a complete story of an event as a present experience,
and to tell a linear story from belated documents.

When the narrator learns that Albertine knows Mlle Vinteuil and her
friend quite well, and that Albertine 'always call[s] them my two big sisters'

(*SG*, p. 702), he recalls the scene in Montjouvain which he witnessed in his childhood, told in 'Combray', which enables him to gain a 'fatal and inevitably painful road of Knowledge' (*SG*, p. 702). He witnessed a 'sapphist' encounter of Mlle Vinteuil and her girl friend (*SW*, pp. 224–33). Brigitte Mahuzier (2003) suggests that Albertine's words:

> like the crumbs of the madeleine, have the powerful effect of bringing back in a flash the Montjouvain scene in which the narrator now imagines Albertine taking the role of Mlle Vinteuil's friend. But, in contrast to the prodigal return of the past brought about by the madeleine, the words make him realize that Albertine will never be in his possession and will always remain an object of suspicion and jealousy. (ibid., p. 141)

Only when the narrator learns that Albertine knew Mlle Vinteuil (this is triggered by Albertine's words) can he remember the lesbian encounter he saw at Montjouvain. But this is the jealous historian inside him who creates a linear narrative (chronology) for Albertine's uncertain lesbianism – that which is a form of otherness.

Narrative: Fixing the Unstable Beauty Spot

The jealous person is like an historian who wishes to tell a linear and coherent narrative of an event for which he has got no supporting document; narrative can be seen as a way of dealing with a fear of lack of evidence, which also arouses jealousy. Linear narrative originates from the same anxiety as a jealous man's fear: this is owing to the unstable nature of desire and the loved object.

After the narrator has been introduced to Albertine and her friend Gisèle, two girls in the group of 'young girls' at the beach of Balbec, he has a short trip from Balbec to Paris with Gisèle, a girl he thinks he is united to by 'a bond of mutual affection' (*BG*, p. 642) At that moment he thinks that 'Albertine no longer attract[s] me' any more. His narrative then turns into an essay. He argues:

> in those periods of my life in which I was not actually in love but desired to be, I carried in my mind not only a physical ideal of beauty which [...] I recognized from a distance in every passing woman far enough away from me for her indistinct features not to belie the identification, but also the mental phantom [...] of the woman who was going to fall in love with me, to take up her cues in the amorous comedy which I had had all

written out in my mind from my earliest boyhood, and in which every attractive girl seemed to me to be equally desirous of playing, provided that she had also some of the physical qualifications required. In this play, whoever the new star might be whom I invited to create or to revive the leading part, the plot, the incidents, the lines themselves preserved an unalterable form. (*BG*, p. 642)

The narrator is not in love at this stage but desires to be. De Rougemont would say his desire is the love of love (1983, p. 42). It is not the beloved but the state of being in love which is desirable. So the beloved object is not necessarily unique to the lover. He desires himself to be in love with certain qualities, which can be attributed to anybody who is 'attractive'. He has decided the qualities his beloved should possess and no matter who she is, 'the plot, the incidents, the lines themselves preserved an unalterable form'. Love is actualized in narrative. Love should take the form of a narration, otherwise it is only 'the desire to be in love'. The beloved may be unstable, but the narrative stabilizes 'the plot, the incidents, the lines'. The very analogy of love to narrative fiction already evokes the beloved as a 'mental phantom', who is not necessarily a specific person. However, as soon as the narrator decides to travel with Gisèle, he immediately recalls the image of Albertine:

Like a wet hen, I had thought to myself, and this view of her hair had induced me to embody in Albertine a different soul from that implied hitherto by her violet face and mysterious gaze. That shining cataract of hair at the back of her head had been for a moment or two all that I was able to see of her, and continued to be all that I saw in retrospect. Our memory is like one of those shops in the window of which is exposed now one, now another photograph of the same person. And as a rule the most recent exhibit remains for some time the only one to be seen. (*BG*, p. 641)

Perhaps jealousy as a passion is like the image on a photo: the most recent exhibit remains for some time the only one to be seen. To say someone is jealous is to see one particular aspect of that person and disavow others. To say the jealous old man is jealous is to extract a particular quality from him, to single out jealousy from other many passions he might have, such as love, hatred, anger, *ressentiment*, and so on.

Or perhaps jealousy is like Barthes' notion of the *studium* of a photograph, that which 'derives from an *average* affect, almost from a certain training', and where 'my sovereign consciousness' (1981, p. 26) is invested, so it is a framed way of reading a photograph, for its cultural messages. And another element is the *punctum*, which is 'that accident which pricks me (but also bruises me, is poignant to me)' (ibid., p. 27) and that which 'breaks (or punctuates) the *studium*' (ibid., p. 26). So the *studium* in a photograph is that which stabilizes reading. To say someone is jealous is to read the *studium* of that person, ignoring the *punctum*. But if jealousy is not one jealousy, then to call someone a jealous old man is to create an allegory out of him, to work within the sphere of the *studium*.[2]

Love is unstable, the beloved is unstable, but narrative stabilizes. In *A Lover's Discourse* Barthes asks:

> But isn't desire always the same, whether the object is present or absent? Isn't the object *always* absent? (1999, p. 15)

The characteristic of desire is always to be unsatisfiable, no matter what the object of desire is. For Barthes, the object is not even there, since photography only confirms absence. This coincides with the narrator's desire. In retrospect, the narrator realizes that Albertine is the product of his imagination. Or to be precise, the name Albertine is assigned to replace his imagined young girls playing at the beach (*BG*, pp. 618–19). To see Albertine's beauty spot, for the narrator, is a marker of a certain stage at which he knows Albertine:

> I once again saw the tiny mole on her cheek, below her eye, marked another stage. (*BG*, p. 618)

It is as if saying the discovery of her having a mole, as a detail about that person, helps to pin down and to shape that unstable person who is fixed the first time for the narrator. He even thinks of Albertine as undergoing 'metamorphosis' (*BG*, p. 619). However, these qualities (of having a beauty mole on the cheek below the eye, for example) are never stable. When the narrator thinks of the 'unstable' beauty spot on Albertine's face, he cannot make up his mind again:

> I might [...] have guessed as much in advance, since the girl on the beach was a fabrication of my own. In spite of which, since I had [...] identified her with Albertine, I felt myself in honour bound to fulfil to the real the promises of love made to the imagined Albertine. [...] Finally, to conclude this account of my first introduction to Albertine, when trying to recapture that little beauty spot on her cheek, just under the eye, I remembered that, looking from Elstir's window when Albertine had gone by, I had seen it on her chin. In fact, when I saw her I noticed that

she had a beauty spot, but my errant memory made it wander about her face, fixing it now in one place, now in another. (*BG*, pp. 621–2)

In order to coalesce the imagined Albertine (who is not necessarily Albertine) with the 'real' Albertine, the narrator has to decide where the unstable beauty spot is. And before he actualizes his ideal lover as 'Albertine', he is free from jealousy because there is no body for him to be jealous of. The desire of fixing the beauty spot is also the desire to narrate, and thus begins jealousy, because jealousy fills the gaps between contradictory events.

Deleuze writes, 'jealousy is the very delirium of signs' (2000, p. 122). He differentiates two kinds of madness, two forms of 'sign-deliria' in *Proust and Signs*: deliriums of a paranoiac type of interpretation, and an erotomaniacal or jealous type of demand. Deliriums of the paranoiac type:

> have an insidious beginning, a gradual development that depends essentially on endogenous forces, spreading in a general network that mobilizes the series of verbal investments. (ibid., p. 179)

And those of the erotomaniac or jealous type:

> begin much more abruptly and are linked to real or imagined external occasions; they depend on a sort of 'postulate' concerning a specific object, and enter into limited constellations; they are not so much a delirium of ideas passing through an extended system of verbal investments as a delirium of action animated by an intensive investment in the object (erotomania [...] presents itself as a delirious pursuit of the beloved, rather than as a delirious illusion of being loved). (ibid., p. 179)

Deleuze's notion of the erotomaniac who deliriously pursues the beloved (rather than thinking s/he is loved), is different from Freud and Lacan's notion of erotomania, which is the illusion of being loved, as discussed in Chapter 2. Lacan's Aimée, it will be recalled, was an erotomaniac who had the illusion that she was being loved.

Deleuze then differentiates paranoiac and erotomaniac (or jealous) types of delirium in terms of narrative types: the paranoiac deliria 'form a succession of finite linear processes', while erotomania or jealous delirium 'first forms radiating circular sets' (2000, p. 179). Deleuze argues that Charlus belongs to the paranoiac type of delirium, as it concerns idea and interpretation. His madness refers to 'communications that must be discovered', and he is the 'master of discourse' (ibid., p. 178). The paranoiac narrates and interprets.

The narrator's delirium is erotomaniacal or jealous, because it comprises action and demand. His problems concern 'individuation itself', writes Deleuze:

> what is specifically hidden is the mystery of her individuation, and this mystery can be fathomed only insofar as the communications are interrupted, forcefully brought to a halt, Albertine made a captive, immured, sequestered. (ibid., p. 178)

The mystery nature of Albertine is suspended when she is sleeping. By seeing Albertine sleeping, the narrator realizes 'the possibility of love':

> Alone, I could think of her, but I missed her, I did not possess her; when she was present, I spoke to her, but was too absent from myself to be able to think of her; when she was asleep, I no longer had to talk, I knew that I was no longer observed by her, I no longer needed to live on the surface of myself. [...] She had called back into herself everything of her that lay outside, had withdrawn, enclosed, reabsorbed herself into her body. In keeping her in front of my eyes, in my hands, I had an impression of possessing her entirely which I never had when she was awake. Her life was submitted to me, exhaled towards me its gentle breath. (*LP*, p. 84)

The perfect mode of love for the narrator is watching a sleeping beloved. A sense of total control and complete possession is established by the feeling of not being under the (imagined) gaze of the beloved. The narrator does not have to live 'on the surface' of himself. Keeping the beloved sleeping is a way of allegorizing her. The idea of Albertine's being 'reabsorbed into her body' reveals his anxiety, that he cannot deal with the 'mystery of her individuation', and can only dream of reducing her to a single, fixed, sleeping being, who is in between present and absent, alive and dead. Towards the end of *La Prisonnière*, after Albertine reminds the narrator to visit her in her bedroom in five minutes, or else she 'shall fall asleep at once, for I am dead', he sees her sleeping, 'It was indeed a dead woman that I saw when, presently, I entered her room' (*LP*, p. 485), and he describes her body as 'that twisted body, that allegorical figure' (*LP*, p. 485). Albertine's body is seen as an allegorical figure of Death, as if saying the dream of a jealous lover is to have seen his beloved's dead body because only a dead body can be kept under control. Deleuze writes:

> There is an astonishing relation between the sequestration born of jealousy, the passion to see, and the action of profaning: sequestration, voyeurism, and profanation – the Proustian trinity. For to imprison is

[...] to put oneself in a position to see without being seen, that is, without the risk of being carried away by the beloved's viewpoint that excluded us from the world as much as it included us within it. Thus, seeing Albertine asleep. To see is indeed to reduce the beloved to the contiguous, noncommunicating aspects that constitute her and to await the transversal mode of communication that these partitioned halves will find the means of instituting. (2000, pp. 140–1)

The Proustian trinity is interchangeable – at least the sequestration and voyeurism are: seeing is imprisoning; and imprisoning is a way of putting the prisoner under the voyeur's gaze. 'To imprison is to put oneself in a position to see without being seen.' Deleuze anticipates Foucault's idea of panopticism, in *Discipline and Punish* (1975), which is derived from Jeremy Bentham's ideal prison 'The Panopticon'. In the Panopticon, prisoners are confined in the cells on the perimeter of the prison, while there is a watch tower at the middle, overlooking the cells. The warden is invisible, whereas the prisoners are visible. This architecture of surveillance is structured in a way that the prisoners do not know whether or not there is a warden stationed in the watch tower. They internalize the warden's gaze. Foucault argues that the mind of the modern subject is structured through panoptical devices at work in society.[3] The warden in the panopticon is in a position to see without being seen. Yet curiously the narrator does not feel that he is free. He has to 'live on his surface' when Albertine is awake. But nevertheless he has the 'impression' that he possesses Albertine, only when she is asleep.

In Search of Sexuality

The narrator is busy investigating what Albertine has done and his jealousy grows after Albertine is dead. His jealousy has to do with Albertine's sexuality, which is beyond his imagination. It is Cottard who arouses the narrator's 'painful unease' (*SG*, p. 264) when he tells him to notice women touching each other. This 'unease' could be of the same sort when the narrator wants to fix the unstable beauty spot on Albertine's face. Although Albertine's sexuality becomes the major obsession for the narrator, it is not he who starts the suspicion: when Albertine and Andrée waltz together, Cottard draws his attention to their dance, from 'the professional point of view of a doctor' without noticing that the two dancing girls whom he is commenting on are the narrator's friends (*SG*, p. 264). After directing him to watch Albertine and Andrée 'waltzing slowly, tightly clasped together' (*SG*, p. 264), Cottard says:

I've left my glasses behind and I can't see very well, but they are certainly keenly roused. It's not sufficiently known that women derive most
excitement through their breasts. And theirs, as you see, are touching
completely. (*SG*, p. 264)

And the narrator then notices that 'indeed the contact between the breasts
of Andrée and of Albertine had been constant' (*SG*, p. 264). He then feels
'sour' (*SG*, p. 264) and he finds that Albertine 'appears to be conveying
some secret and voluptuous thrill' (*SG*, p. 264). Thus begins his jealousy.
The 'voluptuous thrill' he perceives from Albertine and Andrée is also mentioned by Schreber in his *Memoir*, as discussed in Chapter 2, a state of enjoyment associated with a feminine 'State of Blessedness'. Here, the spectacle of
women dancing is framed by Cottard. The effect is like (though much less
intense) Iago's erotic dream which invites Othello to see what Iago wants
him to see. But of course the motive in the narrator's case is different: Cottard may be vicariously enjoying 'the excitement through their breasts'. But
nevertheless the narrator's worry (or obsession?) is circumstantial, as the
two women could be any female couple dancing. His jealousy is aroused
by a doctor whose eyesight is not functioning very well. He is seeing what
Cottard wants him to see.

The tone Cottard uses is very interesting: the phrase 'it is not sufficiently
known' of course means the opposite: he is quoting what *on dit* [they say], he
is framed by ideological discourse, in what Barthes in *S/Z* calls the 'cultural
code' – he actually does not need glasses because he knows, according to a
present knowledge, his knowledge as *déjà vu* (already seen) (1974, p. 20). The
scene is like two voyeurs sharing with each other, constructing the pleasure
they understand in heterosexuality in relation to the two women. And the
narrator's anxiety begins with the piece of 'knowledge' Cottard tells him.
Lesbianism in women is so unknown to the narrator, who cannot bear the
idea that Albertine could enjoy a pleasure which is outside what he can offer:

But in jealousy we have, so to speak, to try out sufferings of every shape
and size, before we arrive at the one which seems fit. And how much
more difficult this is in the case of a suffering such as that of feeling that
she whom we loved is finding pleasure with beings who are different
from us, who give her sensations which we are not capable of giving her,
or who at least by their configuration, their aspect, their ways, represent
to her something quite different from us! Ah, if only Albertine had fallen
in love with Saint-Loup, how much less, it seemed to me, I should have
suffered! (*AD*, p. 735)

This is where we begin to understand what Deleuze means when he says in Proust 'all lies are organized around homosexuality, revolving around their center. Homosexuality is the truth of love. This is why the series of loves is really double' (2000, p. 81). The narrator even hopes that Albertine loves a man, his friend Saint-Loup assuming she has to have an affair with somebody. The Marquis Robert de Saint-Loup belongs to the aristocracy and his intellectual tastes and advanced ideas are all fascinating for the narrator. (His aunt Oriane de Guermantes was the second loved object of the narrator.) Saint-Loup serves as an army officer and dies as a war hero. He was once involved in a love affair with Rachel, whom the narrator saw in a brothel. However, Saint-Loup's repressed homosexuality becomes obvious when he marries Gilberte Swann, the narrator's first love. Also, perhaps because he unconsciously thinks that Saint-Loup may be homosexual, Albertine is not having an affair at all if she loves Saint-Loup. But this is contradicted in *Sodome et Gomorrhe*, when the narrator is asked to accompany Bloch, his friend, to his carriage, leaving behind Saint-Loup and Albertine:

> But I could not bear to leave Albertine in the train with Saint-Loup; they might, while my back was turned, get into conversation, go into another compartment, smile at one another, touch one another; my eyes, glued to Albertine, could not detach themselves from her so long as Saint-Loup was there. (*SG*, p. 682–3)

Though the narrator could not bear the jealousy aroused by leaving Albertine with Saint-Loup, the jealousy aroused by heterosexual infidelity is more acceptable than that which is aroused by the homosexual. Hence Bersani writes:

> The most accurate sexual metaphor for a hopeless pursuit of one's own desire is undoubtedly the heterosexual's jealousy of homosexuality in the other sex. (1986, p. 416)

This is the case of the narrator, who is jealous of (and curious of) the other's sexuality, which, according to Bersani, is the most hopeless pursuit of one's own desire.

On love between women, not 'between men', the narrator writes that it:

> was something too unfamiliar; there was nothing to enable me to form a precise and accurate idea of its pleasure, its quality. [. . .] Now the knowledge that I had of them was internal, immediate, spasmodic, painful. Love is space and time made perceptible to the heart. (*LP*, p. 519)

The love that the narrator mentions depends on his inability to understand the love between women. Women's desire has no history, no record, for it is not understood within the language of patriarchy (the Lacanian Symbolic Order).[4] Jealousy in this sense is the reaction to the realization that one cannot understand the other's desire. The narrator continues:

> As there is no knowledge, one might almost say that there is no jealousy, except of oneself. Observation counts for little. It is only from the pleasure that we ourselves have felt that we can derive knowledge and pain. (*LP*, p. 519)

There is no jealousy except being jealous of oneself, which echoes Swann's idea that:

> the memory of those [jealous] feelings is something that's to be found only in ourselves; we must go back into ourselves to look at it. (*SG*, p. 139)

The knowledge that one acquires is paired with, or rather, followed by, pain. Perhaps that is why Sprinker argues that:

> Jealousy is not a relationship in which one stands to objects, but a condition one must endure in relation to oneself. (1994, p. 151)

Homosexuality and the Truth of Love

Saint-Loup's homosexuality is repressed (perhaps by the narrator) at an early stage in the novel. He is very hostile and violent to a 'shabbily dressed gentleman', who is an 'impassioned loiterer', a 'man of the type', who tries to 'ma[k]e a proposition' (*CG*, p. 243) to him. Saint-Loup beats up the 'impassioned loiterer', and the narrator writes:

> this elaborate display was nothing more than a pummeling which Saint-Loup was administering, the aggressive rather than aesthetic character of which was first revealed to me by the aspect of the shabbily dressed gentleman who appeared to be losing at once his self-possession, his lower jaw and a quantity of blood. He gave mendacious explanations to the people who came up to question him, turned his head and, seeing that Saint-Loup had made off and was hastening to rejoin me, stood gazing after him with an offended, crushed, but by no means furious expression on his face. Saint-Loup, on the other hand, was furious, although he himself

had received no blow, and his eyes were still blazing with anger. [...]
My friend could not get over the audacity of this 'clique' who no longer
even waited for the shades of night to venture forth, and spoke of the
proposition that had been made to him. (*CG*, p. 243)

Saint-Loup's hostility may be a sign of homophobia shown by a repressed
homosexual man. The hostile reaction could well be a variation of 'I (a
man) love him (a man).' Or, it may be an act performed for the narrator.
The narrative is made through the point of view of the narrator, who initially 'concluded that this [the shabbily dressed gentleman] was a personal
friend of Robert' because 'they seemed to be drawing even closer to one
another' (*CG*, p. 242). So if the narrator and Rachel were not there, Saint-
Loup's reaction may not have been so violent. Also, the 'impassioned
loiterer' is 'excusable' because 'that Saint-Loup was beautiful was beyond
discussion' (*CG*, p. 243). (It is interesting to notice that the incident is
framed by the narrator's brief involuntary memory of Gilberte, his first
lover, when he arrives at a corner of the Avenue Gabriel: it foreshadows
Saint-Loup's later marriage with Gilberte.)

Saint-Loup's career, as an army officer who dies as a war hero, may well
be the reaction to a masculinity crisis in repressed male homosexuality, as
argued by Freud in the Schreber Case (1990c) discussed in Chapter 2.
Klaus Theweleit, in *Male Fantasies* (1987), argues that men go to war in
order to resist what is defined as the feminine:

Aside from the animals, all of the love objects [...] are ones [...] in connection with movements of resistance to women as potential love objects.
(ibid., p. 61)

So, for Theweleit, by going to war, men could avoid the feminine; and it also
provides the excuse for satisfying homoerotic attraction between men. But
this homoeroticism is not revealed as homosexuality, as it is repressed and
encoded as comradeship. Theweleit argues that the attraction of homosexuality to the fascist male, is:

its capacity to be associated with power and transgression. [...] [It is] one
of the few remaining gaps through which he can escape the compulsory
coding of feared heterosexuality; it is an escape from normality, from a
whole domain of more or less permissible pleasures – all encoded with
'femininity.' As a homosexual the fascist can prove [...] that he is 'non-
bourgeois' and boldly defiant of normality. His 'homosexuality' is strictly
encoded [...] (ibid., pp. 323–5)

For Theweleit, the army was for the men of the *Freikorps* an escape from normality, and a reaction to the fear of being identified as being 'bourgeois'. Though Saint-Loup is not a fascist, his fear may be the similar to that which is encountered by the fascist male, with his fear of the other. Saint-Loup's sympathies, even in his heterosexual stage are homosocial: he belongs to 'a group of four' which is known as 'the four gigolos':

> These were never asked anywhere separately, they were to be seen riding together, and in country houses their hostesses gave them communicating bedrooms, with the result that [. . .] rumours were current as to the extent of their intimacy. I was in a position to give the lie direct so far as Saint-Loup was concerned. But the curious thing is that if, later on, it was discovered that these rumours were true of all four, each of the quartet had been entirely in the dark as to the other three. And yet each of them had done his utmost to find out about the others, to gratify a desire or (more probably) a grudge, to prevent a marriage or to secure a hold over the friend whose secret he uncovered. A fifth (for in groups of four there are always more than four) had joined this platonic party who was more so than any of the others. (*CG*, p. 555)

So, the idea of hoping Albertine loves Saint-Loup may be the result of the narrator's intuition of Saint-Loup's repressed homosexuality, though at that time he does not realize (or does not want to realize, or represses in the narrative) Saint-Loup's homosexuality – 'I was in a position to give the lie direct so far as Saint-Loup was concerned'. But the narrative is written from a much later standpoint; the narrator has been living in a sanatorium, so Saint-Loup's 'new' aspects actually comprise knowledge held all along, at some level of consciousness, which is now perhaps more fully revealed by writing. Later, he confirms from Jupien that Saint-Loup is unfaithful to Gilberte, 'though not in the fashion which everyone believed, which perhaps she herself still believed, which in any case she alleged' (*AD*, p. 922). The narrator says he later understands:

> what Robert had meant when he said to me [. . .], 'It's a pity your Balbec girlfriend hasn't the fortune that my mother insists upon. I believe she and I would have got on very well together.' He had meant that she belonged to Gomorrah as he belonged to Sodom, or perhaps, if he did not yet belong, that he had ceased to enjoy women whom he could not love in a certain fashion and together with other women. (*AD*, p. 924)

The narrator compares himself with Saint-Loup's 'new orientation' (*AD*, p. 925), without specifying his own sexuality:

On the whole it was the same thing that had given both Robert [Saint-Loup] and myself a desire to marry Albertine – to wit, the knowledge that she was a lover of women. But the causes of our desire, as for that matter its objects, were the reverse of each other. In my case, it was the despair in which I had been plunged by the discovery, in Robert's the satisfaction; in my case to prevent her, by perpetual vigilance, from indulging her predilection; in Robert's to cultivate it, and by granting her her freedom to make her bring her girlfriends to him. (*AD*, p. 925)

Why do the causes of the object of desire reverse for the narrator and Saint-Loup? The comparison of the narrator to a homosexual is extraordinary, as his sexuality has not been revealed to the readers and is therefore ambiguous, although he differentiates himself from Saint-Loup. But there is not much difference, at least at the level of sexuality, between his and Saint-Loup's reactions to Albertine, though we should note that he is speaking for, interpreting, Saint-Loup. Justine O'Brien, in 'Albertine the Ambiguous' (1949)[5] argues that Proust 'transposes' Albertine's sex, making a real Albert become Albertine in the novel, so as to conceal Proust's own sexual orientation, on the assumption that the narrator is a fictional version of Proust:

In endowing Albertine with lesbian impulses Proust was acting quite intentionally and logically. [...] If Albertine had been named Albert and Marcel had been homosexual, Marcel would have suffered intensely from Albert's relations with women. In order for the transposition of sexes to be consistent, Albertine had to be bisexual. (ibid., p. 945)

O'Brien's argument is reductive, and cannot avoid an autobiographical argument about Proust's 'suspected homosexuality', which cannot be proved, and even if it could, would still beg the question 'what is the link between the author and the narrator?'. She slights the novel's interest in women; nonetheless, the narrator's sexuality may not be necessarily heterosexual. Even if the friendship of Saint-Loup does not count, another example showing the narrator's ambiguous sexuality is Charlus, who offers to guide his life, who is 'induced and touched' by the narrator's polite reply, and decides 'to do a great deal for you [the narrator]' (*CG*, p. 387). In response to his 'instinctive gesture of denial' of remembering Charlus' 'declaration' of feeling a 'certain liking for you' (*CG*, p. 760), Charlus is very angry:

[D]o you mean to pretend that you did not receive my message – almost a declaration – that you were to remember me? [...] Could there have been a clearer way of saying to you: 'Forget me not'? (*CG*, pp. 760-1)

Perhaps Charlus looks and acts 'queer', but it has not been shown by the narrator that he has mistaken any homosexual man as heterosexual in the whole novel.

We have discussed Saint-Loup's repressed homosexuality and have also posited a question about the narrator's ambiguous sexuality. We will look in detail about how the narrator is obsessed with others' sexuality. After he witnesses the encounter of Charlus and Jupien in the beginning of *Sodome et Gomorrhe*, the novel turns into a long essay on the issue of homosexuality. A speculative example follows of a non-relationship between a man and a woman:

> The young man [...] was so evidently a woman that the women who looked upon him with desire were doomed [...] to the same disappointment as those who in Shakespeare's comedies [i.e. *Twelfth Night*] are taken in by a girl disguised as a youth [man]. The deception is mutual, the invert is himself aware of it, he guesses the disillusionment which the woman will experience once the mask is removed, and feels to what an extent this mistake as to sex is a source of poetical imaginings. Moreover it is in vain that he keeps back the admission 'I am a woman' even from his demanding mistress [...] when all the time, with the cunning, the agility, the obstinacy of a climbing plant, the unconscious but visible woman in him seeks the masculine organ. (*SG*, p. 29)

A homosexual man is feminine, a 'man-woman' or perhaps unconsciously a woman, certainly not announcing 'I am a woman' (*SG*, p. 28). It is the 'unconscious but visible woman' behind the man who 'seeks the masculine organ' (*SG*, p. 29), but not under the threat of castration as the source of homosexuality, which Freud argues in 'Fetishism' (1991b). Freud suggests that fetishism is the reaction to castration anxiety, when a boy sees the lack of the penis in a woman's body:

> the fetish is a substitute for the woman's (the mother's) penis that the little boy once believed in and [...] does not want to give up. (ibid., p. 352)

And the fetish:

> remains a token of triumph over the threat of castration and a protection against it. It also saves the fetishist from becoming a homosexual, by endowing women with the characteristic which makes them tolerable as sexual objects. (ibid., p. 353)

For Freud, the fetish induces heterosexuality because of its success in disavowing the castration threat aroused by the absence of the penis perceived in women's bodies. So, homosexuality is the result of the failure of fetishism. In contrast, the homosexual man has got the masculine organ and the 'woman' inside him seeks the 'masculine organ', voluntarily. Such seeking is not fetishistic, perhaps contrary to what Freud suggests.

The Proustian non-fetishistic nature of homosexuality is suggestive, putting homosexuality outside phallocentrism and patriarchy, and challenging the idea that homosexuality is the sign of an extreme masculinity. And it suggests that homosexuality is the acceptance of a woman's position, not the refusal of the feminine. The idea of a woman inside the body of a man challenges the man/woman, or heterosexual/homosexual binary oppositions. But afterwards the narrator complicates the issue by identifying two sorts of men who love men: one sort excludes woman entirely apart from 'conversation, flirtation, intellectual loves' (*SG*, p. 30), whereas:

> the second sort seek out those women who love other women, who can procure for them a young man, [...] better still, they can, in the same fashion, take with such women the same pleasure as with a man. Whence it arises that jealousy is kindled in those who love the first sort only by the pleasure which they may enjoy with a man, which alone seems to their [male] lovers a betrayal, since they do not participate in the love of women, have practiced it only out of habit and to preserve for themselves the possibility of eventual marriage, visualizing so little the pleasure that it is capable of giving that they cannot be distressed by the thought that he whom they love is enjoying that pleasure; whereas the other sort often inspire jealousy by their love-affairs with women. For, in their relations with women, they play, for the woman who loves her own sex, the part of another woman, and she offers them at the same time more or less what they find in other men, so that the jealous friend suffers from the feeling that the man he loves is riveted to the woman who is to him almost a man, and at the same time feels his beloved almost escape him because, to these women, he is something which the lover himself cannot conceive, a sort of woman. (*SG*, pp. 30–1)

This astonishingly difficult passage involves men taking women for men, and men for men, and liking men for what is womanly in them, or women for what is manly in them. It shows an ability to speculate on forms of same and other sex desire which always ends with one theme: jealousy. In 'On Narcissism: an Introduction' (1984d), Freud comments that:

The complaints [of being watched, of hearing criticism] made by para-noiacs also show that at bottom the self-criticism of conscience coincides with the self-observation on which it is based. Thus the activity of the mind which has taken over the function of conscience has also placed itself at the service of internal research, which furnishes philosophy with the material for its intellectual operations. This may have some bearing on the characteristic tendency of paranoiacs to construct speculative systems. (p. 91)

The passage in Proust is, like many others where the narrator spells out his reasons for jealousy, an example of a drive towards constructing a 'specula-tive system' (which is also present in the way Schreber constructs his system of thought). The narrator is not paranoid, but there is something sympto-matic in the way the passage is put together which suggests the impossibility of ever seeing any kind of 'normative' sexuality. Or, of ever having under-standing or knowledge of the other.

We can try to interpret the passage: for the homosexual lover of the first sort, it is only the love-affairs with other men which inspire jealousy, because the beloved man enjoys pleasure with other men. But the jealous lover of the second sort suffers a double jealousy, because, firstly, the woman is almost a man for the beloved homosexual lover, and therefore the beloved seems as if he is having an affair with another man, which is the same fear felt by the first sort (who only loves other men). And the jealous lover feels that it is the woman inside his beloved which the other women love, and it is the fail-ure of understanding which arouses jealousy. He feels his beloved 'escapes' him, in the sense that the second sort not only escapes him sexually, but also escapes understanding, that is to say, escapes knowledge.

Both the men of the second sort and the women whom the second sort love are actually bisexual. But they are bisexual in different senses. It is because although the men of the second sort engage in relationships with both sexes, it is with the man as acted by the woman that he loves, and therefore he is still homosexual in this sense. And for the woman, she is bisexual only because she has relationships with both sexes: if we apply the same logic to her as to the beloved man, she is a lesbian, because what she wants is the woman as acted by the man. It implies that the whole idea of heterosexuality can be understood in terms of homosexual love, as argued by Deleuze in *Proust and Signs* (2000). For Deleuze, the truth of love is that what we think is the most intimate relationship is in fact a relationship with oneself. The truth of love is discovered by the narrator, who is jealous of the others' sexu-ality. To understand the truth of love, whether or not it is heterosexual love, is to realize that the other is unknowable.

The truth of love is that any gender and sexual position is not 'normal', and only when we realize this 'double series of loves', can we understand the truth of love. The truth of love is this: there is no single truth of love, so heterosexuality becomes the love of (single) 'truth'. Or 'truth', by which we mean non-phallocentric truths, is the non-narcissistic love the homosexual man has. The love of the masculine organ is thus non-phallocentric. This is 'queer theory' before the letter.[6]

The love of homosexuality becomes the love of otherness, or of heterogeneity. Homosexuality is the truth of love, in the sense that homosexuality is the heterogeneous threat to heterosexuality. The truth of love is the realization that one's sexuality is not even known to oneself, and love is the emotion which responds to this opacity. So love is the relationship to the other, and therefore is bound to be plural. Swann's love is Swann's jealousy towards an unknown beloved. The narrator's love is his anxiety towards his beloved's homosexuality, and in turn towards his own sexuality. Homosexuality is the truth of love. The existence of other sexualities challenges the dominant sexuality, or what Adrienne Rich calls 'compulsory heterosexuality', and it makes both sexualities 'queer' (1993, pp. 203–24).

Perhaps the otherness of oneself is a source of jealousy, and its self destructiveness is brought out by Nietzsche using the image of a scorpion:

> Each virtue is jealous of the others, and jealousy is a terrible thing. Virtues too can perish of jealousy. Surrounded by the flame of jealousy, one will in the end, like the scorpion, turn one's poisonous sting against oneself. (1968, I.5.149)

Jealousy, outside and inside each emotion, has the power to destroy everything, including the person who is jealous. It works as the opposite to a desire for self-protection. Thus the idea of being self-jealous could be understood as 'metajealousy'. The reason for one's jealousy and the reason for one's anger is that: I am jealous that I am jealous. In this case no identity (and thus no unique sexuality) can be claimed, as in Freud's Schreber Case (1990c), in which the statement 'I (a man) *love* him (a man)' can be a translation of 'I am jealous of myself being jealous.' Also, if we cannot understand either other people's or our own desire (instanced in the case of the narrator and Albertine), the beloved's desire can never be matched. Sexuality depends on an allegorical reading of the beloved, and to explain this, I will turn to Walter Benjamin. Benjamin's idea of allegory reveals the problematic nature of sexuality, as it reveals the problematic nature of symbolism: the insistence of fixing meaning to signs.

Allegorizing Sexuality

We must take a detour through Benjamin's discussion of allegory before we continue the discussion of sexuality. 'Allegory' appears in Benjamin's studies on the German 'mourning play', in *Ursprung des deutschen Trauerspiels* [The Origin of German Tragic Drama] (1996), where it is argued that in allegory:

> Any person, any object, any relationship can mean absolutely anything else. (p. 175)

In contrast to symbolism, in which the fixed relation between signs and meaning is assumed, however ideologically, Benjamin points out that the relationship between allegorical signs and meaning breaks down. Allegory is often seen as the personification of an abstract quality. For example, Love is personified as a character and is represented so as to signify Love. In Bronzino's *An Allegory of Venus and Cupid* (c. 1540–50), Love is personified as a Cupid. Allegory assumes that abstract qualities, such as Envy or Love, are known and well defined, so that the task of the allegorist is to represent a quality in a standard way. I have said that to call Carrizales *El celoso extremeno* [The jealous old man from Extramadura] is to allegorize him. But Benjamin draws attention to the constructedness of allegory (in Greek 'speaking other'). There is no transcendental reason for a green colour to signify jealousy. Nor is there an objective sign for a particular abstract quality; red roses need not symbolize Love.

But the arbitrary nature of allegory is a reminder that each quality depicted associates with its opposite. And perhaps nothing can act knowingly as the allegory of a particular quality. Giotto's allegorical paintings in the Arena Chapel in Padua, where Virtues and Vices are depicted on frescoes facing each other, such as Charity/Envy, Justice/Injustice, are commented on in *Du côté de chez Swann*. The narrator remembers his parents' kitchenmaid, 'whose pregnancy had swelled and stoutened every part of her, even including her face and her squarish, elongated cheeks' (*SW*, p. 111), and he thinks she resembles the virtue of Charity as personified by Giotto:

> For just as the figure of this girl [the kitchenmaid] had been enlarged by the additional symbol which she carried before her, without appearing to understand its meaning, with no awareness in her facial expression of its beauty and spiritual significance, as if it were an ordinary, rather heavy burden, so it is without any apparent suspicion of what she is about that

the powerfully built housewife who is portrayed in the Arena chapel beneath the label 'Caritas'. (*SW*, p. 111)

The kitchenmaid is not conscious of her facial expression, nor does she appear to understand the symbolism of her pregnancy. That unawareness makes her the perfect example of Benjamin's allegory. The painting labelled 'Caritas' [Charity]:

> embodies that virtue, for it seems impossible that any thought of charity can ever have found expression in her vulgar and energetic face. [...] she is trampling all the treasures of the earth beneath her feet, but exactly as if she were treading grapes in a wine-press to extract their juice, or rather as if she had climbed on to a heap of sacks to raise herself higher; and she is holding out her flaming heart to God, or shall we say 'handing' it to him, exactly as a cook might hand up a corkscrew through the skylight of her basement kitchen to someone who has called down for it from the ground-floor window. (*SW*, p. 111)

So Giotto's Charity is not self-conscious of herself as being allegorical. She is opposite to 'Invidia' [Envy], which:

> should have had some look of envy on her face. But in this fresco, too, the symbol occupies so large a place and is represented with such realism, the serpent hissing between the lips of Envy is so huge, and so completely fills with wide-opened mouth, that the muscles of her face are strained and contorted, like those of a child blowing up a balloon, and her attention [...] is so utterly concentrated on the activity of her lips as to leave little time to spare for envious thoughts. (*SW*, pp. 111–12)

There are some details on the face of Envy which makes it so 'real' that the allegorical figure is not allegorical any more. When one is aware of being envious, the allegorical image lacks validity. The personification of the figures does not look like the various qualities that the pairs of Virtues and Vices of Padua are supposed to represent. The narrator could not find any pleasure in reproductions of the Virtues and Vices, hung on the walls of his classroom:

> Charity devoid of charity, that Envy who looked like nothing so much as a plate in some medical book, illustrating the compression of the glottis or the uvula by a tumour of the tongue or by the introduction of the operator's instrument, a Justice whose greyish and meanly regular features

were identical with those which characterized the faces of certain
pious, desiccated ladies of Combray whom I used to see at mass and
many of whom had long been enrolled in the reverse forces of Injustice.
(*SW*, p. 112)

The ladies of Combray (with greyish and meanly regular features) who go
to church every Sunday, can be labelled as Charity. But they can just as
easily be captioned as 'the reverse forces of Injustice', because of their
actual lack of charity. One picture can have alternative and opposite meanings: realism, as conveying one meaning only, is defeated, as always in
Proust. The narrator says he later understands why:

> the arresting strangeness, the special beauty of these frescoes derived from
> the great part played in them by symbolism, and the fact that this was
> represented not as a symbol (for the thought symbolized was nowhere
> expressed) but as a reality, actually felt or materially handled, added
> something more precise and more literal to the meaning of the work,
> something more concrete and more striking to the lesson it imparted.
> (*SW*, p. 113)

So even a symbol has not a symbolic value, but seems 'real', outside symbolism. It seems that an allegorical representation must include something
other in itself, which is different from what meaning could be attributed to
it, and this makes it indeed the art of 'speaking other'.[7] So, even jealousy
includes in it non-jealousy. And to admit to jealousy is to admit jealousy to
the other. It seems, on the basis of the Giotto pictures, that such other qualities must be unconscious. When the narrator tries to show that he is not
jealous (when he wishes to leave soon because of Albertine), he denies it by
saying that he does not even know what jealousy is. Ironically, perhaps he is
right to say that he does not know, as no single abstraction can express fully
what it is meant to define.

The crisis in representation put forward by Benjamin also threatens the
knowledge of sexuality. If we treat 'sexuality' as an abstract, the claim to
possess any sexuality – Hysteria, Homosexuality – would turn that sexuality into an allegory. In *The History of Sexuality* (1976), Foucault argues that
confession is the practice of the production of the 'truth of sex' while there is
no truth. Through confession, a particular character type is produced. And
the one who confesses becomes 'perverse'. Foucault writes:

> What if sex in our society, on a scale of several centuries, was something
> that was placed within an unrelenting system of confession? The transfor-
> mation of sex into discourse, [...] the dissemination and reinforcement of

heterogeneous sexualities, are perhaps two elements of the same deploy-
ment: they are linked together with the help of the central element of a
confession that compels individuals to articulate their sexual peculiarity.
(ibid., p. 61)

By the repeated practice of confession, the individual's sexuality is reified
into a personification. If someone commits homosexual acts, he becomes,
as happened in the nineteenth century, the homosexual, 'the invert'. The
allegorization or reification of sexuality feeds the will to knowledge, forcing
the individual to cease to be a plural subject, but, to be constituted as 'perverse'. The Proustian narrative frustrates the idea of defining anything, and
the allegorization of sexuality is an example of it.

The relationship of the love affairs between the second sort of homosexual
man (who seeks out those women who love other women) and the women
who love other women requires an allegorical (Benjamin-inspired) reading
of sexuality. The condition for such a relationship to exist does not require
the beloved to offer or to act the opposite sex, but rather, requires a reading
technique for them: reading allegorically. I would suggest that all relationships require reading the other allegorically, to see the other as both male
and female, and not to confine the reading of the other person to a single
gender. To read allegorically is the ability to see otherness in the other's
gender, to embrace the heterogeneous within genders. That entails seeing
that the very notion of strangeness is ideological and therefore one position
is as strange as any other.

But this is not the whole story. The ultimate ability to read signs is the
ability not simply to make reversals, but to realize the mobility of signs and
desire. Also, the ability to read allegorically is necessary for sexuality, reducing the significance of whether the beloved is a male or a female, refusing to
see that the beloved cannot be confined to one of two genders. The narrator
contemplates, after his witnessing the encounter between Charlus and
Jupien in the beginning of *Sodome et Gomorrhe*, a scene which is 'stamped
with a strangeness, or if you like a naturalness' (*SG*, p. 6). Perhaps any
notion of naturalness is strange. In *Gender Trouble* (1999), Judith Butler
goes so far as to say:

Gender is always a doing, though not a doing by a subject who might be
said to pre-exist the deed. (p. 33)

This is Butler's application of Nietzsche. If there is no essence for the subject,
only the deed of the subject counts. If there is no pre-existing gender position, any gender position claimed is 'queer'.

Having said that, for the sake of clarity, if we confine ourselves to the two sorts of homosexual men whom the narrator was contemplating, Saint-Loup (and possibly the narrator too) belongs to the second sort, who 'seeks out those women who love other women, who can procure for them a young man' (*SG*, pp. 30–1); whereas it is more difficult to say what sort Charlus belongs to. We cannot even say definitely that his homosexuality comes to the surface after the death of his wife. In speaking of Morel, Charlus says:

> I can't go out with him to a restaurant without the waiter bringing him notes from at least three women. [...] He's become so beautiful, he looks like a sort of Bronzino. (*LP*, p. 284)

It is as if Charlus' love for Morel depends on Morel's appeal to other women. And by comparing Morel to 'a sort of Bronzino', Charlus is allegorizing him as a figure (not Venus?) in Bronzino's paintings – possibly his *Allegory of Venus and Cupid*. There might not be a depth in Charlus, only a surface, or persona. We cannot define what Charlus' sexuality is, even if we say he is homosexual. If sexuality is allegorical, any declaration of sexuality is also 'speaking other'. And any claim about one's own sexuality installs its own dissimilarity. The person is, and only is, a persona. There is no essence for a person. In allegory everything can mean anything and therefore no 'normal' sexuality can be claimed. Every sexuality is differently 'queer'.

Chapter Eight

Revenge: Almodóvar's *Carne Trémula*

The Anatomy of Jealousy and the Jealousy of Anatomy

Another title of this book could have been *The Anatomy of Jealousy*. 'Anatomy' could mean the logical dissection, cutting up or the logical investigation of the subject 'jealousy', alluding to what Robert Burton (1577–1640) did for melancholy: *The Anatomy of Melancholy: What it is, with all the Kinds, Causes, Symptoms, Prognostickes, and Seuerall Cures of it. In Three Partitions: with their Several Sections, Members & Subsections. Philosophically, Medically, Historically Opened and Cut Up* (2001). The 'anatomy of jealousy' also means the anatomy *done by* jealousy. To be jealous is also to anatomize, to have a close look at a subject (and thus turning it into an object), to open up the beloved. The psychiatrist Peter van Sommers writes, 'The jealous commit a double crime: treating people as objects and claiming private possession of them.' Jealous men are not just guilty of treating people as objects, they are 'guilty' of anatomizing, and therefore, opening up the beloved (1988, p. 3).

The practice of anatomy as a science came into being in the sixteenth century. Anatomy can simply mean 'dissection' (*OED*), which derives from the Greek word ανατομη (ανα, up; τομ-, cut). The 'objective', scientific knowledge of human body, can only be established through anatomy, which cannot do without the development of the microscope, a typical device of an ocularcentric culture, which also begins to revalue curiosity, like that of Anselmo's. For example, the Dutch microscopist Antonie van Leeuwenhoek first described the spermatozoa of humans in 1674. His microscope enabled him to see the structure of muscles and nerves, and a new way of seeing and therefore thinking about the body was created. Since then, the human body has been discussed as a machine and doctors who get the power to 'open up' human bodies can formulate a body of knowledge. Medical science has denied or forgotten that knowledge through anatomy can only be achieved when the body is opened up, that is to say, when it is dead. Marie-Francois Xavier Bichat marks the turning point of perceptions within medicine at the end of the eighteenth century, from a position of working with symptoms, in which diseases were thought of as independent of bodies, to an alternative perception which addressed itself to tissues, which therefore demanded the practice of anatomy. Foucault, in *The Birth of the Clinic* (1963), quotes Bichat's *Anatomie générale*:

> for twenty years, from morning to night, you have taken notes at patients' bedsides on affections of the heart, the lungs, and the gastric viscera, and all is confession for you in the symptoms which, refusing to yield up their meaning, offer you a succession of incoherent phenomena. Open up a few corpses: you will dissipate at once the darkness that observation alone could not dissipate. (quoted in Foucault 1973, p. 146)

Foucault adds ironically that 'The living night is dissipated in the brightness of death' (ibid.). The will to knowledge objectifies, or anatomizes, and it works with the assumption that the only knowledge which is secure is where life and process have been arrested. The culture of Western civilization is the culture of anatomy. (Not to consider related words like encyclopedia, dictionary, glossary, history and so on, there are altogether 349 entries of titles starting with 'The Anatomy of' in the library of the University of Hong Kong, including *The Anatomy of Architecture*, *The Anatomy of Love*, *The Anatomy of Knowledge*, and so on.) And an 'anatomy culture' seeks power over the object, dreams of opening up the object, and yet disguises itself through the excuse of achieving objective knowledge through reasoning and observation. Jeremy Tambling comments on Foucault's analysis of the change in perceptions of medicine in '*Middlemarch*, Realism and *The Birth of the Clinic*':

> The desire [of opening up corpses] is for a total interpretation, and if the corpse may, to post-deconstruction eyes, offer the fitting commentary on what the fulfilment of that desire would mean, it also, in historical terms, marks a change in perceptions of life and death. [...] There is a discontinuity marked out at the level of perception; a new investment was being made in searching beneath the surface of the corpse. (1990b, p. 942)

The 'new investment' can include jealousy, which, as a desire for objective knowledge of the other, also contains a desire to 'search beneath the surface of the corpse'. Since 'anatomy' also means 'human body', the body is seen as a single unit which can be opened up. It involves not only the taboo of cutting up a human body, but also a kind of body politic: the body is a single unit which consists of 'inside' and 'outside'. Descartes' famous saying 'I think therefore I am' is at the beginning of the modern differentiation of the mind and the body. The body becomes objectified. Three centuries after Descartes, Freud declares that:

> The ego is first and foremost a bodily ego; it is not merely a surface entity, but is itself the projection of a surface. (1991a, p. 364)

Subjectivity is thus not as firm as Descartes understands it. Descartes constructs the subject by making it to be the rational mind and objectifying the body, Lacan and Freud return to the body's importance.

Francis Barker, in his *The Tremulous Private Body* (1984), questions the concept of the individual as the 'foundation of value and meaning'. He writes, 'our personhood – and its vicissitudes – is historical' (ibid., p. v). Barker argues that the idea of the ethical, spiritual, epistemological and ontological sense of the individual influences all the cultural aspects of Western modernity. He challenges the notion of human subjectivity by arguing that the idea of personhood is historical. Thus the idea of becoming a person is ideological. The very word 'personal' reveals that individuality has to do with privacy, for 'personal' means 'private', turning a 'person' into an adjective.[1] To quote Barker:

> Aristotle remarked that it is easy to become a human being you just have to be born, but to become a person takes hard work. Perhaps the harder work is not to be a person? (ibid., p. x)

Although anatomy results in a new understanding of the human body, it is, paradoxically, the desire to find something new about the body, making the idea of the body different. The body in this study is understood as the 'bourgeois body', which is unified, fixed and therefore, dead. Anatomizing is treating what one deals with as dead. It is invested with the desire to look underneath the surface of a body, an ideology which it regards as a mere object.

The Detours of Revenge

In response to Desdemona's potential infidelity, Othello says to Iago 'I'll tear her all to pieces!' (III.iii.434), and later still, 'I will chop her into messes! Cuckold me!' (IV.i.196).[2] Here, Othello's revenge takes up the form of violence to cut Desdemona into pieces, to open her up, look at the body, anatomize her. His revenge is not just to cut her up physically, but to turn her body into a dead body so he can deal with it. Also, in Shakespeare's time anatomy was the equivalent of using a mirror, to hold the mirror up to nature. In this last chapter, I want to consider a film which does not seem on the surface to be particularly about jealousy, but where it seems to be a mirror used in order to give a tightly constructed view of how jealousy works. I will therefore treat Almodóvar's *Carne Trémula* [Live Flesh] (1997) as a case-history showing both how jealousy segues into what is its extension: revenge, or how (since this film also shows optimism) people can move beyond jealousy. *Carne Trémula* (a film adaptation of Ruth Rendell's novel *Live Flesh* (1986)) is my last Spanish text, among Cervantes' two novellas and Buñuel's *El*.

The film is prefaced by an episode showing the birth of Victor Plaza by a prostitute in a bus rushing to a hospital in 1970. It reopens about twenty years later with two policemen, Sancho and David de Paz, in a car patrolling Madrid. Sancho is the supervisor, telling David that he has discovered his wife seeing someone whom he claims he does not know. Sancho is an alcoholic and is on the verge of being divorced by his adulterous wife Clara, whom he used to abuse physically. The camera cuts to Elena Benedetti, refusing to meet Victor Plaza because she is waiting for a drug dealer, although she has met Victor a fortnight before and promised to meet him again. After having a circular ride in a bus which Victor Plaza is entitled to travel free of charge for life, he breaks into Elena's apartment. Sancho and David happen to be around and rescue her but end up in a fake 'accident', in which David is shot by Victor. David becomes Elena's husband after he has been paralysed, while Victor Plaza is imprisoned, and Sancho remains unaffected. Victor's mother Isabel Plaza Caballero dies of cancer when he is in prison.

After six years in jail, Victor encounters Clara at the funeral of Elena's father, and he later has sex with her. In a confrontation at the place where Elena works, Victor tells David that it was Sancho who was literally forcing his hand to shoot David on purpose, in order to take revenge on him for his affair with his wife, Clara. After Elena learns that David has slept with Clara (even if it was before he knew her), she spends a night making love with Victor. David shows the photographs he took of Victor and Clara, in order to make Sancho jealous. Sancho ends up shooting Clara and committing suicide in front of Victor, in his apartment left by his mother. The film starts with the birth of Victor Plaza in a bus at Christmas, and ends with the birth of his and Elena's son.[3]

There are several beginnings in the film: the preface shows an unjust enforcement of an 'emergency article' limiting the freedom of the citizen in Spain in 1970. The film opens with words on the screen: 'A state of emergency has been declared throughout the country. The Articles affecting freedom of speech, freedom of residence, freedom of association, and habeas corpus have been suspended', followed by 'Madrid, January 1970', and then the radio announces, with Isabel's caretaker Doña Centro listening to it while she is spinning:

> Minority actions systematically carried out, in order to disturb public order in Spain, have been occurring in recent months, and are obviously part of an international plot. The defence of peace and progress in Spain, and of the right of Spaniards as desired by all sectors of society, obligates the government to take urgent measures, which will bring an end to these outbreaks. Therefore, invoking the powers set out by law, in particular those contained in the following articles ...

The radio announces a policy which is paranoid in nature, a reminder of the unjust political situation. The plot of the film is deceptive, since it veils what is happening and shows to the audience one perspective as perceived by one of the characters. No full understanding of the plot is possible at the moment of watching. The ending of the film echoes what happens to Victor 26 years ago, the difference being that he is accompanied by Elena, who is going to hospital to have a baby, and the city is represented as safe and rich, directly in contrast to the opening when state repression was at its highest. He talks to his not-yet-born son, saying that the birth doesn't need to be too rushed, as if commenting on his own birth, which was untimely. (His mother, Isabel Plaza, accompanied by Doña Centro, gave birth to him in a bus which was looping the city, showing a dark and prison-like space.)

'Looping' is in a sense what all the characters do: Victor is granted by the bus company a life-long pass, and he is shown taking the circular bus looping from the telephone kiosk where he could see Elena in her balcony, and going back to where he was. The job of the two policemen is to patrol the city – another kind of looping. The marriage of Sancho and Clara is also looping in the same pattern: she is physically abused by her husband. She commits adultery and is discovered repeatedly – first with David, and later with Victor. Sancho's reactions toward Clara's adultery are the same: wanting revenge on the men who sleep with his wife, by shooting them.

Sancho's alcoholic addiction, Elena's drug addiction, David's wheelchair basketball shooting, and Victor's sexual encounters are types of compulsion to repeat. Also, Elena's line 'I have tortured myself enough' implies a sense of recurrence. There are repeated motifs of gun pointing and shooting, such as Elena to Victor, and later Clara to Sancho. The recurrence of motifs is described by Rikki Morgan-Tamosunas as the ' "fort/da" mechanics of desire' (2002, p. 189), alluding to Freud's notion of the 'fort/da game' in 'Beyond the Pleasure Principle' (1984a).[4] Certainly repetition structures the film, and suggests both the compulsiveness of jealousy, and of revenge, for the looping narrative evokes the nature of revenge as that which is repetitive, for revenge is by definition a reaction to something that happened earlier. The prefix 're' for the word 'revenge' evokes a sense of repetition, reaction and, perhaps, regret.

Revenge: the Cure for Jealousy?

As Othello takes revenge, and similarly there are several examples of revenge in Proust, the film is a study of revenge and its relationship with jealousy, since revenge is inseparable from it. It seems that all men in this film are in crisis: Sancho is older and is on the verge of marital breakdown, David is paralysed and sexually impotent, made so by Sancho. Victor's 'revenge plan' is actually a disguise for affirming his masculinity: he is called the 'jerk-off' by Elena, and all he wants is to assure his machismo. The film is full of motifs of 'balls' – basketball, soccer and testicles – symbols of masculinity. Victor is not the figure of jealousy, and he is not revengeful, although he acts so, while the 'buddy' policemen are both characterized by jealousy and vengeance. Perhaps David is envious, as he is envious of Victor who could make love with Clara. He wants something which the other gets. But if that were the case it does not matter whether the loved object is a particular person or not, as what he longs for is something which he can no longer offer: his sexual potency. This masculinity crisis takes the form of taking revenge and appears as a reaction to jealousy. Perhaps revenge is a reaction to a masculinity crisis, but it results in feminizing the revenger.

There are five moments of revenge activated by jealousy in the film. First, Sancho's revenge for Clara and David's adultery, which is shown in the second opening. Second, Victor's against Sancho, for Sancho's putting him into jail, as the result of the first revenge. But it turns out not to be revenge because his intention of sleeping with Clara is 'to learn how to make a woman feel pleasure', and he does not know she is Sancho's wife at the time when he tries to seduce her. (Of course we should bear in mind that the camera might have concealed the intention of Victor, by showing them meeting randomly in front of his mother's grave.) Third, Elena's revenge for David's adultery with Clara. Fourth, David's revenge on Victor (who sleeps with Elena, as a result of the third revenge) by telling Sancho who Clara is sleeping with. And fifth, Sancho's revenge against Victor towards the end of the film, which turns out to be his suicide after killing Clara.

From these instances, it seems that moments of revenge are moments of jealousy, as if saying one is synonymous with the other. Or perhaps the crisis in the male characters creates both jealousy and the desire to revenge. Revenge is jealousy uncured.

The first revenge is set in Edurado Dato where Elena and her father live. It is taken by a policeman (Sancho), who is supposed to be on the side of law, as if saying in the beginning there was injustice. After the accident, Elena marries David, who is impotent. Elena marries dead flesh: the English translation of the Spanish title *Carne trémula* is the original title of Ruth Rendell's novel, *Live Flesh*, from which the film is adapted. Trembling, quivering or flickering are bodily reactions which are out of the subject's control. The English 'original', *Live Flesh*, suggests that flesh which is live has its own life independent from the mind. The title, and the film's attention to the body, especially the deformed body, evokes a sense its own independent being is an object separated from the control of the mind, as Descartes suggests. Perhaps trembling flesh is the affirmation of the body, taken against the mind.

Later in the film, Elena commits adultery with Victor (the third revenge) after she learns that David had slept with Clara, which is the apparent 'cause' of the 'accident'. Here we have a female revenger, who seems to be jealous of David's adultery. Elena's response can be revenge out of jealousy, not in the sense that she is jealous of David, but that she is jealous of herself, being so repressed that she did not commit adultery with Victor after her marriage. She sleeps with Victor, but it can be a way of compensating for her own unsatisfying sex life – 'I have tortured myself enough' – and for her 'guilt complex'.

Before the first act of revenge (Sancho to David), when Elena faints after Victor shoots, the television shows a woman shot in a room with the window broken, from Luis Buñuel's 1955 black and white film *Ensayo de un crimen* [Rehearsal for a Crime] or *La Vida criminal de Archibaldo de la Cruz* [The Criminal Life of Archibaldo de la Cruz]. The Buñuel film is as if commenting on Sancho's revenge: the protagonist in *Ensayo de un crimen* (Archibaldo de la Cruz) thinks of committing a crime (taking revenge on a woman) but every time he is about to execute it the 'victims' are 'punished' by other reasons. The person in question is 'punished' but the 'revenge' is not actualized. There is no more than a 'rehearsal' for the crime: the burning of a plastic woman model, which represents the 'victim'. This moment from Bunuel's film fails to be an apotropaic for the 'crime' Sancho is about to commit.

The Appropriated Life

I will now discuss the last act of revenge in the film. Sancho is the least endearing character: he is not sympathetic – he is associated with drink, he hits his wife, he is old (not in years, but rather in the sense that he is like Carrizales the jealous old man), he is jealous and he is spiteful. He knows before the film starts that his lieutenant, David, has committed adultery with his wife Clara.

If Sancho were a modern-day Spanish Othello, would David be his Iago (the name 'Iago' is Spanish, so Iago is a foreigner in Venice), and would Clara be Desdemona? But Sancho is also Iago, because he plans the death of David, shooting him in the leg/groin (where Iago wounds Cassio, in an act of revenge inseparable from jealousy). Both Sancho and Othello kill their wives and commit suicide. But Sancho takes a long detour before he kills Clara and himself. (Instead of killing Clara, the detour goes this way: first, Sancho forces Victor to shoot David; second, Victor commits adultery with Clara, for an ambiguous reason; third, David tells Sancho after he learns that his wife Elena has slept with Victor; finally, Sancho tries to kill Victor and is prevented by Clara.) Sexual lieutenancy, place-holding, holds with David and Sancho, but the person who really takes Sancho's place and David's 'place' is Victor Plaza (whose surname means place).

Although Sancho is under-represented and off-centred, his contradictory character is worth noting. After killing his wife he says:

Dragging myself towards you . . . this sums up my life.

This self-mocking statement, which echoes Othello's last gestures, also suggests Iago in its ironizing of the self. But if we take Sancho as the figure of jealousy, that is to say, as someone who is a victim of bourgeois ideology, we miss out his radical statement in response to Victor's anger against him before Sancho commits suicide:

> **Victor**: You stole six years of my life.
> **Sancho**: You stole much more from me.
> **Victor**: Your wife didn't belong to you.
> **Sancho**: Your life didn't belong to you.

Apart from seeing Sancho as articulating bourgeois ideology's belief in possession (that 'my wife is my life'), we can see him as a radical figure if we read his words in another way, evoking the sense of life as an event, which I will explain with the help of Derrida and Heidegger.

If Victor's words 'your wife didn't belong to you' were used to justify his affair with Clara, he is no more than a man who believes in justice and revenge. However, if 'your wife didn't belong to you' means also 'the husband does not own his wife': that is a summary of part of this book, that possession is an illusion, a *engaño*, and jealousy is the disillusion(ing), *desengaño*, of love. Although Victor claims that 'your wife didn't belong to you', he still thinks that his life was stolen by Sancho, whose reply is surprising. If Sancho's words are taken literally, that one's life does not belong to oneself, the idea of belonging needs to be considered. It could mean that Victor's body does not belong to himself. It could also mean that life as lost time (six years in prison) is not something which could be owned. As with Proust, Victor is in search of lost time, but this is inaccessible, except through 'involuntary' processes, memory, which is also creation. As discussed in Chapter 3, possessive individualism is the basic assumption in jealousy. The trick, the 'illusion' of jealousy, is the belief that one can possess. If my life does not belong to me, the concept of jealousy needs to be reconsidered. The cure for jealousy would be the undoing of the concept of possession. It is not be possible for us to read Don Quixote's book, *Desengaño de celos* [The Cure of Jealousy], but if we understand the entirety of *Don Quixote* as the cure for jealousy, it suggests that apart from death, going mad (but not into paranoia) might be another way to prevent jealousy. Francisco in *El* is a counter-example, as he is still jealous even after he goes mad. Don Quixote and his servant Sancho Panza are not figures of jealousy. Or, if we take the novel as self-reflexive, as about writing a novel, the cure for jealousy is in writing, which is a way of opening oneself to the other. This point draws Cervantes and Proust together, both stress the novel's fictional character.

Paranoia leads to suicide. But it is necessary to distinguish the suicides of Sancho and that of his wife Clara. Of course strictly speaking they do not commit suicide, as they shoot each other, Sancho shooting himself after he is shot by Clara, who dies from his wounding her. But Clara knows that she is going to die and she still points her gun (actually Sancho's gun) at him, trying to kill him and inviting him to shoot her back. On suicide and murder, Derrida, discussing Hegel, writes in *Glas* (1986), of:

> the absolute equivalence or continuity of murder and suicide. I affect myself specularly by what I affect the other by. The nearly undecidable suspense about which we were speaking – the lynching rope hanging between life and death or the unstable balance of a funambulist – leaves each consciousness to an absolute solitude in the very instance of the recognition. But this suicide solitude places two lives – and the other – in play. Let us imagine rather two bodies, gripped by one another, on

the edge of a cliff: it is impossible for the one who presses the other not to be *drawn* by the void. He desires this fall (his desire is the pressure of this fall), clings to it as to himself in the act of falling, tends toward it without knowing which of the two can protect [*garder*] the other – that is, see the other dead. There is no other definition of suicide. In the Jena *Realphiloso-phie*, in the chapter on the 'Struggle for Recognition (*Der Kampf des Aner-kennens*)' [by Hegel]: 'There appears to consciousness as consciousness that it aims at (goes for) the other's *death*; but also at (for) its very own: it is a suicide (*Selbstmord*) as it exposes itself to *danger*.'

The suspense of the *Aufhebung* is these singularities, let us not forget, that it thus holds in the air in the absolute contradiction or equivalence of the contraries, that is also to say, in indifference. (p. 140)

So murder and suicide, argues Derrida, are not separable. The 'continuity of murder and suicide' implies that to murder the other is to commit suicide, because I depend on the other for recognition, even though I affirm wholly my own singularity. And seeing the other dead is to see my own death, as I need the other's recognition: my consciousness depends on the other, is reflected from the other (note the specular, the mirroring effect from the other). Derrida uses the image of two men standing on the edge of a cliff with their bodies gripped together. One of them desires the other to fall: seeing the other's death in murder is thus inseparable from desiring my own death, as I will lose the other's recognition which contributes to my singularity. My singularity is a contradiction because it depends on the other. Derrida's comparison may illuminate the death of Bradley Headstone with Rogue Riderhood in Dickens' *Our Mutual Friend* (Part 4, chapter 15, p. 781).

Two men (*dos amigos*) fighting are more or less the same as Sancho and Clara – husband and wife – pointing a gun at each other. So Derrida would say that they are both murdering and committing suicide. However, Sancho's 'suicide' is like Othello's; both of them treat their suicide as a way of fixing their own identity: Othello demands (and creates) a narrative that can 'speak of me as I am' (V.ii.341). After Sancho is shot by Clara, he tells Victor, 'this sums up my life: dragging myself towards her [Clara]', and then he shoots himself, with Clara's dead hand on the trigger. The demand is for 'recognition': for Sancho, recognition from Clara; for Clara, from Victor.

The suicide of Sancho at the end of the film could be understood as the fixing of his identity. Clara's death, although technically not a suicide, could be understood as a kind of sacrifice, since she identifies herself being a mother figure to Victor, she even writes him a letter (itself a symbol of absence) and strengthens her will of being his mother/lover by protecting him. So another possibility for Victor sleeping with Clara is that she could be a mother figure for him. In the good-bye letter to Victor written not long before she points the gun toward Sancho, Clara writes:

I would like you to keep this note among the things you like most.

Both women in fact write to Victor before they think that they are going to die. The letter is the remainder of death, a proper death, which is affirming the notion of life which could be owned, and Clara does mention that her life was 'expropriated and destroyed'. But the film shows something which is contradictory to her own understanding of her life: she has been committing adultery twice (at least), and Sancho has been beating her for years. And she wants to be the replacement of Victor's mother especially when she is shown towards the end kissing Victor's Bible.

To say that 'your life didn't belong to you' is to subvert the notion of ownership, if not the notion of possessive individualism. The *OED* defines 'belong' in terms of 'appropriate': 'to go along with, or accompany, as an adjunct, function, or duty; to be the proper accompaniment, to be appropriate, to pertain to'. To 'appropriate' is 'to make (a thing) the private property of any one, to make it over to him as his own; to set apart' (*OED*), so to *ap*propriate is to *ex*propriate. In *Carne Trémula* the word 'expropriate' is used twice:

1. Victor tells Clara that the estate where he lives is going to be 'expropriated', and a new shopping mall is to be built on the site.
2. In the letter Clara writes to Victor telling him 'to keep this note among the things you like most', [a point which shows her desire to perpetuate her identity] and she says that she knew that her life was to be 'expropriated and destroyed' once she starts having the affair with him.

To 'expropriate' is 'to dispossess (a person) of ownership' (*OED*), or to 'to put (a thing) out of one's own control'. Both expropriate and appropriate mean to take from the other and make it one's possession. This might imply the loss of ownership. Jealousy is the fear of being expropriated or appropriated. In this sense, 'appropriation' is desiring 'place-holding', the lieutenancy, the standing-in for the other. Victor blames Sancho for Sancho's appropriation of his life. Although Victor thinks that a husband and a wife do not belong to each other, he still believes in possessing his life. Life, for Victor, is like property, something which could be expropriated. But for Heidegger, life is not property. He discusses *Dasein* [Being] in terms of *Ereignis* [appropriation] in 'The Way to Language' (1982). Heidegger writes:

There is nothing else from which the Appropriation itself could be derived, even less in whose terms it could be explained. The appropriating event is not the outcome (result) of something else, but the giving yielding whose giving reach alone is what gives us such things as a 'there is,' a 'there is' of which even Being itself stands in need to come into its own as presence. (ibid., p. 127)

Being is not owning, but rather, an 'appropriating event' which 'gives us such things as a "there is"' [*es gibt*: there is, it gives]'. Charles Spinosa comments that *Ereignis* is 'the tendency of the revealing of language to reveal particular things in the mode that is best suited to the kind of thing they are' (1992, pp. 271–97). So Sancho's claim 'your life does not belong to you' could be understood as Heideggerian, that life unfolds in events in which the subject has no autonomy. If life is a 'there is' in which 'even Being itself stands in need to come into its own as presence', identity becomes a series of standings in, and life is not a life of somebody's but 'there is', instead, life:

Appropriation grants to mortals their abode within their nature, so that they may be capable of being those who speak. If we understand 'law' as the gathering that lays down that which causes all beings to be present in their own, in that is appropriate for them, then Appropriation is the plainest and most gentle of all laws. (1982, p. 127)

Sancho's statement contradicts his earlier statement 'As long as I love you, you are not leaving me' as a claim of possessive individualism, which promotes emotions like jealousy, envy, *ressentiment*. Sancho kills himself and Victor gets married. But if only death could cure jealousy (in fact, death is a non-cure), how to be in love without being jealous still remains unanswered.

We could conclude by saying that if 'life' is that which is owned and possessed, that concedes everything to patriarchal and logocentric ideology. Derrida suggests an alternative in 'Freud and the Scene of Writing' (2002):

Life must be thought of as the trace before Being may be determined as presence. This is the only condition on which we can say that life is death, that repetition and the beyond of the pleasure principle are native and congenital to what which they transgress. (p. 203)

If life is seen as the 'trace', it is not wholly 'present' to be possessed, and the expropriation of life means not to take away ownership, but rather, to build death into the concept of life, and create a new concept which Derrida calls 'life death'. Repetition is part of the 'trace' in which life and death are not wholly distinguishable, but constitute being as absence and presence at the same time. Revenge, which claims to be a single action responding to another single action, can only exist within a pattern of repetition, which Derrida places inside life as the 'trace'. We cannot take revenge as a unique future act, thinking that it will complete an action and establish the presence of the revenger; in the beginning there was both revenge and jealousy, so that any act of revenge is a repetition of what has gone before. The repetition of narrative in *Carne Trémula* is not apparent to the characters but only visible at the level of structure. They encounter something already repeating itself, so that their jealousies or revenges cannot be unique acts. But when the idea of life as repetition begins to take hold, we can also see that repetition always gives something new, which makes jealousy futile: it brings about what Derrida thinks of as the return of the different. There is a little glimpse of the return of the different at the end of the film, and that makes it optimistic, suggesting that this return is the cure of jealousy.

Bibliography

Adorno, Theodor. *In Search of Wagner*. Trans. Rodney Livingstone. London: New Left Books, 1981.

Allen, Don Cameron. 'Symbolic Color in the Literature of the English Renaissance', *Philological Quarterly* 15 (1936), pp. 81–92.

Armas Wilson, Diane de. ' "Passing the Love of Women": The Intertextuality of *El curioso impertinete*', *Cervantes* 7 (1987), pp. 9–28.

Augustine, St. *Confessions*. Trans. Henry Chadwick. New York: Oxford University Press, 1991.

Barker, Francis. *The Tremulous Private Body: Essays on Subjection*. London: Methuen, 1984.

Barthes, Roland. *S/Z*. Trans. Richard Miller. New York: Hill and Wang: The Noonday Press, 1974.

——. *Fragments d'un discours amoureux* [A Lover's Discourse]. Paris: Éditions du Seuil, 1977.

——. *Camera Lucida: Reflections on Photography*. Trans. Richard Howard. New York: Hill and Wang, 1981.

——. *A Lover's Discourse: Fragments*. Trans. Richard Howard. New York: Hill and Wang, 1999.

Bataille, George. 'The Psychological Structure of Fascism', in *Visions of Excess*. Trans. and ed. Allan Stoekl. Minneapolis: University of Minnesota Press, 1985, pp. 137–60.

——. 'Madame Edwarda', in *My Mother, Madame Edwarda, The Dead Man*. Trans. Austryn Wainhouse. London: Marion, 1995, pp. 135–60.

Baudelaire, Charles. 'The Painter of Modern Life' (1863), in *The Painter of Modern Life and Other Essays*. Trans. and ed. Jonathan Mayne. London: Phaidon Press, 1964, pp. 1–40.

Beckett, Samuel. *Proust*. New York: Grove Press, 1970.

Benedict, Barbara M. *Curiosity: a Cultural History of Early Modern Inquiry*. Chicago: University of Chicago Press, 2001.

Benjamin, Walter. *Illuminations*. Trans. Harry Zohn. London: Fontana Press, 1970.

——. 'Theses on the Philosophy of History', in *Illuminations*. Trans. Harry Zohn, ed. Hannah Arendt. London: Fontana Press, 1973a, pp. 255–67.

——. 'Some Motifs in Baudelaire', in *Illuminations*. Trans. Harry Zohn, ed. Hannah Arendt. London: Fontana Press, 1973b, pp. 152–86.

——. *The Origin of German Tragic Drama*. Trans. John Osborne. London: Verso, 1996.

——. *Charles Baudelaire: a Lyric Poet in the Era of High Capitalism*. Trans. Harry Zhon. London, New York: Verso, 1997.

Benveniste, Emile. *Problems in General Linguistics*. Trans. Mary Elizabeth Meek. Florida: University of Miami Press, 1966.

Benvenuto, Bice and Roger Kennedy. *The Works of Jacques Lacan: an Introduction*. London: Free Association, 1986.

Bersani, Leo. 'The Culture of Redemption': Marcel Proust and Melanie Klein', *Critical Inquiry* 12.2 (Winter 1986), pp. 399–421.

Biondi, Cavalier Giovanni Francesco. *Eromena, or, Love and Revenge*. Trans. James Hayward. London: printed by Richard Badger, for Robert Allot, 1632.

Black, Michael. *The Literature of Fidelity*. London: Chatto & Windus, 1975.

Blake, William. *Blake: Complete Writings, with Variant Readings*, e. Geoffrey Keynes. London: Oxford University, 1966.

Blumenberg, Hans. 'Curiosity Is Enrolled in the Catalog of Vices', in *The Legitimacy of the Modern Age*. Trans. Robert M. Wallace. Cambridge, MA: The MIT Press, 1991, pp. 309–23.

Bowie, Malcolm. *Freud, Proust and Lacan: Theory as Fiction*. Cambridge: Cambridge University Press, 1987.

Bradley, A. C. *Shakespearean Tragedy: Lectures on Hamlet, Othello, King Lear, Macbeth*. London: Macmillan, 1904.

Bray, Alan. *Homosexuality in Renaissance England*. London: Gay Men's Press, 1998.

Brooks, Peter. *Reading for the Plot: Design and Intention in Narrative*. Oxford: Clarendon Press, 1984.

Brooks, Thomas. *A Golden Key to Open Hidden Treasures, or, Several Great Points that Refer to the Saints Present Blessedness and Their Future Happiness, with the Resolution of Several Important Questions* (London: Dorman Newman, 1675) Early English Books Online, 11 Nov 2000 ⟨http://wwwlib.umi.com/eebo/image/66517/1⟩.

Bryson, Norman. 'Géricault and 'Masculinity', in *Visual Culture: Images and Interpretations*. Ed. Norman Bryson, Michael Ann Holly and Keith Moxey. Hanover, NH: University Press of New England, 1994, pp. 228–59.

Burgin, Victor. *In/Different Spaces: Place and Memory in Visual Culture*. Berkeley: University of California Press, 1996.

Burton, Robert. *Anatomy of Melancholy: What it is, with All the Kinds, Causes, Symptoms, Prognostickes, and Scucrall Cures of It. In Three Partitions: with Their Several Sections, Members & Subsections. Philosophically, Medically, Historically Opened and Cut Up* (1621). Ed. Holbrook Jackson. New York: New York Review Books, 2001.

Buss, David M. *The Dangerous Passion: Why Jealousy is as Necessary as Love and Sex*. New York: The Free Press, 2000.

Butler, Judith. *Bodies that Matters: On the Discursive Limits of 'Sex'*. New York and London: Routledge, 1993.

——. *Gender Trouble: Feminism and the Subversion of Identity*. London: Routledge, 1999.

Canetti, Elias. *Crowds and Power*. Trans. Carol Stewart. New York: Seabury Press, 1978.

Caravaggio, Michelangelo Merisi da. *The Incredulity of Saint Thomas*. 1601–1602. Oil on canvas. 107 × 146 cm, Sanssouci, Potsdam.

Carne Trémula [Live Flesh]. Dir. Pedro Almodóvar. Writ. Pedro Almodóvar, Jorge Guerricaechevarria, Ray Loriga, Ruth Rendell (novel). Perf. Javier Bardem (David),

Francesce Neri (Elena), Liberto Rabal (Victor Plaza), Angela Molina (Clara), Jose Sancho (Sancho). 1997. DVD, MGM/UA Studios, 2004.

Cascardi, Anthony J. *The Bounds of Reason: Cervantes, Dostoevsky, Flaubert.* New York: Columbia University Press, 1986.

Cervantes Saavedra, Miguel de. *Don Quixote.* Trans. J. M. Cohen. Harmondsworth: Penguin, 1950.

——. *Exemplary Stories.* Trans. C. A. Jones. Harmondsworth: Penguin, 1972.

——. *The Portable Cervantes* (1949). Trans. Samuel Putnam. Harmondsworth: Penguin, 1976.

——. 'The Jealous Old Man from Extremadura', in *Exemplary Novels III.* Trans. Michael and Jonathan Thacker. Warminster: Aris & Phillips Ltd, 1992, pp. 1–56.

——. *Don Quixote* (1742). Trans. Charles Jarvis, ed. E. C. Riley. Oxford: Oxford University Press, 1998a.

——. *Exemplary Stories.* Trans. Lesley Lipson. Oxford: Oxford University Press, 1998b.

——. *Don Quixote.* Trans. Burton Raffel, ed. Diana de Armas Wilson. New York: W.W. Norton, 1999.

——. *Don Quixote.* Trans. John Rutherford. Harmondsworth: Penguin, 2000.

——. *Don Quijote de la Mancha.* Ed. Francisco Rico. Barcelona: Crítica, 2001.

——. *Don Quixote.* Trans. Edith Grossman. New York: Vintage, 2005.

Chanskey, J 'Schopenhauer and Platonic Ideas: a Groundwork for an Aesthetic Metaphysics', in von der Luft, E. (ed.) *Schopenhauer.* Mellen, 1988, pp. 67–81.

Chaucer, Geoffrey. *The Canterbury Tales: The First Fragment.* Ed. Michael Alexander. Harmondsworth: Penguin, 1996.

——. *The Riverside Chaucer.* Trans. Larry D. Benson. Oxford: Oxford University Press, 1988.

Clark, Roger and Andy Gordon, *Ian McEwan's* Enduring Love: *a Reader's Guide.* London: Continuum, 2003.

Dalí, Salvador. *The Collected Writings of Salvador Dalí.* Trans. and ed. Haim Finkelstein. Cambridge: Cambridge University Press, 1998.

De Man, Paul. *Allegories of Reading: Figural Language in Rousseau, Nietzsche, Rilke, and Proust.* New Haven and London: Yale University Press, 1979.

De Rougemont, Denis. *Love in the Western World.* Trans. Montgomery Belgion. Princeton: Princeton University Press, 1983.

Deleuze, Gilles. *Proust and Signs: the Complete Text.* Trans. Richard Howard. Minneapolis: University of Minnesota Press, 2000.

——. and Félix Guattari. *Anti-Oedipus: Capitalism and Schizophrenia.* Trans. Robert Hurley, Mark Seem and Helen R. Lane. London: Athlone Press, 1984.

Derrida, Jacques. 'Difference', in *Margins of Philosophy.* Trans. Alan Bass. Sussex: Harvester Press, 1982a.

——. 'Signature Event Context', in *Margins of Philosophy.* Trans. Alan Bass. Sussex: Harvester Press, 1982b. pp. 274–307.

——. 'White Mythology', in *Margins of Philosophy.* Trans. Alan Bass. Sussex: Harvester Press, 1982c. pp. 207–72.

——. *Glas*. Trans. John P. Leavey, Jr and Richard Rand. Lincoln and London: University of Nebraska Press, 1986.

——. *Aporias*. Trans. Thomas Dutoit. Stanford , CA : Stanford University Press, 1993.

——. 'Freud and the Scene of Writing', in *Writing and Difference*. Trans. Alan Bass. London and New York: Routledge, 2002. pp. 246–91.

——. 'Plato's Pharmacy' (1972), in *Dissemination*. Trans. Barbara Johnson. London: Continuum, 2004. pp. 67–186.

Dickens, Charles. *Our Mutual Friend*. Ed. Adrian Poole. Harmondsworth: Penguin, 1997.

——. *Little Dorrit*. Ed. Angus Easson. London: Everyman, 1999.

Duby, Georges. *A History of Private Life*. Trans. Arthur Goldhammer, ed. Antoine Prost and Gérard Vincent, 5 vols. Cambridge, MA: The Belknap Press, 1991.

Dyer, Richard. 'Resistance through Charisma: Rita Hayworth and *Gilda*', in *Women in Film Noir*. Ed. E. Ann Kaplan. London: British Film Institute, 1998, pp. 115–29.

Eco, Umberto. *A Theory of Semiotics*. Bloomington: Indiana University Press, 1979.

Eitner, Lorenz E.A. *Géricault: His Life and Work*. London: Orbis, 1983.

El [This Strange Passion]. Dir. Luis Buñuel. Writ. Luis Buñuel and Luis Alcoriza. Perf. Arturo de Córdova (Francisco Galvan de Montemayor), Delia Garcés (Gloria Milalta). Prod. Oscar Dancigers. 1952. VHS. Hen's Tooth Video, 1989.

El Saffar, Ruth. *Beyond Fiction: The Recovery of the Feminine in the Novels of Cervantes*. London: University of California Press, 1984, pp. 67–71.

Eliot, T.S. 'Shakespeare and the Stoicism of Seneca', in *Selected Essays*. London: Faber and Faber, 1951, pp. 126–40.

Ellison, David. *The Reading of Proust*. Oxford: Blackwell, 1984.

Evans, Peter William. *The Films of Luis Buñuel: Subjectivity and Desire*. Oxford: Clarendon Press, 1995.

Ferrand, Jaques, Dr. of Physick. *Erotomania, or A Treatise Discoursing of the Essence, Causes, Symptomes, Prognosticks, and Cure of Love, or Erotique Melancholy*. Oxford: printed for Edward Forrest, 1640.

Fineman, Joel. 'The Sound of O in Othello: The Real of the Tragedy of Desire', in *The Subjectivity Effect in Western Literary Tradition: Essay Toward the Release of Shakespeare's Will*. London: The MIT Press, 1991, pp. 143–64.

Finkelstein, Haim. *Salvador Dali's Art and Writing, 1927–1942: the Metamorphoses of Narcissus*. Cambridge: Cambridge University Press, 1996.

Forcione, Alban K. '*El celoso extremeño* and the Classical Novella: the Mystery of Freedom', *Cervantes and the Humanist Vision: a Study of Four Exemplary Novels*. Princeton: Princeton University Press, 1982, pp. 31–92.

Foucault, Michel. *The Birth of the Clinic: an Archaeology of Medical Perception*. Trans. A. M. Sheridan Smith. New York: Vintage Books, 1973.

——. 'Introduction', in *Herculine Barbin*. New York: Pantheon, 1980.

——. *The History of Sexuality: Volume I: An Introduction*. Trans. Robert Hurley. New York: Vintage Books, 1990.

——. *Discipline and Punish: the Birth of the Prison*. Trans. Alan Sheridan. New York: Vintage Books, 1995.

Frank, Lawrence. *Charles Dickens and the Romantic Self*. Lincoln: University of Nebraska Press, 1984.

Freud, Sigmund. 'The Antithetical Meaning of Primal Words' (1910). *Five Lectures on Psycho-analysis: Standard Edition 11*. Trans. James Strachey et al. London: Hogarth Press, 1953–74, pp. 153–612.

——. 'Notes upon a Case of Obsessional Neurosis' (The 'Rat Man') (1909). *Penguin Freud 9: Case Histories II*. Trans. James Strachey et al., ed. Angela Richards. Harmondsworth: Penguin Books, 1979, pp. 31–128.

——. 'Beyond the Pleasure Principle' (1920). *Penguin Freud 11: On Metapsychology*. Trans. James Strachey et al., ed. Angela Richards. Harmondsworth: Penguin, 1984a, pp. 269–338.

——. 'Instincts and their Vicissitudes' (1915). *Penguin Freud 11: On Metapsychology*. Trans. James Strachey et al., ed. Angela Richards. Harmondsworth: Penguin, 1984b, pp. 113–38.

——. 'Mourning and Melancholia' (1917). *Penguin Freud 11: On Metapsychology*. Trans. James Strachey et al., ed. Angela Richards. Harmondsworth: Penguin, 1984c, pp. 245–68.

——. 'On Narcissism: an Introduction' (1914). *Penguin Freud 11: On Metapsychology*. Trans. James Strachey et al., ed Angela Richards. Harmondsworth: Penguin, 1984d, pp. 59–98.

——. The Economic Problem of Masochism' (1924). *Penguin Freud 11: On Metapsychology*. Trans. James Strachey et al., ed. Angela Richards. Harmondsworth: Penguin, 1984e, pp. 409–26.

——. 'Moses and Monotheism' (1939). *Penguin Freud 13: The Origin of Religion*. Trans. James Strachey et al., Ed. Angela Richards. Harmondsworth: Penguin, 1985, pp. 237–386.

——. 'Criminals from a Sense of Guilt' (1916). *Penguin Freud 14: Art and Literature*. Trans. James Strachey, ed. Albert Dickson. Harmondsworth: Penguin, 1990a, pp. 317–19.

——. 'Dostoevsky and Parricide' (1928 [1927]). *Penguin Freud 14: Art and Literature*. Trans. James Strachey, ed. Albert Dickson. Harmondsworth: Penguin, 1990b, pp. 435–60.

——. 'Psychoanalytic Notes on an Autobiographical Account of a Case of Paranoia (Dementia Paranoides)' (Schreber Case, *SC*) (1911). *Penguin Freud 9: Case History II*. Trans. James Strachey et al., ed. Angela Richards. Harmondsworth: Penguin, 1990c, pp. 131–223.

——. 'The Theme of the Three Caskets' (1913). *Penguin Freud 14: Art and Literature*. Trans. James Strachey, ed. Albert Dickson. Harmondsworth: Penguin, 1990d, pp. 133–248.

——. 'The "Uncanny"' (1919). *Penguin Freud 14: Art and Literature*. Trans. James Strachey, ed. Albert Dickson. Harmondsworth: Penguin, 1990e, pp. 335–76.

——. 'The Ego and the Id' (1923). *Penguin Freud 11: On Metapsychology*. Trans. James Strachey et al., ed Angela Richards. Harmondsworth: Penguin Books, 1991a, pp. 350–407.

——. 'Fetishism' (1927). *Penguin Freud 7: On Sexuality*. Trans. and ed. James Strachey et al. Harmondsworth: Penguin, 1991b, pp. 347–57.

——. 'Jokes and Their Relationship to the Unconscious' (1905). *Penguin Freud 6: Case Histories I*. Trans. and ed. James Strachey et al. Harmondsworth: Penguin, 1991c, pp. 147–51.

——. 'On the Universal Tendency to Debasement in the Sphere of Love (Contributions to the Psychology of Love II)' (1912). *Penguin Freud 7: On Sexuality*. Trans. James Strachey et al., ed. Angela Richards. Harmondsworth: Penguin, 1991d, pp. 243–60.

——. 'Some Psychical Consequences of the Anatomical Distinction between the Sexes' (1925). *Penguin Freud 7: On Sexuality*. Trans. James Strachey et al., ed. Angela Richards. Harmondsworth: Penguin, 1991e, pp. 321–43.

——. 'Three Essays on the Theory of Sexuality' (1905). *Penguin Freud 7: On Sexuality*. Trans. James Strachey et al., ed. Angela Richards. Harmondsworth: Penguin, 1991f, pp. 31–169.

Genette, Gerard. *Narrative Discourse: An Essay in Method*. Ithaca: Cornell University Press, 1980.

Genster, Julia. 'Lieutenancy, Standing in and *Othello*', *EHL* 57 (1990), pp. 785–809.

Ghazoul, Ferial J. 'The Arabization of Othello', *Comparative Literature* 50.1 (Winter 1998), pp. 1–31.

Gilda. Dir. Charles Vidor. Writ. Jo Eisinger, E. A. Ellington. Perf. Rita Hayworth (Gilda), Glenn Ford (Johnny Farrell), George Macready (Ballin Mundson). 1946. DVD, Columbia/Tristar Studios, 2004.

Girard, René. *Deceit, Desire & the Novel: Self and Other in Literary Structure*. Trans. Yvonne Freccero. Baltimore: The Johns Hopkins University Press, 1976.

Grange, Kathleen M. 'Pinel and Eighteenth-century Psychiatry', *Bulletin of the History of Medicine* 35 (1961), pp. 442–53.

Green, André. *The Tragic Effect: Oedipus Complex and Tragedy*. Trans. Alan Sheridan. Cambridge: Cambridge University Press, 1979.

——. 'Logic of Lacan's *object (a)* and Freudian Theory: Convergences and Questions', in *Psychiatry and the Humanities Volume 6: Interpreting Lacan*. Ed. Joseph H. Smith and William Kerrigan. New York: Yale University Press, 1983, pp. 161–91.

——. '*Othello*: A Tragedy of Conversion: Black Magic and White Magic', In *Shakespearean Tragedy*. Ed. John Drakakis. London: Longman, 1992, pp. 316–52.

Greenblatt, Stephen. *Renaissance Self-fashioning: From More to Shakespeare*. Chicago: University of Chicago Press, 1980.

Happy Together. Dir. and writ. Wong Kar-wai. Phot. Christoher Doyle. Perf. Tong Leung (Lai Yiu-fai), Leslie Cheung (Ho Po-wing), and Chang Chen (Chang). 1997. DVD, Articical Eye, 1999.

Hahn, Jürgen ' "*El curioso impertinente*" and Don Quijote's Symbolic Struggle Against "*Curiositas*" ', *Bulletin of Hispanic Studies* 49.2 (April 1972), pp. 128–40.

Hall, Jonathan. *Anxious Pleasures: Shakespearian Comedy and the Nation State*. Cranbury, NJ: Associated Universities Press, 1995, pp. 208–314.

Hamilton, Charles. *William Shakespeare and John Fletcher: Cardenio or The Second Maiden's Tragedy*. Lakewood: Glenbridge, 1994.

Hart, Thomas R. 'Frustrated Expectations: *El celoso extremeño*', in *Cervantes' Exemplary Fictions: a Study of the* Novelas ejempares. Lexington: the University Press of Kentucky, 1994.

Hauser, Arnold. *Mannerism: The Crisis of the Renaissance and the Origin of Modern Art*, 2 vols. Trans. Arnold Hauser and Eric Mosbacher. London: Routledge & Kegan Paul, 1965.

Hegel, G. W. F. *Phenomenology of Spirit*. Trans. A.V. Miller. Oxford: Oxford University Press, 1977.

Heidegger, Martin. 'The Way to Language', in *On the Way to Language*. Trans. Peter D. Hertz. San Francisco: Harper & Row, 1982, pp. 111–58.

Herbert, Sir Thomas. *A Relation of Some Yeares Travels into Divers Parts of Asia and Afrique*. London: printed by R Bip [for Iacob Blome and Richard Bishop], 1638.

Hobbes, Thomas. *Leviathan*. Ed. C. B. MacPherson. Harmondsworth, Penguin, 1985.

Howard, Donald R. *The Three Temptations: Medieval Man in Search of the World*. Princeton, NJ: Princeton University Press, 1966.

Irigaray, Luce. *This Sex Which is Not One*. Trans. Catherine Porter. New York: Cornell University Press, 1985.

Jay, Martin. *Downcast Eyes: The Denigration of Vision in Twentieth-Century French Thought*. Berkeley, Los Angeles, London: University of California Press, 1994.

Joyce, James. *Ulysses*. Ed. Hans Walter Gabler. London: Bodley Head, 1993.

Kamen, Henry. *Philip of Spain*. New Haven and London: Yale University Press, 1997.

Kinder, Marsha. 'Reinventing the Motherland: Almodóvar's Brain-dead Trilogy', in *Film Quarterly* 58.2 (2005), pp. 9–25.

King, Adele. *Proust*. London: Oliver and Boyd, 1968.

Klein, Melanie. 'Envy and Gratitude'(1957), in *Envy and Gratitude and Other Works 1946–1963*. London: Vintage, 1997, pp. 176–235.

Knight, G. Wilson. 'The *Othello* Music', in *The Wheel of Fire: Interpretations of Shakespeare Tragedy*. London: Methuen & Co Ltd. 1978, pp. 97–119.

Kofman, Sarah. 'Baubô: Theological Perversion and Fetishism', in *Nietzsche's New Seas: Explorations in Philosophy, Aesthetics and Politics*, ed. Michael Allen Gillespie and Tracy B. Strong. Chicago: The University of Chicago Press, 1988, pp. 175–202.

Kojève, Alexandre. *Introduction to the Reading of Hegel: Lectures on the Phenomenology of Spirit*. Trans. James H. Nichols, Jr, ed. Allan Bloom. London: Cornell University Press, 1969.

Kristjánsson, Kristján. *Justifying Emotions: Pride and Jealousy*. London and New York: Routledge, 2002.

Kristeva, Julia. *Powers of Horror: An Essay on Abjection*. Trans. Leon S. Roudiez. New York: Columbia University Press, 1982.

Kubler, George. *Building the Escorial*. Princeton, NJ: Princeton University Press, 1982.

Lacan, Jacques. *Écrits*. Trans. Alan Sheridan. London and New York: Routledge, 1989.

——. *Television: a Challenge to the Psychoanalytic Establishment*. Trans. Denis Hollier, Rosalind Krauss and Annette Michelson. New York: Norton, 1990.

——. *The Ethics of Psychoanalysis 1959–1960: The Seminar of Jacques Lacan Book VII*. Trans. Dennis Porter, ed. Jacques-Alain Miller. London: Routledge, 1992.

——. *The Psychoses 1955–1956: The Seminar of Jacques Lacan, Book III*. Trans. Russell Grigg, ed. Jacques-Alain Miller. London: W.W. Norton & Company Ltd, 1993.

——. 'God and Woman's Jouissance', *On Feminine Sexuality, the Limits of Love and Knowledge, 1972–1973*. Trans. Bruce Fink. Ed. Jacques-Alain Miller. New York and London: W. W. Norton & Company, 1998a, pp. 64–77.

——. *The Four Fundamental Concepts of Psychoanalysis*. Trans. Alan Sheridan. Ed. Jacques-Alain Miller. New York: W. W. Norton & Company, 1998b.

——. *Feminine Sexuality. Jacques Lacan and the Freudienne*: Trans. Jacqueline Rose, eds Juliet Mitchell and Jacqueline Rose. London: Macmillan, 1982.

Laing, R. D. *The Divided Self: an Existential Study in Sanity and Madness*. London: Penguin Books, 1993.

Lambert, A. F. 'The Two Versions of Cervantes' *El celoso extremeño*: Ideology and Criticism', *Bulletin of Hispanic Studies* 57.3 (July 1980), pp. 219–32.

Lancashire, Anne. *The Second Maiden's Tragedy*. Manchester: Manchester University Press, 1978.

Laplanche, Jean and Jean-Bertrand Pontalis. *The Language of Psychoanalysis*. London: Karnac Books, 1973.

Leavis, F. R. 'Diabolic Intellect and the Noble Hero: or The Sentimentalist's Othello', in *The Common Pursuit*. London: Chatto & Windus, 1972, pp. 136–59.

Levinas, Emmanuel. *Totality and Infinity*. Trans. Alphonso Lingis. Pittsburgh: Duquesne University Press, 1969.

Lewis, C. S. *The Allegory of Love: a Study in Medieval Tradition*. London: University Press, 1953.

Lewis-Smith, Paul 'The Two Versions of *El celoso extremeño*: a Reconsideration of the Questions of Authorship and Authorial Intent', *Neophilologus* 74.4 (October 1992), pp. 559–68.

——. 'Free-Thinking in *El celoso extremeño*', A Companion to Cervantes', in *Novelas Ejemplares*, ed. Stephen Boyd. Woodbridge: Tamesis, 2005, pp. 191–206.

Livers, J. E. *Proust and the Art of Love: The Aesthetics of Sexuality in the Life, Times, and Art of Marcel Proust*. New York: Columbia University Press, 1980.

Lloyd-Goldstein, Robert. 'De Clérambault On-line: A Survey of Erotomania and Stalking from the Old World to the World Wide Web', in *The Psychology of Stalking: Clinical and Forensic Perspectives*. Ed. J. Reid Meloy. San Diego: Academic Press, 1998, pp. 193–224.

Luckhurst, Nicola. *Science and Structure in Proust's Á la recherche du temps perdu*. Oxford: Clarendon, 2000.

Lupton, Julia Reinhard. '*Othello* Circumcised: Shakespeare and the Pauline Discourse of Nations', *Representations* 57 (Winter 1997), pp. 73–89.

McKendrick, Melveena. 'Calderón and the Politics of Honour', *Bulletin of Hispanic Studies* 70.1 (January 1993), pp. 135–46

Macey, David. *Lacan in Contexts*. London, New York: Verso, 1988.

MacPherson, C. B. *The Political Theory of Possessive Individualism: Hobbes to Locke*. Oxford: Oxford University Press, 1962.

Mahuzier, Brigitte. 'Proust in a Gender Studies Course: What to Do with Montjouvain', in *Approaches to Teaching Proust's Fiction and Criticism*. Ed. Elyane Dezon-Jones and Inge

Crosman Wimmers. New York: The Modern Language Association of America, 2003, pp. 140–43.

Miller, J. Hillis. *Charles Dickens: The World of his Novels*. London: Oxford University Press, 1958.

Moi, Toril. 'Jealousy and Sexual Difference', *Feminist Review* 11 (Summer 1982), pp. 53–68.

——. *What is a Woman?* Oxford: Oxford University Press, 1999.

Morgan-Tamosunas, Rikki. 'Narrative, Desire and Critical Discourse in Pedro Almodóvar's *Carne trémula* (1997)', in *Journal of Iberian and Latin American Studies* 8.2 (2002), pp. 185–99.

Morón-Arroyo, Ciriaco. 'Cooperative Mimesis: Don Quixote and Sancho Panza', *Diacritics* 8.1 (Spring 1978), pp. 75–86.

Muller, John P. and William J. Richardson. *Lacan and Language: a Reader's Guide to* Écrits. New York: International University Press, 1982.

Mulvey, Laura. 'Visual Pleasure and Narrative Cinema', *Screen* 16.3 (1975), pp. 6–18.

Neill, Micahel. 'Opening the Moor: Death and Discovery in *Othello*', in *Issues of Death: Mortality and Identity in English Renaissance Tragedy*. Oxford: Clarendon Press, 1997, pp. 141–67.

Nelson, T.G.A. and Charles Haines. 'Othello's Unconsummated Marriage', *Essays in Criticism* 33.1 (Jan 1983), pp. 1–18.

Niederland, William. *The Schreber Case: Psychoanalytic Profile of a Paranoid*. New York: New York Times Book Co., 1974.

Nietzsche, Friedrich. *Genealogy of Morals*. in *The Birth of Tragedy* and *The Genealogy of Morals*. Trans. Francis Golffing. New York: Anchor Books, 1956.

——. *Gay Science*. Trans. Walter Kaufmann. New York: Vintage, 1974.

——. *Thus Spoke Zarathustra*. in *The Portable Nietzsche*. Trans. Walter Kaufmann. Harmondsworth: Penguin, 1968.

——. 'On the Utility and Liability of History for Life', in *Unfashionable Observations*. Trans. Richard T. Gray. Stanford: Stanford University Press, 1995, pp. 83–168.

——. 'On the Uses and Disadvantages of History for Life' in *Untimely Meditations*. Trans. R.J. Hollingdale, ed. Daniel Breazeale. Cambridge: Cambridge University Press, 1999. pp. 57–124.

O'Brien, Justine. 'Albertine the Ambiguous: Notes on Proust's Transposition of Sexes', *PMLA* 64.5 (Dec 1949), pp. 933–52.

Panofsky, Erwin, *Studies in Iconology: Humanistic Tthemes in the Art of the Renaissance*. New York, Hagerstown, San Francisco, London: Harper & Row, 1972.

Parker, Deborah. *Bronzino: Renaissance Painter as Poet*. Cambridge: Cambridge University Press, 2000.

Parker, Patricia. 'Shakespeare and Rhetoric: "Dilation" and "Delation" in Othello', in *Shakespeare and the Question of Theory*. London: Methuen, 1985, pp. 54–74.

Peeping Tom. Dir. Michael Powell. Writ. Leo Marks. Perf. Karlheinz Böhm (Mark Lewis), Moira Shearer (Vivian). DVD. Criterion Collection, 1960.

Perriam, Chris. *Stars and Masculinity in Spanish Cinema: from Banderas to Bardem*. Oxford: Oxford University Press, 2003.

Pevsner, Nikolaus. 'The Architecture of Mannerism', *The Mint* 1 (1946), pp. 116–38.

Pines, Ayala Malach. *Romantic Jealousy: Causes, Symptoms, Cures*. New York: Routledge, 1998.

Pierson, Peter. *Philip II of Spain*. London: Thames and Hudson, 1975.

Proust, Marcel. *À la recherche du temps perdu* [In Search of Lost Time]. Trans. C. K. Scott Moncrieff, Terence Kilmartin and D.J. Enright, 6 vols. New York: The Modern Library, 1998–99.

Puig, Manuel. *Kiss of the Spider Woman*. Trans. Thomas Colchie. New York: Vintage, 1991.

Rich, Adrienne. 'Compulsory Heterosexuality and Lesbian Existence', in *Poetry and Prose: Poems, Prose, Reviews, and Criticism*. Ed. Barbara Chartesworth Gelpi and Albert Gelpi. New York: W. W. Norton, 1993. pp. 203–24.

Riley, E.C. *Don Quixote*. London: Allen & Unwin, 1986.

Robbe-Grillet, Alain. *Jealousy*. Trans. Richard Howard. London: John Calder Publishers, 1957.

Roudinesco, Elisabeth. *Lacan & Co.: a History of Psychoanalysis in France, 1925–1985*. Trans. Jeffrey Mehlman. Chicago: The University of Chicago Press, 1990.

Rudnytsky, Peter. 'The Purloined Handkerchief in *Othello*', in *The Psychoanalytic Study of Literature*. Ed. Joseph Reppen and Maurice Charney. New Jersey: The Analytic Press, 1985, pp. 169–90.

Said, Edward. *Orientalism: Western Conceptions of the Orient*. London: Penguin Books, 1995.

Salber, Linde. *Dalí*. Trans. Anne Wyburd. London: Haus, 2004.

Santner, Eric. *My Own Private Germany: Daniel Paul Schreber's secret history of modernity*. Princeton, NJ: Princeton University Press, 1996.

Sass, Louis. *The Paradoxes of Delusion: Wittgenstein, Schreber, and the Schizophrenic Mind*. Ithaca, NY: Cornell University Press, 1994.

——. 'Schreber's Panopticism: Psychosis and the Modern Soul', *Social Research* 54 (1987), pp. 101–47.

Saussure, Ferdinand de. *Course in General Linguistics*. Trans. Wade Baskin, eds Charles Bally et al. London: Peter Owen Limited, 1960.

Sawday, Jonathan. *The Body Emblazoned: Dissection and the Human Body in Renaissance Culture*. London: Routledge, 1995.

Scheler, Max. *Ressentiment*. Trans. William H. Holdheim. New York: Free Press, 1960.

Schiesari, Julia. *The Gendering of Melancholia: Feminism, Psychoanalysis, and the Symbolics of Loss in Renaissance Literature*. Ithaca: Cornell University Press, 1992.

Schreber, Daniel Paul. *Denkwürdigkeiten eines Nervenkranken* [Memoirs of My Nervous Illness]. Trans. Ida Macalpine and Richard A. Hunter. New York: New York Review Books, 2000.

Sedgwick, Eve Kosofsky. *Between Men: English Literature and Male Homosocial Desire*. New York: Columbia University Press, 1985.

——. *Epistemology of the Closet*. Berkeley: University of California Press, 1990.

Segal, Hanna. *Introduction to the Work of Melanie Klein*. London: The Hogarth Press, 1975.

Seneca, 'On the Shortness of Life', *Moral Essays vol. 2*, trans. John W. Basore. Cambridge, MA: Harvard University Press, 1932.

Shakespeare, William. *The Tragedy of Othello: the Moor of Venice*. Ed. Alvin Kernan. New York: The New American Library, 1963.

——. *Othello*. Eds Celia Hilton and R.T. Jones. London: Macmillan Education, 1984.

Othello (Arden Shakespeare). Ed. E.A.J. Honigmann. London: Thomas Nelson & Sons, 1997.

——. *Othello*. Ed. Michael Neill. Oxford: Oxford University Press, 2006.

——. *Shakespeare's Sonnets*. Ed. Stephen Booth. New Haven and London: Yale University Press, 2000.

Shattuck, Roger. *Proust*. London: Collins, 1974.

——. *Proust's Way: A Field Guide to In Search of Lost Time*. New York: W.W. Norton, 2000.

Shelley, Percy Bysshe. *Shelley's 'The Triumph of Life': A Critical Study: Based on a Text Newly Edited from the Bodleian Manuscript*. Ed. Donald H. Reiman. Urbana: University of Illinois Press, 1966.

Spinosa, Charles. 'Derrida and Heidegger: Iterability and *Ereignis*', in *Heidegger: a Critical Reader*. Ed. Hubert Dreyfus and Harrison Hall. Oxford: Blackwell, 1992, pp. 271–97.

Splitter, Randolph. *Proust's Recherche: A Psychoanalytic Intepretation*. London: Routledge, 1981.

Sprinker, Michael. *History and Ideology in Proust:* Á la recherche du temps perdu *and the Third French Republic*. Cambridge: Cambridge University Press, 1994.

Stern, Sheila. *Marcel Proust: Swann's Way*. Cambridge: Cambridge University Press, 1989.

Stone, Lawrence. *The Family, Sex and Marriage in England 1500–1800*. London: Weidenfeld and Nicolson, 1977.

Szondi, Peter. *An Essay on the Tragic*. Trans. Paul Fleming. Stanford, CA: Stanford University Press, 2002.

Tambling, Jeremy. *Confession: Sexuality, Sin, the Subject*. New York: Manchester University Press, 1990a.

——. 'Middlemarch, Realism and the Birth of the Clinic', *ELH* 57 (1990b), pp. 939–60.

——. *Dickens, Violence and the Modern State: Dreams of the Scaffold*. Basingstoke, Hampshire: Macmillan, 1995.

——. *Opera and the Culture of Fascism*. Oxford: Clarendon Press, 1996.

——. *Becoming Posthumous: Life and Death in Literary and Cultural Studies*. Edinburgh: Edinburgh University Press, 2001a.

——. *Lost in the American City: Dickens, James, and Kafka*. New York: Palgrave, 2001b.

——. 'Monomania of a Whale Hunter: "Moby-Dick"', *English* 52 (2003a), 101–23.

——. *Wong Kar-wai's* Happy Together. Hong Kong: Hong Kong University Press, 2003b.

——. *Blake's Night Thoughts*. London: Palgrave Macmillan, 2005.

Theweleit, Klaus. *Male Fantasies: Women, Floods, Bodies, History*. Trans. Stephen Conway, Erica Carter and Chris Turner. Cambridge: Polity Press, 1987.

2046. Dir. and writ. Wong Kar-wai. 2004. DVD, Block 2 Pictures, 2005.

Trollope, Anthony. *He Knew He was Right* (1869). Harmondworth, Penguin, 1994.

Van Sommers, Peter. *Jealousy: What is It and Who Feels It?* Harmondsworth: Penguin, 1988.

Viti, Elizabeth Richardson. *Mothers, Madams, and 'Lady-like' Men*. Birmingham: Summa Publication, Inc., 1994.

Wells, Stanley and Gary Taylor. *William Shakespeare: a Textual Companion*. Oxford: Clarendon Press, 1987.

Wey-Gómez, Nicolás. 'The Jealous and the Curious: Freud, Paranoia and Homosexuality in Cervantes's Poetics', in *Cervantes and His Postmodern Constituencies*. Eds J. Cruz, Carroll B. Johnson. New York: Garland, 1999, pp. 170–200.

Whittock, Trevor. *A Reading of the Canterbury Tales*. London: Cambridge University Press, 1968.

Wigley, Mark. *The Architecture of Deconstruction: Derrida's Haunt*. Cambridge, MA: MIT Press, 1993.

Woods, Evelyn A. and Eric T. Carlson. 'The Psychiatry of Philippe Pinel', *Bulletin of the History of Medicine* 35 (1961), pp. 14–29.

Notes

Introduction

1. Quoted in David M. Buss, (2000), p. 27. Throughout this book, see the Bibliography for editions used for primary texts.
2. Quoted in Barthes (1977), p. 171 (my translation).
3. Kristján Kristjánsson, *Justifying Emotions: Pride and Jealousy* (2002) and Peter van Sommers, *Jealousy: What is It and Who Feels It?* (1988).
4. For *desengaño* see Thomas R. Hart (1994), p. 89.
5. See Sigmund Freud, 'The Antithetical Meaning of Primal Words' (1953–74), and 'The "Uncanny" ' (1990e).
6. On this, see Alan Bray (1998).
7. Bronzino, *An Allegory of Venus and Cupid*, 1540–50, The National Gallery, London. See Deborah Parker (2000), pp. 128–76.
8. See also Peter William Evans (1995), pp. 111–33. For Lacan's admiration for *El*, which evokes Buñuel's relationship to Dali and his work on paranoia, see Lacan 'Kant with Sade', trans James R. Swerson jr. *October* 21 (1989): 104n.
9. See Freud, 'Some Psychical Consequences of the Anatomical Distinction between the Sexes' (1991e). For the gender of jealousy, especially female jealousy, see Toril Moi (1982).

Chapter One

1. See also Toril Moi (1999) for a feminist critique of Girard.
2. On homosexuality in *Happy Together*, see Jeremy Tambling (2003b), ch. 6.
3. See also Lacan (1998b), pp. 105–19, especially p. 116.
4. See Ayala Malach Pines (1998).

Chapter Two

1. When quoted in the text this edition will be referred to as *SC*.
2. See also pp. 41–3 for a discussion of the Schreber Case.

3. The word 'monomania' was coined by Esquirol, while Pinel calls it melancholia. See Lorenz E. A. Eitner (1983), p. 354, note 29. Also Jeremy Tambling (2003): pp. 101–23.

4. Esquirol, *Traité des maladies mentales*, quoted in David Macey (1988), p. 183.

5. Contrast this Oedipal reading of Schreber with Deleuze and Guattari (1984), p. 297.

6. For a critical account on Lacan's Aimée case, see Bice Benvenuto and Roger Kennedy (1986), p. 43. Erotomania is usually thought of as feminine. See Juliana Schiesari (1992), pp. 96–7. See also Kathleen M. Grange (1961) and Evelyn A. Woods and Eric T. Carlson (1961), pp. 14–29, especially p. 20.

7. See also Jacques Lacan and the *Ecole Freudienne* (1982), p. 94.

8. Piera Aulagnier-Spairani et al., 'Points', *Le Désir et la perversion* (1981), quoted in Macey (1988), p. 184.

9. See Roger Clark and Andy Gordon (2003).

10. See Freud, 'The Economic Problem of Masochism' (1984e).

11. For a discussion of *Our Mutual Friend*, see J. Hillis Miller (1958), Lawrence Frank (1984), and Jeremy Tambling (1995).

Chapter Three

1. Lipson's translation (1998b) is referred to as L here; C. A. Jones's (1972) will be J, then the relevant page numbers.

2. There are two versions of the story (either 1604 or 1606, which is the manuscript called the 'Porras version', and 1613, the published version), but only the later version was translated by Lipson and Jones. In the Porras version, Leonora (called Isabela) commits adultery with Loaysa, who dies not because of going to the Indies, but in a gun accident. This alters the question of the punishments of Carrizales, Loaysa and Leonora (and the duennas). A. F. Lambert argues that in the Porras version the links between Loaysa and Carrizales are not as obvious as in the published version (in which they both go to the Indies), and also that the Porras versions is more moralistic, whereas the published version shows that people are more complex. A. F. Lambert maintains that the published version make *El celoso extremeño* a tragedy, which reflects 'a tragic flaw in the protagonist's character' (1980, p. 562). The issue of Leonora's 'free will' (as she chooses to end up in a convent, instead of following Carrizales' will), which was important in the seventeenth century, has become important in the criticism of *El celoso extremeño*. See A. F. Lambert (1980) and Paul Lewis-Smith (1992) and (2005). See also Alban K. Forcione (1982) and Cervantes, 'The Jealous Old Man from Extremadura' in *Exemplary Novels III*, trans. Michael and Jonathan Thacker (1992) for another translation and for a discussion of what 'exemplary' means.

3. See Paul Lewis-Smith (2005) and Boyd's 'Introduction' to this work, especially pp. 36–7. See also pp. 3–4 and pp. 27–31 in the 'Introduction' for a discussion of the title '*Novelas Ejemplares*' [Exemplary Stories].

4. See also Lawrence Stone (1977), p. 31.

5. For Blake see Tambling (2005), ch. 4.

6. See Henry Kamen (1997), p. 186.

7. The original is in Nikolaus Pevsner (1946), p. 137.

8. Jacques Lacan (1989), p. 5.

9. See Jeremy Tambling (2001b), especially the section 'Lying Architecture' in 'City Spaces: *Martin Chuzzlewit*', in which Tambling writes, 'architectural facades indicating that no reality is being constructed' (p. 61).

10. See also Tambling (2001b, p. 207). James D. Chanskey's 'Schopenhauer and Platonic Ideas: a Groundwork for an Aesthetic Metaphysics' (1988), quotes Alexis Philomenko (*Schopenhauer, Une Philosophie de la Tragedie* (Paris: Verim, 1980)), who makes 'the tantalising suggestion' that '*l'architecture est l'art du ressentiment*' (1988, p. 150).

11. Derrida is quoting Seneca, 'On the Shortness of Life' (1932), Book 10, section 3, pp. 1–4.

Chapter Four

1. Quotations from Jarvis's translation are noted as J. Translations from Raffel are referred to as R. On 'The Curious Impertinent', see Jonathan Hall (1995), pp. 208–314.

2. The complete 'Cardenio and Dorotea' narrative is found in different parts of the novel (I. 23–4, 27–9, 36). For an account of the interpolated story, 'Cardenio and Dorotea', see Ruth El Saffar (1984), pp. 67–71. For a discussion of its structure, see E. C. Riley (1986), p. 80, who also argues that *El curioso impertinente* has a 'Shakespearean tragedy' quality. In the light of this, it should be noted that the anonymous English play (probably by Thomas Middleton), *The Second Maiden's Tragedy* (1610–11), has as plot of the story of 'Cardenio and Dorotea' and as subplot, *El curioso impertinente*. It seems equally probable that Shakespeare and John Fletcher were joint authors of a play called *Cardenio*. (Charles Hamilton (1994) even claims that *The Second Maiden's Tragedy* was actually Fletcher and Shakespeare's lost play *History of Cardenio* (performed in 1614). This has not been generally accepted.) *El curioso impertinente* was translated into French in 1608, and the whole text was translated into English in 1612. See the Introduction to Hamilton, *William Shakespeare and John Fletcher: Cardenio or The Second Maiden's Tragedy* (1994). For a discussion of the source of this play, in relationship with *El curioso impertinente*, see Anne Lancashire (1978), p. 30. See also Stanley Wells and Gary Taylor (1987), pp. 132–3. For an analysis of the two interpolated stories in relationship with *Don Quixote*, see Ciriaco Morón-Arroyo, (1978), pp. 75–86, especially pp. 83–4. Since there are at least two plays containing the plot of *El curioso impertinente* and 'Cardenio and Dorotea', the impact of the material of *El curioso impertinente* should be considered in relationship to English Renaissance drama (e.g. Middleton's *A Mad World, My Masters*). See my chapter on *Othello* following.

3. Melveena McKendrick remarks that honour is seen as an aspect of self-consciousness, See McKendrick (1993), pp. 135–46.

4. Diana de Armas Wilson suggests that *El curioso impertinente* is a 'frank intruder' in the whole *Don Quixote*, whereas Camila's 'little drama' is a 'fiction-within-a-fiction-within-a-fiction'. See Armas Wilson (1987), p. 28.

5. In *Orlando Furioso*, Ludovico Ariosto uses this motif between Orlando and Rinaldo. Shakespeare's *The Two Gentlemen of Verona*, *Much Ado about Nothing*, and *The Winter's Tale*, are also versions of the *dos amigos*. Diana de Armas Wilson discusses the issue of homosexuality in *El curioso impertinente* by referring to subtexts using the motif of *Los dos amigos*. See de Armas Wilson (1987), pp. 9–28.

6. Adorno quotes Benjamin, 'disgust [is] the fear of being thought to be the same as that which is found disgusting' (1981, p. 24). For a discussion of disgust in relationship with the fear of the other, see Jeremy Tambling (1996), p. 29.

7. For an interpretation of these lines see also Trevor Whittock (1970): 'the carpenter's jealousy is a sin against truth, and against the enjoyment of God's plenty' (p. 80).

8. Jürgen Hahn argues that in fact the doubting Thomas motif recurs in the whole Don Quixote, see Hahn (1972) especially 138, n.1.

9. For a discussion of truth as a woman and on Baubô, see Sarah Kofman (1988), especially 191–200.

10. Kreeger, 'Envy preemption in small and large groups', *Group Analysis* 25.4 (1992): 391–408, quoted in Pines (1998), p. 8.

Chapter Five

1. See André Green (1978 and 1992) and Wilson Knight (1978).

2. See especially Lecture 6.

3. See André Green (1979).

4. See also T.S. Eliot, 'Shakespeare and the Stoicism of Seneca' (1951), p. 130.

5. For a discussion of the concepts of self-fashion and confession in the making of subject, and a critical analysis of Othello's identity, see Tambling (1990), pp. 192–200.

6. See also Rudnytsky (1985), p. 181.

7. On a comparison of *Othello* and *El curioso impertinente* see Anthony J. Cascardi (1986), pp. 244–51 and p. 240.

8. For the various puns on 'turn', see Neill (ed.) (2006), *Othello* 339, note at IV.i.244–6.

9. 'Who do you identify with?' is the question Valentin asks Molina in Manuel Puig's *Kiss of the Spider Woman*. They are a version of *Los dos amigos*, with Molina a homosexual who is good at telling stories. See Puig (1991), p. 25. The point is a reminder of Lacan's idea about the 'mirror stage', in which identity is taken up by identifying with the phantasized other.

10. See also Michael Neill's Introduction to *Othello* (2006), pp. 147–58, in which he discusses the resonance among place, office and occupation.

11. The Quarto and Folio read 'topped', and Honigmann (1997) follows in the new Arden. 'Tupped' was adopted in the eighteenth century to ensure the echo of I.i.89.
12. See especially pp. 85 and 87.
13. See for a discussion of this theme, Patricia Parker (1985).

Chapter Six

1. For the English title of Proust's *À la recherche du temps perdu*, there are two versions: *Remembrance of Things Past* and later *In Search of Lost Time*. *Remembrance* is given originally in the C. K. Scott Moncrieff edition (1919). Terence Kilmartin, in his revised edition of Scott Moncrieff in 1981, preserved the title. The reworking of Kilmartin's edition by D. J. Enright in 1992 was published under the title *In Search of Lost Time*. The most recent translation of Proust is the new Penguin translation, general editor Christopher Prendergast, 6 vols (2002), also published under the title *In Search of Lost Time*. But I have generally preferred to quote from the edition *In Search of Lost Time*, trans. C. K. Scott Moncrieff, Terence Kilmartin and D. J. Enright, 6 vols (1998–99). The following abbreviations are used throughout in the present study:

SW	*Du côté de chez Swann*	[Swann's Way]
BG	*À l'ombre des jeunes filles en fleurs*	[Within a Budding Grove]
CG	*Le Côté de Guermantes*	[The Guermantes Way]
SG	*Sodome et Gomorrhe*	[Sodom and Gomorrah]
LP	*La prisonnière*	[The Captive]
AD	*Albertine disparue*	[The Fugitive]
TR	*Le temps retrouvé*	[Time Regained]

They are referred to as abbreviation plus page number. Although *La Prisonnière* [The Captive] and *Albertine disparue* [The Fugitive] are collected in Volume 5, entitled *The Captive and the Fugitive* in the Modern Library translation, different abbreviations are used in order to match the original French title. So *LP* and *AD* refer to different French titles, but are collected in the same volume in the Modern Library translation. For a comment on translation, see Roger Shattuck (2000), pp. 177–92. See for an introduction, Shelia Stern (1999). For a discussion on the issue of lesbianism, see Nicola Luckhurst (2000). For an analysis of the narrative, see Gerard Genette (1980). For a psychoanalytic analysis, see Randolph Splitter (1981). See also David Ellison (1984); J. E. Livers (1980); and Samuel Beckett (1970).

2. See Benjamin (1973a), pp. 255–67, especially p. 260.
3. Consider Derrida's discussion of the siglum, a letter or an initial used to denote words or abbreviations. A siglum does not belong to any system, and is not even a proper sign. Sigla are private, incomplete, and fragmentary. Derrida thinks of a signature as a siglum, and since the signature signifies death, we are left with no more than unrelated fragments of the other. See Derrida (1986), p. 19.

4. For a discussion of paranoia and surrealism see Haim Finkelstein (1996), especially the section on Dalí's *Le Mythe tragique de l'Angélus de Millet* [The Tragic Myth of Millet's *Angelus*].

5. See Lacan (1989), p. 181. Ferdinand de Saussure defines 'in language there are only differences without positive terms'. See Saussure (1960), p. 120.

6. Charles Baudelaire, in *Peintre de la vie moderne* [The Painter of Modern Life] (1860), also quotes Augustine's phrase *amabam amare* to describe a 'minor artist', Constantin Guys (1802–92), his idea of the painter of modern life, ' "*Amabam amare*", said St. Augustine. "I am passionately in love with passion," Monsieur G. might well echo' (1964, p. 9). See Baudelaire (1964), pp. 1–40.

Chapter Seven

1. See Paul de Man's discussion of this (1979, pp. 57–78).

2. For discussion of earlier representations of human qualities as allegories, see C. S. Lewis' discussions of personification allegory in *The Allegory of Love: a Study in Medieval Tradition* (1953).

3. See Michael Foucault (1995), Part III, Chapter 3.

4. Lacan writes, 'There is a jouissance that is hers (*à elle*), that belongs to that 'she' (*elle*) that doesn't exist and doesn't signify anything' (1998a, p. 74).

5. For a brief review of the issue of women's influence on Proust's writings, and an introduction to the debate of Albertine as a man in disguise, see Viti (1994), pp. 1–7.

6. There are homosexual men who are fetishistic, and there is a possibility for a man to think of himself as woman. Also, there are homosexual men who hate women, as Theweleit argues in *Male Fantasy* (1987). For discussion and application of Theweleit's thesis, see Jeremy Tambling (1996), pp. 53–7. On queer theory, see Judith Butler (1993).

7. For a comparable discussion of Giotto, see Paul de Man (1979), ch. 3.

Chapter Eight

1. Also see Georges Duby (1991), vol. 5, ch. 2.

3. Jonathan Sawday refers to Shakespeare's *Othello*, *The Winter's Tale*, and especially *Romeo and Juliet*, for its stresses on the 'dead' body of Juliet as 'an hymn to erotic death' (1995, p. 45, also ch. 3).

3. See Chris Perriam (2003), pp. 104–10, for a critical reading of the film. On Almodóvar, see Marsha Kinder (2005).

4. On Freud's '*Beyond the Pleasure Principle*' (1984a), see Peter Brooks, 'Freud's Master Plot', in *Reading for the Plot: Design and Intention in Narrative* (1984).

Index

The index mainly comprises names, but topics as well when their place for discussion in the text cannot be easily deduced from the mention of the names.